DATE DUE

GAYLORD			PRINTED IN U.S.A.

Civic Education for Diverse Citizens in Global Times

Rethinking Theory and Practice

The **Rutgers Invitational Symposium on Education** Series

Belzer, Ed.
Toward Defining and Improving Quality in Adult Basic Education: Issues and Challenges

Rubin/Giarelli, Eds.
Civic Education for Diverse Citizens in Global Times: Rethinking Theory and Practice

O'Donnell/King, Eds.
Cognitive Perspectives on Peer Learning

Vitello/Mithaug, Eds.
Inclusive Schooling: National and International Perspectives

Golbeck, Ed.
Psychological Perspectives on Early Childhood Education: Reframing Dilemmas in Research and Practice

Shimahara/Holowinsky/Tomlinson-Clarke, Eds.
Ethnicity, Race, and Nationality in Education: A Global Perspective

O'Donnell/Hmelo-Silver/Erkens, Eds.
Collaborative Learning, Reasoning, and Technology

For more information on titles in the Rutgers Invitational Symposium on Education series visit **www.routledge.com**

Civic Education for Diverse Citizens in Global Times

Rethinking Theory and Practice

Edited by

Beth C. Rubin

James M. Giarelli

LEA Lawrence Erlbaum Associates

Taylor & Francis Group

New York   London

Lawrence Erlbaum Associates
Taylor & Francis Group
270 Madison Avenue
New York, NY 10016

Lawrence Erlbaum Associates
Taylor & Francis Group
2 Park Square
Milton Park, Abingdon
Oxon OX14 4RN

© 2008 by Taylor & Francis Group, LLC
Lawrence Erlbaum Associates is an imprint of Taylor & Francis Group, an Informa business

Printed in the United States of America on acid-free paper
10 9 8 7 6 5 4 3 2 1

International Standard Book Number-13: 978-0-8058-5159-5 (Hardcover)

Library of Congress Cataloging-in-Publication Data

Civic education for diverse citizens in global times : rethinking theory and practice /
   Beth C. Rubin, James M. Giarelli, [editors].
      p. cm. -- (Education)
   Includes bibliographical references.
   ISBN 0-8058-5159-3 (cloth : alk. paper) 1. Citizenship--Study and teaching--United
   States. 2. Civics--Study and teaching--United States. 3. Social sciences--Study
   and teaching--United States. 4. Pluralism (Social sciences)--United States. 5.
   Education--Social aspects--United States. I. Rubin, Beth C. II. Giarelli, James M.,
   1950-

LC1091.R83 2007
323.6'07073--dc22   2006101920

Visit the Taylor & Francis Web site at
http://www.taylorandfrancis.com

and the LEA and Routledge Web site at
http://www.routledge.com

Contents

FOREWORD

The chapters in this book provide both historical summaries of citizenship education and descriptions of a host of current programs. They point out that problems abound in the field of citizenship education, and many are discussed here explicitly. Others are implicit in the exposition of general issues. This brief foreword highlights a few issues for readers to consider.

Social studies teachers today are asked to extend their work well beyond the traditional problems of American democracy into the domain of global education. How this should be done, however, is a matter of considerable debate. For example, how should we present the topic of *globalization*? We may well agree that it should not be presented dogmatically, but we face a big task in gathering the information required to present it fairly. Teachers need to read widely in economics, cultural studies, politics, and environmental studies. If our views on globalization are more negative than positive, we may want to distinguish carefully among terms such as globalization, global studies, global awareness, and *global citizenship*. For example, we may be enthusiastic about teaching for global awareness even though we are critical of globalization.

Can we reasonably advocate global citizenship? What do we mean by this term? Thomas Paine was one of the earliest supporters of the idea: "My country is the world; to do good is my religion." Many of us admire this statement, but years after it was made, Theodore Roosevelt referred to Paine as "that filthy little atheist." This is not the reaction of an admirer! Serious questions arise out of the tension between national and global citizenship and, in times of conflict, global citizenship may well be scorned. Can global citizenship be defined in a way that reduces this tension? Should national citizenship be redefined to moderate nationalistic patriotism? Does one have to express a belief in God in order to qualify as a political leader in this democratic society?

As we try to stretch our students' knowledge and understanding to issues of global concern, we have to acknowledge that many similar matters remain controversial within our own national boundaries. We live in an age when tolerance is much touted. But how far should tolerance be extended in a liberal democracy? How should our democracy respond to the illiberal and intolerant groups within it? One general answer is to allow such groups freedom of expression but to deny them public support. Some feminist political philosophers have even suggested that the Catholic church be denied tax exemption because of its discrimination against women. Similarly, the problem of school vouchers is complicated by that same question: Should public monies be directed to groups whose rules and customs (e.g., on the role of women) undermine or violate the agenda of our liberal democracy?

On the global level, we often have difficulty interacting with illiberal or undemocratic governments. Indeed, our own government sometimes adopts an evangelical attitude on democracy, insisting that "we" must spread democracy over the whole world. How should teachers lead discussions on this sensitive issue? Should it be discussed at all in our social studies courses?

In the past couple of decades, multiculturalism has become an important topic in social studies education. Tolerance and respect for immigrants have been effectively supplemented with much information about the customs of immigrants and their contributions to our democratic way of life. Cultural pluralism has been celebrated. However, today we face a dangerous escalation of bad feeling toward illegal immigrants. How should this problem be discussed? Is it simply a matter of obeying or disobeying the law? Can the issue be discussed without inflaming passions? Can pluralism be preserved as we promote unity? Does the United States bear some responsibility for the economic problems that drive so many to enter our country illegally?

One of the toughest tasks facing social studies teachers (perhaps all teachers) is to help students gather information, analyze, and evaluate arguments. The idealistic temptation is to take sides quickly and muster arguments to defend the chosen side. But many topics need deep, open-minded exploration: the effects of globalization on poor populations (Are they always exploited?), the building of dams and diversion of waterways (Is the practice sometimes beneficial to local populations?), the exercise of eminent domain (When does it violate democratic principles?), and the questionable behavior of our own nation (How far should we go with criticism?). Can we achieve an honest balance on these issues—one that preserves commitment, but avoids both cynicism and naïve idealism?

We should also recognize that citizenship is learned through democratic interaction, not only through formal studies. John Dewey said that democracy is not simply a form of government, but also a "mode of associated living." If we believe this, then we should look beyond our formal curriculum to the structure of school life. Today, under the pressures of standardized testing, many schools are cutting back on extracurricular activities. But these activities provide a rich setting for democratic practice. As students elect leaders, set agendas, carry out plans of action, and evaluate their success, they are learning something important about democracy as a mode of associated living.

Similarly, when students are allowed substantial choices among rich, well-organized courses of study, they are getting a start on freedom of choice, the most cherished right of democratic life. That choice should, of course, be well-informed and supported by rational dialogue. Those educators and policymakers who believe that students must be coerced into studies that "will give them opportunities" ignore the very foundations of liberal democracy—free choice and the rational dialogue that ensures well-informed choice. The opportunity to engage in such dialogue and to make sound choices is one to be supported and encouraged.

This volume should initiate the sort of rational dialogue we cherish. Readers will find many more substantial issues to debate and, I am sure, welcome the opportunity to do so.

Nel Noddings

PREFACE

The conference that formed the initial basis for this book was held in October 2002, a little more than a year after September 11. Although it seemed then that the country was at a new height of civic anxiety, it could be argued that discomfort and dissent on civic issues have only risen since that time. War in Iraq, potential violations of civil liberties at home, and the status of illegal immigrants, these are just a few of the many issues that have captured the attention of U.S. citizens, involving us in contentious discourse around perennial issues in American life. What does it mean to be an American citizen? How should this country situate itself among the other nations of the world? Who is worthy of citizenship, and what benefits should citizenship entail? In the newspaper, on television, in classrooms, and around kitchen tables, discussion resonates on these themes. Educators, in general, and social studies educators, in particular, can play a pivotal role in the formation of this discussion.

Yet, despite the potential these issues hold for inciting relevant learning and discourse in social studies classrooms, something is missing. Despite heated interest in both national and international civic topics, we are not shocked when students describe their social studies classes as boring. There is a gap between theory and practice in social studies education; although social studies researchers call for teachers to nurture skills of analysis, decision making, and participatory citizenship, students in social studies classrooms are often found participating in passive tasks (e.g., quiz- and test-taking, worksheet completion, listening to lectures), rather than engaging critically with the curriculum. This book, directed at students, researchers, and practitioners of social studies education, seeks to engage this divide by gathering together a collection of work that puts practice at the center of research and theory.

This book seeks to situate civic education amidst pressing current concerns. The social studies have long been a forum for the discussion and promotion of civic values and competences. At the center of this mission has been an enduring commitment to teach children the historical, social, and ethical understand-

ings that will inform citizens, as well as the skills of reflective and critical thinking to make this knowledge constructive. Whereas this core mission of public
education is more important than ever, changing local, national, and international contexts raise new questions about the meaning of social studies and civic
education, and the curriculum and methods most appropriate to accomplish it.

Although our schools and our country are more diverse than ever before,
traditional concepts of U.S. citizenship often do not allow for, take into account,
or value cultural, racial, linguistic, and gender diversity. Teachers and schools
struggle to cope with the dilemmas of diversity and citizenship. Recent events
have made painfully real the oft-repeated assertions about the increasingly interconnected nature of global cultures and economies. Social studies educators are
charged with helping students to understand the rapidly changing international
scene in order to prepare youth for a competitive global economy. These are the
concerns—national diversity, global interconnectedness, and the implications of
these trends for civic research and practice — that are central to this collection
of work.

This collection represents the collaboration of researchers and practitioners
of civic education from a wide variety of fields. In October 2002, a diverse
group of experts on civic and democratic education gathered to discuss past and
future trends in the field as part of the Rutgers Invitational Symposium on Education (RISE), an annual series sponsored by the Graduate School of Education
at Rutgers, the State University of New Jersey. The group included academics
from a variety of disciplinary backgrounds: philosophy, history, political science, Middle Eastern studies, social and cultural studies, American studies, social education, psychology, as well as practitioners from innovative public
schools. Each participant prepared a paper. On the first day of the conference,
the invited chapter writers thoroughly discussed and critiqued this work, along
with the general ideas raised in the papers. On the second day of the conference,
participants presented their papers to an audience of teachers, researchers, activists, and policymakers, further enriching the dialogue. Presentations by teachers
and students participating in promising civic education programs lent a sense of
hope and immediacy to the second conference day, serving as both illustration
and counterpoint to the more academic presentations.

This volume, comprised of the papers prepared for the conference with a
few relevant additions, represents the fruit of these discussions. It is organized
around four interrelated themes: rethinking civic education in light of the diversity of U.S. society, reexamining these notions in an increasingly interconnected
global context, reconsidering the ways that civic education is researched and
practiced, and taking stock of where we are currently through use of an historical understanding of civic education.

Part I of the book challenges readers to think more inclusively about the
civic body and the ways that civic education might evolve to serve it. It includes
a chapter focusing on issues of gender and sexuality in the social studies
(Crocco, chap. 2), and a study of differences in civic knowledge and attitude by

gender, race and socioeconomic status (Hahn, chap. 4). Chapter 3, by Chi and Howeth, highlights the endeavors of a diverse urban elementary school that puts civic education and service learning at the center of its mission. Part II of the book encourages readers to consider the implications for civic education in a world that is rapidly globalizing in all arenas: economic, social, and political. This section includes a study of conceptions of citizenship held by students in six democratic countries (Richardson & Torney-Purta, chap. 5), and a chapter examining the limitations of traditional approaches to democratic educational theory given the current global context (Cahill, chap. 6). Another chapter highlights the efforts of an exciting university–public school collaboration, Global Citizen 2000, that engages students with global issues through hands-on projects and electronic communication with youth in other countries (Davis, chap. 7).

Part III presents innovative approaches to research and practice in civic education. It includes a chapter proposing new ways of conducting civic education directed at correcting students' misconceptions of the U.S. political system (Hibbing & Rosenthal, chap. 8), and a study of programs designed to promote civic involvement among students at two different public schools (Kahne and Westheimer, chap. 9). Another chapter argues for a reconceptualization of our understanding of civic learning and engagement based on a sociocultural approach that considers the impact of students' daily civic experiences on their development as citizens (Rubin, chap. 10).

Part IV situates the previous chapters in a larger framework. One chapter reviews the ramifications of our current state of civic anxiety (Giroux, chap. 11), and the last contextualizes current efforts to remake U.S. civic education amidst the long history of debate over the meaning, purpose, and method of the endeavor (Justice, chap. 12).

It is our hope that this volume will, in some small way, help to shape understandings of civic education as we move deeper into the 21st century. More importantly, however, we hope that the collection will be of use to civic educators and researchers who are working to create a social studies education that reaches the subject's great potential for stimulating critical thought, passionate interest, and civic connection in students.

ACKNOWLEDGMENTS

As noted earlier, this book grew out of a 2-day conference organized under the auspices of the Rutgers Invitational Symposium on Education with the theme "Social Studies for a New Millennium: Re-envisioning Civic Education for a Changing World." We would like to thank the Dean of the Graduate School of Education at that time, Louise Wilkinson, for her encouragement, and the current Dean of the Graduate School of Education, Richard De Lisi, for his continuing support. We are grateful to the Office of Continuing Education and Global Programs at the GSE, especially Executive Director Darren Clarke and his staff, Jana Curry, Joyce Carlson, and Joan Melillo for taking care of the many detailsthat made the conference a success. Special thanks also to our colleagues at the Eagleton Institute of Politics—Susan Sherr, John Weingart, Alan Rosenthal, and Ruth Mandel—who hosted the participants for a preconference day of discussion and dialogue. Special thanks to Lin Zhitongy for his excellent and efficient preparation of the manuscript and to Brian Hayes for making this a better book with his proofreading and index preparation. Our editors, Naomi Silverman, at Lawrence Erlbaum Associates, and Mimi Williams at Taylor & Francis, have been gracious and patient guides to our work.

This volume has been a long time coming. We appreciate the patience of all our contributors and hope the wait was worth the while. Thanks.

—Beth C. Rubin
—James M. Giarelli

About the Authors

William Cahill teaches in Edison Township High School in New Jersey. He is also a part-time lecturer in the Graduate School of Education at Rutgers University.

Bernadette Chi received her doctorate from the Graduate School of Education, University of California at Berkeley in Policy, Organization, Measurement, and Evaluation. She is the former Director of the Institute for Citizenship Education and Teacher Preparation at the East Bay Conservation Corps (EBCC) and member of the School Development Team for the K-5 EBCC Charter School. She now works as Director of Evaluation forSports4Kids in Oakland, CA.

Margaret Smith Crocco is Professor of Social Studies and Education at Teachers College, Columbia University. She also coordinates the Program in Social Studies. Her research interests include gender, sexuality, and citizenship education; social studies in urban secondary schools; technology use in social studies; and women's history. She has written or edited six books, and has published numerous articles in *Theory and Research in Social Education, Social Education, Journal of Computing in Teacher Education*, and *Journal of Curriculum Studies*, among others. She is currently working on a book, *Teaching U.S. Women's History* with historians Carol Berkin and Barbara Winslow, which will be published by Oxford University Press.

Eric Davis is Professor of Political Science at Rutgers University, New Brunswick, New Jersey, where he specializes in the comparative politics of the Middle East and theories of democratic transitions, with particular reference to Iraq. Professor Davis is the past director of the Rutgers University Center for Middle Eastern Studies. During the 2004–2005 academic year, Professor Davis held a grant from the U.S. Institute of Peace to write a book on post-Baathist Iraq, *Taking Democracy Seriously in Iraq*. During the 2006–2007 academic year, he was awarded a grant from The American Academic Research Institute in Iraq (TAARI) to conduct research on democratization and civil society building in post-Baathist Iraq. Professor Davis is particularly interested in the relationship of historical memory, political identity, and democratization in the Arab world.

James M. Giarelli is Professor and Chair of the Department of Educational Theory, Policy, and Administration at the Graduate School of Education, Rutgers University. He serves as an Associate Editor of *Educational Theory*, on the Executive Board of the Philosophy of Education Society, and as faculty director of the Graduate School of Education South African Initiative. He has published widely in social philosophy, ethics, civic, and moral education.

Henry A. Giroux currently holds the Global TV Network Chair Professorship at McMaster University in the English and Cultural Studies Department. He has published numerous books and articles. His recent books include: *The Terror of Neoliberalism* (Paradigm, 2004), *Against the New Authoritarianism* (Arbeiter Ring, 2005), *Take Back Higher Education* (coauthored with Susan Giroux, Palgrave, 2006), *America on the Edge: Henry Giroux on Politics, Culture and Education* (Palgrave, 2006), *Beyond the Spectacle of Terrorism* (Paradigm, 2006), and *Stormy Weather: Katrina and the Politics of Disposability* (Paradigm, 2006). His primary research areas are cultural studies, youth studies, critical pedagogy, popular culture, media studies, social theory, and the politics of higher and public education.

Carole L. Hahn is the Charles Howard Candler Professor of Educational Studies at Emory University. Her research in cross national studies of citizenship education, gender issues and social studies, and controversial issues discussion and classroom climate has earned her many awards, including the 1996 Exemplary Research Award from the National Council for the Social Studies (NCSS), the 1998 Jubilee Award from the Danish Secondary Teachers' Union, and in 2006, the Jean Dresden Grambs Distinguished Career Research in Social Studies Award from NCSS. She is past President of NCSS and currently the National Research Coordinator for the U.S. portion of the Civic Education Study being conducted under the auspices of the International Association for the Evaluation of Educational Achievement (IEA).

John Hibbing is the Foundation Regents University Professor of Political Science at the University of Nebraska-Lincoln. He is the author of several books including *Stealth Democracy: Americans' Beliefs about How Government Should Work*, Cambridge University Press, 2002 with Elizabeth Theiss-Morse and *Republic on Trial*, Congressional Quarterly Press, 2002, with Alan Rosenthal, Karl Kurtz, and Burdett Loomis. He has edited the *Legislative Studies Quarterly*, served as President of the American Political Science Association's Legislative Studies Section, won the Fenno Prize and been a NATO Fellow in Science and Senior Fulbright Fellow.

Tim Howeth is a National Board Certified Teacher who has taught second, third and fourth grade in public schools in Virginia and California for 14 years. He received his BFA and has a Multiple Subject Credential with a supplementary authorization in Art from California State University, Long Beach. During the 2001–2002 school year, Mr. Howeth served as the Fourth Grade Teacher and Lead Teacher in Technology at the EBCC Charter School.

Benjamin Justice is an Assistant Professor of Education at Rutgers University in New Jersey. He has written numerous articles and book chapters on the history of American education, and is the author of *The War That Wasn't: Religious Conflict and Compromise in the Common Schools of New York, 1865–1900* (SUNY, 2005). He is a 2005 National Academy of Education/Spencer Post-Doctoral Fellow.

Joseph Kahne holds the Kathryn P. Hannam Chair and is the Director of the Doctoral Program in Educational Leadership at Mills College, where he is also the Research Director for the Institute for Civic Leadership. Professor Kahne publishes regularly on the democratic purposes of education and on urban school reform. He is currently conducting a statewide study of the civic/democratic commitments, capacities, and activities of high school students in California and of the distribution and impact of school-based opportunities that aim to shape those outcomes. He can be reached at jkahne@mills.edu.

Wendy Klandl Richardson is an independent consultant specializing in research, evaluation, and professional development for teachers in the areas of social studies and civic education. She is a former Faculty Research Associate and doctoral student in the Department of Human Development, College of Education, at the University of Maryland, College Park, where she worked on analysis and dissemination of the IEA Civic Education Study. Her dissertation on the topic of adolescent civic engagement and political discussion earned the 2004 Bruce H. Choppin Award, which is awarded to an outstanding dissertation using IEA data.

Alan Rosenthal is Professor of Public Policy at the Eagleton Institute of Politics at Rutgers University. His field of study is state politics and state legislatures. His latest book is *Heavy Lifting: The Job of the American Legislature* (CQ Press, 2004).

Beth C. Rubin is Assistant Professor of Education at Rutgers, the State University of New Jersey. A former high school social studies teacher, her research focuses on better understanding the intersection of classroom life, students' daily experiences in school, and larger structures of inequality. She has published in journals, including the *American Educational Research Journal, Teachers College Record, Excellence and Equity in Education,* and *Theory Into Practice,* and has authored numerous book chapters and two edited books. She is a 2003 Spencer Foundation/National Academy of Education Postdoctoral Fellow and mother of two.

Judith Torney-Purta holds a BA from Stanford University in Psychology and a PhD from the University of Chicago in Human Development. She has been Professor of Human Development in the College of Education at the University of Maryland at College Park since 1981. She was awarded the Nevitt Sanford Prize by the International Society for Political Psychology (2001) and the Decade of Behavior Research Award in Democracy (2005). Her long-term research interest has been developmental and educational psychology as it can be applied to political socialization and the civic engagement of youth. Her first book, *The Development of Political Attitudes in Children,* was published in 1967 (and was recently reissued). From 1994 until 2004 she served as the Chair of the International Steering Committee of the Civic Education Study of IEA (the International Association for the Evaluation of Education Achievement, Amsterdam). Phase 1 of this study included the development of case studies and the content framework on which the test and survey were based. During Phase 2, representative samples totaling 140,000 respondents at two age levels were surveyed. *Citizenship and Education in Twenty-Eight Countries: Civic Knowledge and Engagement at Age Fourteen (*by Torney-Purta, Lehmann, Oswald, and Schulz) was published by IEA in March 2001, as was a volume reporting results from upper secondary students in 16 countries in July 2002. Secondary analysis of the data is continuing. The Website for information about the study is www.wam.umd.edu/~iea/

Joel Westheimer is University Research Chair in Democracy and Education, Professor of the Social Foundations of Education, and Co-Director of Democratic Dialogue: Inquiry into Democracy, Education, and Society (www.DemocraticDialogue.com) at the University of Ottawa. He teaches and writes on democracy, social justice, youth activism, and community service learning. Westheimer is a former New York City public school teacher and musician. He lives in Ottawa, Ontario where in winter he ice skates to and from work. He can be reached by e-mail at joelw@uottawa.ca

Civic Education for Diverse Citizens in Global Times: Rethinking the Theory and Practice

Beth C. Rubin and James M. Giarelli
Rutgers, The State University of New Jersey

During a classroom discussion in an urban middle school, students engaged in a lively discussion of the Pledge of Allegiance:

Amber:	We [loudly] are the one nation, under God. One nation.
Jessica:	When the Pledge of Allegiance says "under God," it can't actually say that and expect people to pledge allegiance to the flag. Because there's other races that really don't BELIEVE in God. So if you don't believe in God why would you pledge allegiance to the flag that states "under God?" You won't . . . it's . . .
Angelica:	Well, me and her [referring to another student, LaShawn] were discussing. She said that it's not one nation because of segre . . . , like we had segregation, all this stuff, all this hate. But you're not pledging to the people IN America, you're pledging to AMERICA itself.

One brief snippet of classroom conversation displays a wealth of grounded complexity around key civic issues. Who is the "one nation" invoked in the Pledge? Does our nation's history of segregation and "all this hate" provide a challenge to this notion? Can all Americans be expected to agree to a pledge that invokes belief in a deity? What about those "other races" who don't believe in God; can they be expected to make the same pledge? Amber, Jessica, Angelica, and LaShawn, African American and Latina eighth-grade students at a middle school in a low-income urban area, energetically pursued such questions, pondering the implications of the Pledge in a diverse society amidst a global context.

1

Civic education research and practice can no longer focus on the civic workings of the United States in isolation; nor can it continue to assume a unified, monolithic citizenry. In today's diverse society and interconnected world, the whole notion of civic knowledge and engagement must be reworked to include global dimensions and multiple perspectives. Fortunately, there is a growing body of work that does just that. This collection provides a sampling of such work, aiming to move in the direction of an approach to civic research and practice that is situated more firmly in the diverse and interconnected reality of life in the 21st century. The chapters herein foreshadow the possibility of a civic education that is more relevant, engaging, motivating, and, ultimately, broadly enfranchising than that provided before.

This collection is divided into four thematic parts, but there are additional themes that run through many of the chapters: the tension between empowering students and giving them realistic expectations so they aren't disappointed, the struggle to integrate civic education into a social studies curriculum dominated by transmission of historical facts, the limitations of current research on civic education and attempts to rectify this. Each of the first three parts includes at least one empirical chapter that tests new ideas in the field. The work of K–12 practitioners is highlighted in the collection as well. The following describes each section and its chapters.

PART I: RETHINKING CIVICS AND CITIZENSHIP IN A DIVERSE DEMOCRACY

Part I brings issues of race, class, gender, and sexual diversity to the foreground (other chapters that incorporate these issues are Davis, chap. 7; Kahne and Westheimer, chap. 9; and Rubin, chap. 10). In "Reimagining Citizenship Education: Gender, Sexuality and the Social Studies," Crocco writes (chap. 2) about ascriptive characteristics that define shifting notions of citizenship in America and draws our special attention to silences about gender and sexuality in the discourse of citizenship in the social studies literature. Based in part on interviews with beginning social studies teachers, Crocco argues that the constraints and obstacles that inhibit the kind of teaching that promotes civic competence present an urgent challenge to social studies educators. "Social studies educators," she holds, "can make a difference" in this area, and the nature of our democracy is at stake.

In "Service Learning as a Strategy to Promote Citizenship Education and Civic Engagement in an Urban Elementary Grammar School" (chap. 3), Chi and Howeth, founders of and teachers at the East Bay Conservation Corps Charter School in northern California, describe a diverse urban elementary school in which service learning and youth civic engagement are central to its mission. The authors describe how service-learning projects both within and beyond the classroom were employed to create a "culture of civic engagement" in the school. Other practices, including schoolwide meetings, peer mediation, and a new discipline policy, spread this culture of civic engagement throughout the school. The authors conclude that students, predominantly students of color from low-income families, reaped both personal and academic gains through this approach, and are involved in an educational experience quite different from that experienced by their peers in other urban schools.

In Chapter 4, "Gender and Civic Education," Hahn asks how we might better prepare all young people to be "engaged citizens in a multicultural democracy in an integrated global society", the core question of this volume, and turns her attention to gender, a variable that she points out is often overlooked in discussions of civic education. Reviewing studies using nationally representative samples of students, she finds that boys and girls differ in their civic and political attitudes, and argues that qualitative research is needed to better understand the source and nature of these differences. She also notes that there appear to be differences in students' political knowledge, attitude, and experiences by race/ethnicity and socioeconomic background, and stresses the importance of including this dimension in any exploration of student civic engagement.

PART II: RETHINKING CIVICS AND CITIZENSHIP IN A GLOBAL CONTEXT

Part II offers views on civic education and practice in light of an increasingly interconnected world. In chapter 5, "Connections Between Concepts of Democracy, Citizen Engagement and Schooling for 14-Year Olds Across Countries," Richardson and Torney-Purta compare concepts of democracy and civic engagement among students from six different countries. They take up the question of the connection between students' understandings of democracy, political engagement, civic knowledge, and trust and their intention to participate actively as adults. Based on IEA Civic Education Study data from Chile, Estonia, Finland, Greece, Switzerland, and the United States, the authors suggest that students' understandings of democratic concepts are less connected to their intent to participate than their understandings of good citizenship. This chapter decenters the United States in its consideration of students' civic knowledge and engagement; we are part of a larger democratic world struggling with similar issues of connecting young people to the processes that make our political systems work.

The rhetoric of globalization had become the hegemonic vocabulary in educational policy discourse by framing a way of thinking about the connections among persons, institutions, and knowledge. Chapter 6, "A Primer on Democracy and Education in the Era of Globalization" is written by Cahill, a high school English teacher and historian of education. Cahill worries about the constraints this rhetoric has—with its emphasis on economic competitiveness, the commodification of knowledge, and persons as human capital—on the theory and practice of civic, democratic education. The author first traces the long history of attention to internationalism in American education, beginning at least as early as the Centennial, up through the 1960s and 1970s. Against this background, Cahill explores more contemporary approaches to democratic educational theory, which he calls "utopian" or "liberal democratic," as alternatives to the dominant human capital approach.

Davis (chap. 7), a political scientist, raises critical questions about global citizenship in a post- September 11, 2001, world, and asks "What types of pedagogy need to be developed to make global citizenship a salient concept to the current generation of American citizens?" His chapter, "Global Citizenship: Theoretical and Pedagogical Perspectives," describes Global Citizen 2000, an exemplary effort at extending "global citizenship" education to K–12 classrooms. Global Citizen 2000, and its offshoot, Citizens Across Borders: The Student Initiative in Global Citizenship in the Wake of September 11, 2001, involve students in hands-on projects in which they generate their own understandings of their roles in a global society and exhibit their creative representations of these roles. This project also creates connections between U.S. students and students in eight foreign countries through e-mail and videoconferencing. These creative, interdisciplinary, and active approaches to incorporating global issues into K–12 classrooms are unique and promising.

PART III: NEW APPROACHES TO CIVIC RESEARCH AND PRACTICE

Part III highlights ways of thinking about civic education research and action distinct from how these topics have traditionally been approached. Political scientists Hibbing and Rosenthal begin "Teaching Democracy Appreciation" (chap. 8), with a dramatic claim: Civic education in the United States is failing. According to the authors, media, political campaigns, reform efforts, issue campaigns, and the complexities of the legislative process all contribute to these misconceptions. Civic education, however, bears the brunt of the blame for not correcting these misconceptions, and the authors take schools to task for not providing a civic education that is relevant to current democratic practices or that is taught in an engaging manner. They propose an approach to civic education in which experiential exercises and contact with local legislators are used to enhance students' understandings of the workings of the legislative process at state and national levels, and how the different values, interests, and priorities of our diverse citizenry are represented within this process.

In chapter 9, "The Limits of Efficacy: Educating Citizens for a Democratic Society," Kahne and Westheimer analyze two programs, one in a suburban and the other in an urban school, designed to involve students in civic experiences. In the former setting, the program was structured to ensure that students' encounters with government agencies were efficacious, and students reported that they felt they had "made a difference," and would engage in civic activities in the future. In the latter setting, students had frustrating experiences with local agencies, and experienced a decline in confidence as civic change agents and in their commitment to future civic involvement. Echoing concerns raised by Hibbing and Rosenthal, the authors note that opportunities for young people to experience civic and political efficacy must be mixed with opportunities for students to "learn about and experience the barriers and constraints they and other civic actors face."

In chapter 10, "Civics and Citizenship in Students' Daily Lives: Towards a Sociocultural Understanding of Civic Knowledge and Engagement," Rubin considers the possibility of enriching the current civic education literature through a broader conceptualization of civic learning and engagement. In particular, she suggests that sociocultural, interpretive investigation of how civic *identities* take shape might shed light on troubling findings within the current literature, such as race and class-linked patterns of civic knowledge and engagement. Traditional research approaches are unable to illuminate the nature and source of these disparities. An understanding of civic identity as shaped by context and experience might allow the development of a fuller understanding of how diverse students become citizens and civic beings.

PART IV: CIVIC EDUCATION IN A CHANGING WORLD

Part IV, the final section of the book, features two chapters that look more broadly at the issues at hand, taking stock of both the current moment and the historical trajectory that preceded it. In "Public Time Versus Emergency Time After September 11th: Democracy, Schooling, and the Culture of Fear" (chap. 11), Giroux questions the notion that after the attacks of September 11, 2001, the country has experienced a resurgence in "patriotism, community, and public spiritedness". He argues that, on the contrary, the notion of "emergency time" invoked by the presidential administration after the attacks effectively impinges on the public deliberation and critical civic engagement fundamental to a thriving democracy. Giroux holds that to counter the dangers of living in emergency time, "educators and others need to reclaim a notion of politics and pedagogy that embraces a notion of public time, one that fosters civic engagement and public intelligence".

In chapter 12, "Looking Back to See Ahead: Some Thoughts on the History of Civic Education in the United States", Justice reminds us that there have been other moments in the history of American education defined by efforts to "re-envision civic education". Although the present is never the past writ large or small, Justice defines three themes (tradition vs. truth, conflict vs. compromise, rhetoric vs. reality) that have coursed through American educational history from the colonial to contemporary eras and have structured debates around civic education.

CONCLUSION

Justice concludes the volume by noting that it is a healthy sign of our democracy that there are so many alternative ways to understand citizenship and civic education. According to Justice, "the lack of consensus over the meaning of civic education is a good thing". We agree and offer this collection as another contribution to the continuing conversation of democratic public education. When this project started, our aim was to bring together a diverse set of scholars around a common set of questions for conversations about theory, research, and practice in civic and social studies education and, especially, new directions for the future. In addition, we aimed to assemble a collection that would honor the perspectives and possibilities of each particular view, while situating them in tension with alternative approaches. Our aim was coherence without consensus, balance without boundaries. John Dewey once wrote that the intellectual function of trouble is to make us think. We agree and offer this collection as a prod and occasion for thinking about the civic and social aims of public education. In a diverse, yet interconnected world, there is no more important item on the public agenda.

PART I

RETHINKING CIVICS AND CITIZENSHIP IN A DIVERSE DEMOCRACY

Chapter 2

Reimagining Citizenship Education: Gender, Sexuality, and the Social Studies

Margaret Smith Crocco
Columbia University

> *We may continue to permit undirected social changes to dictate what takes place in the educational system, or we must think and act upon the assumption that public education has a positive responsibility to shape those habits of thought and action which in turn shape organized conditions of social action. The latter course cannot be undertaken without profound and courageous will to consider the real meaning of the American experiment and of American life; the obstacles that stand in the way of realizing this meaning; and the means by which the basic ideals can be continuously promoted. I see no other way of rendering education in fact, and not just in name, the foundation of social organization. —Dewey (cited in Boydsten, 1987, p. 23)*

In "Education for Democratic Citizenship," Mitchell (2001) states that allegiance to the concept of multiculturalism has, over the last 50 years, become firmly established as a "cornerstone of mid-twentieth century liberalism and a fundamental and ongoing national narrative in both Canada and the United States" (p. 55). Educators, no less than politicians, are abundantly aware of this fact. One of the most tangible examples of the acceptance of multiculturalism within education can be found in the textbooks so pervasively used in social studies courses.

Beginning in the mid-1990s, a teacher or teacher educator attending a professional conference and visiting the exhibit area could scarcely ignore the widespread promotional efforts of publishers trumpeting the multicultural content of their wares. Whether textbook authors incorporated multi-cultural content in a superficial or transformative fashion was, of course, another question entirely. Nevertheless, mainstream publishers' marketing efforts clearly heralded the arrival of multiculturalism as a norm for the educational enterprise. The value of diversity, at least as manifest in text-books, national standards for teaching, and for teacher education, achieved legitimacy in both education and politics by the dawn of the new millennium. As Nathan Glazer (1997) famously put it, "We are all multiculturalists now".

What Mitchell's article and Glazer's book suggest is that civic culture, and by extension, education for democratic citizenship, now acknowledge multiculturalism as part of the national narrative. Such inclusion—or exclusion—contributes to what legal scholar Smith (2001) calls the "politics of people-building". According to a line of reasoning made famous by political theorist Anderson's (1983) concept of "imagined communities," such national narratives help constitute a sense of national identity and are among "the most basic of political processes" (p.74). These stories, like all political processes, are dynamic. Eighteenth century Americans composed a story of self-creation emphasizing abrogation of affection and attachment to a despotic monarchy, the contribution of divine providence to shaping an American people, and more generous inclusion of ethnic and religious groups in its citizenship status than any other country at that time. Nevertheless, the United States was also a nation whose history was characterized by the maintenance of class, race, ethnic, and gender exclusions in voting long after other nations had abandoned them (Keyssar, 2000). From the beginning, the boundaries between citizen and noncitizen reflected deep-seated cultural beliefs: "An independent American people would not include Indians, but only citizens who could be trusted to strive to protect the interests of European-descended colonists against Indians; and the American people would not be savages, but rather bearers of a civilization of superior worth" (Smith, 2001, p. 80).

As part of its politics of people building, American society elaborated the "story of American freedom" (Foner, 1998). Despite the paradoxes and contradictions of such a claim in the face of constitutionally sanctioned slavery, this characterization about the American past could be interpreted as more aspiration than reality. The ideal did, however, gradually undermine the very politics of exclusion the narrative may have ignored. Still, "change was neither linear nor uncontested" (Keyssar, 2000, p. 2), whether one takes the history of citizenship, voting, or civil rights as the critical measure of progress (Shklar, 1991).

By the late 19th century, science and social science provided new intellectual rationales for hierarchies related to race, ethnicity, gender, and sexual identity:

A history of sexuality reveals how categories of deviant and non-deviant behavior are created and change over time. The idea of the homosexual, as a social category, was only proposed in the United States and Europe during the late nineteenth century, most historians agree. Earlier, homosexuality was a sexual practice that anyone could engage in . . . But science, mainly medical science, sought to distinguish, classify, describe, and promote or remedy health and morbidity. That process paralleled other scientific projects at the time to name, order, and govern places, races, and genders at home and abroad. The disciplining of sexuality, like the science of race and gender, was conditioned by assumptions and values prevalent during the latter part of the nineteenth century. That was evident in the naming of homosexuality as "deviant" sexual behavior by medical scientists, who focused upon a range of deviant gender behavior called "sexual inversion" as early as 1870. (Okihiro, 2001, p. 94)

In the early 20th century, the social studies field developed out of the modernist faith that educational expertise could be used to fashion a more cohesive American society in the face of an increasingly unfamiliar, perhaps even unassimilable, population. School subject matter aimed at citizenship education would help bring African Americans and the "new immigrants" into the body politic. Since that time, social studies educators have served as the chief purveyors of citizenship education in American schools, in theory at least, rehearsing the values, attitudes, and dispositions necessary to support the activities of citizens in a democratic republic.

Writing at about the same time as social studies' founding, Dewey (1916) saw education not as preparation for life, but as life itself. His work reveals sympathy for education's role in the politics of people building and in creating imagined communities. Thus, it is no surprise that Mitchell (2001) calls on Dewey's ideas as the framework for her consideration of the relationships among multiculturalism and democratic education. Dewey offered a vision of democracy and education that continues to challenge Americans who believe in schools' responsibility for maintaining and nurturing democracy. Mitchell describes Dewey's vision in these terms:

A mutually constitutive process, democracy expands the nation as the nation expands democracy. In the lived experience and conjoint decision making of the "American experiment," democracy is realizable; at the same time, the narrative of the nation as the open, tolerant, and egalitarian community is ceaselessly performed and supplemented through the democratic practices. (p. 53)

This chapter argues that we need to recapture Dewey's commitment to the democratic possibilities of education, especially social studies education. Tackling diversity remains problematic for the field, which continues to view difference with ambivalence and sometimes promulgates a national narrative that "silences the past" (Trouillot, 1995). I believe that such silences most often exist these days in the areas of gender and sexuality within the social studies curriculum.

In making a case for greater attention to these topics, I rely on a vision of educational possibility consonant with Dewey's, which believes diversity to be of educational value in and of itself, thus embracing what Walter Parker (1996) has called "advanced ideas about democracy". As we move through the 21st century, sustaining the promises of American citizenship will mean that students must learn how to practice a set of civic competencies resting heavily on attributes of tolerance, rational deliberation, and acceptance of the norms of American democratic life. Social studies education, in particular, must work steadfastly to inculcate the knowledge, habits, and dispositions necessary to defend "advanced ideas about democracy" in a world that is both shrinking and fractured along multiple fault lines, including religion, nationalism, race and ethnicity, material wealth, gender, and sexuality.

In reflecting on difference and its place within the social studies, I rely on new scholarship about citizenship, democracy, and democratic education. Testimonial evidence of beginning teachers' efforts and the obstacles they recount in introducing gender and sexuality into their curriculum are provided. Suggestions are made for introducing these topics into social studies education, based on a rationale rooted in contemporary thinking about civic education and the civic competencies necessary for dealing productively with all forms of difference in a globalizing world.

NEW HISTORIES AND THEIR IMPLICATIONS FOR CIVIC EDUCATION

In *American Citizenship*: *The Quest for Inclusion*, political scientist Shklar (1991) cautions that "citizenship is not a notion that can be discussed intelligibly in a static and empty space" (p. 9). Thus, it would seem important to situate citizenship in its proper time and place.

When the National Council for the Social Studies was founded in 1921, the 19th Amendment granting women the right to vote was only a year old. A few years later, proposals for literacy requirements to restrict voting by new immigrants were being widely circulated across the states (Keyssar, 2000). Even earlier, racial intimidation and Jim Crow laws had conspired to end voting by African Americans in the South. These facts indicate the contradictory paths taken by the franchise in American history, expanding and contracting its progress at the same time.

Shklar (1991) gives four meanings to citizenship: social standing within a society, that is, the right to vote and work; nationality or legal standing; active participation in civic life and a sense of obligation to the body politic; and the republican ideal of full and direct engagement in civic life (see also, Crocco, 2000). The last meaning of citizenship was carried out by a few males in Greek city-states thousands of years ago, but is out of touch with the realities of modern life, according to Shklar (p. 54).

The history of American society reveals that persons denied access to citizenship tend to be those who most value its prerogatives:

> The significance of the two great emblems of public standing, the vote and the opportunity to earn, seems clearest to those excluded men and women. They have regarded voting and earning not just as the ability to promote their interests and to make money but also as the attributes of an American citizen. And people who are not granted these marks of civic dignity feel dishonored, not just powerless and poor. They are also scorned by their fellow citizens. (Shklar, 1991, p. 3)

Denial of citizenship status in any of Shklar's senses has, in American history, rested on "ascriptive identity characteristics"—that is, race, ethnicity, gender, and sexual orientation (Smith, 1997). One of the most sobering conclusions drawn from reviewing a history of citizenship rights in this country is that "neither the possession nor the fresh achievement of greater equality can guarantee against later losses of status due to renewed support for various types of ascriptive hierarchy" (Smith, 1997, p. 471). Two traditions have competed over the course of this nation's past: one liberal and expansive in nature, and the other continuously reinscribing exclusionary hierarchies even after their formal, albeit incomplete, repudiation has occurred during more liberal periods (Crocco, 2000, p. 54). Thus, rights once granted can, in time, become rights denied, and often the basis for this denial is the suspect nature of the identity category to which one belongs.

Focusing on the history of voting yields insights comparable to those reached from reviewing the history of citizenship:

> The history of suffrage in the United States is certainly distinctive in many ways, several of which merit bold headlines. The United States was indeed the first country in the western world to significantly broaden its electorate by permanently lowering explicit economic barriers to political participation. . . . The United States

also was exceptional, however, in experiencing a prolonged period during which the laws governing the right to vote became more, rather than less restrictive. Finally, despite its pioneering role in promoting democratic values, the United States was one of the last countries in the developed world to attain universal suffrage. (Keyssar, 2000, pp. xxiii-xxiv)

The right to vote is, of course, only one of a constellation of rights accorded democratic citizens in this country. A further example of uneven progress in gaining full rights of democratic citizenship even after achievement of suffrage can be found in women's history or African American history. Women won property rights in almost all states by the late 19th century and the franchise in 1920. Nevertheless, they still suffered discrimination, including loss of citizenship upon marriage to a foreigner until well into the 20th century in certain states, and the inability to sit on juries and be judged by a jury of their peers until the 1930s or later in some states (Kerber, 1998).

Kessler-Harris has argued that inequities in the Social Security program and restrictions on women's freedom to work continue to undermine women's full participation in "economic citizenship." This concept echoes the emphasis of political scientists on the centrality of employment to citizenship in a modern economy. Kessler-Harris (2001) writes:

> I use [the term] more broadly to suggest the achievement of an independent and relatively autonomous status that marks self-respect and provides access to the full play of power and influence that defines participation in a democratic society. The concept of economic citizenship demarcates women's efforts to participate in public life and to achieve respect as women (sometimes as mothers and family members) from the efforts of men and women to occupy equitable relationships to corporate and government services. (p. 12)

In analyzing the history of social welfare policy since the 1930s, Kessler-Harris finds a powerful "gendered imagination" at work, one that operates on the sexist and heterosexist assumption that women will find protection as economic citizens through the agency of their spouses. She examines the ways in which "seemingly neutral policies like unemployment and old age insurance acted out gendered assumptions" and then considers "how these assumptions broke down in the postwar years" (p. 16). Widespread social change for women, rising divorce rates, the intersections of race and class, difficulties in gaining recognition of same-gender partnerships, and the survival demands of a rapidly evolving global economy helped to expose the anachronistic views of women and gender relations written into so much public policy (p. 294).

One can teach the national narrative as the "quest for inclusion," as Shklar does, or "the story of freedom" as Foner does. Still, social educators must acknowledge the exclusions that have also characterized American history, the ways in which these exclusions have been operationalized in public policy, and the silences that have pervaded social studies curriculum. Both the celebratory, as well as the cautionary, aspects of this picture need to be included in democratic citizenship education if we intend to create citizens prepared to defend democracy for all the nation's citizens.

Tragedies like Mathew Shepard's murder, violence against women and girls, racial hate crimes, the treatment of Black voters' ballots in Florida in the 2000 election, and the staggering circumstances surrounding 9/11, all indicate that we continue to confront challenges to citizenship rights today: especially the uncontested right to live, work, vote, speak freely, and be treated equitably by fellow citizens and even the government. Thus far, the field of social studies has been characterized by a "missing discourse on gender and sexuality" (Crocco, 2001). Normalizing discussion of these topics as part of an ongoing discussion of the significance of identity attributes to this democracy will contribute to democratic discourse about citizenship education.

These reflections are motivated by the belief that social studies education can and does have an important influence on the "habits of thought and action which in turn shape organized conditions of social action" (Dewey, in Boydsten, 1987, p. 235). If we wish education to yield social action characterized by tolerance, democratic deliberation, and inclusiveness, then we need to muster the "profound and courageous will to consider the real meaning of the American experiment and of American life; the obstacles that stand in the way of realizing this meaning; and the means by which its basic ideals can be continuously promoted" (Dewey, 1987, p. 23).

GENDER, SEXUALITY, AND THE SOCIAL STUDIES: AS IT IS

Recent commentary concerning the place of gender and sexuality in the social studies describes the situation in this way:

> Missing from almost all discussions of gender in school social studies is reference to the lives and history of lesbians and gay men. . . . In effect, the assumption is that all persons mentioned in the social studies curriculum are heterosexual until proven other-

wise. The same animus that fuels anti-woman sentiments . . . also fuels anti-gay sentiments. . . . It seems fair to say that homopho-bia—directed at women and men, girls and boys—as well as the achievements of lesbian and gay people are not even blips on the social studies radar screen. (Thornton, 2002, p. 179)

My own research confirms this state of affairs. Now halfway through a longitudinal study of beginning teachers, I have investigated their ability to infuse diversity into their teaching as one dimension of my inquiry. I asked about race, class, gender, and sexuality both on questionnaires and in inter-views to form a richer impression of what these teachers had done during their first year as social studies professionals. The subjects of this study (approximately 20) had all been required to take coursework in diversity and the social studies curriculum as part of their preservice master's and certification program (see Crocco, 2002), and are now (except for one) teaching in secondary schools in the New York metropolitan area, arguably one of the most liberal regions of the country.

I recognize that these teachers are all untenured, which clearly shapes their sentiments about what they can and cannot do. Still, I was disap-pointed by the array of excuses they voiced for avoiding these topics. Their responses provide evidence of what Cornbleth (2001) refers to as "climates of constraint/restraint of teachers and teaching" (p. 73). Cornbleth uses the words "constraint" and "restraint" because she finds that teachers engage in self-censorship resulting from "social and structural obstacles" that under-mine their ability to enact "progressive curriculum and instructional re-form" (p. 73). A dynamic interaction ensues between these obstacles and teachers' sense of possibilities for their teaching, both in terms of content and method. Of significance to this chapter is the fact that Cornbleth also finds that the processes of constraint/restraint inhibit just the kind of teach-ing necessary to promote citizenship competence, that is, critical thinking, diverse perspectives, and connections between new information and stu-dents' prior knowledge.

The list of problems my interview subjects enumerated as obstacles to progressive pedagogy addressing gender, sexuality, and other diversity top-ics provide tangible evidence for Cornbleth's conclusions. In my admittedly unscientific sample, certain patterns can be discerned. Six of the 20 teachers indicated that they had regularly addressed the four aspects of diversity I had used as a prod: race, class, gender, and sexuality. Three admitted they had given little or no attention to diversity of any kind in their teaching the past year. Four focused their efforts on race, religion, immigration, and lan-guage differences, but did not deal with gender and sexuality. Five others mentioned attention to gender issues specifically, but nothing else. Whether their recollections are accurate cannot be determined. My hunch is that most of them probably did even less than the little that they offered in response to my questions.

What may be more enlightening in these responses are the reasons given for avoidance of these topics. Several individuals cited what they perceived as the rushed and scripted nature of the Regents curriculum, which in their judgment allowed little room for discussions of diversity. In fact, it was clear that in a few of their schools, these new teachers' favorable ratings as professionals would depend directly on how their students did on the Regents' exams. A refrain was repeated: "If it isn't on the Regents, then I don't teach it." Nonetheless, a few found small opportunities for injecting mention of diversity issues, including gender and sexuality, into American History and World History. Several new teachers cited the pressures of tenure and the homophobic climate of their schools as their reasons for avoiding teaching this material, although they did indicate that they countered homophobic slurs directly when they were expressed in their classrooms. One teacher indicated that at her urban middle school this problem was so severe that a social worker was called in to address the subject of homophobia with the entire student body (Franck, 2002). These last two instances suggest the degree to which problems of sexual harassment and homophobia occur in spaces outside classrooms (Bickmore, 2002; Crocco, 2002), social actions that are encouraged by the implicit curriculum of heterosexism, and the null curriculum of silence concerning issues of social justice for gays and women (Thornton, 2002).

These responses provide evidence that social studies teachers wishing to take up the topic of diversity need to work around/between/through the explicit curriculum. Whether one faults the standards and accountability movement, the conservatism of schools and administrators, the fears of untenured teachers, or the lack of leadership by teacher educators in bringing this subject matter into social studies teacher education, the silences remain deafening. Bringing about change, however, can begin as simply as including references to gender and sexual orientation along with race and ethnicity whenever issues of respect, toleration, diversity, and difference are mentioned in classrooms (Roy, 1997). Admittedly, even mentioning these matters may be seen in some quarters as trampling on family values or religious belief systems. Within the civic space of public education, however, we should be respectful of these viewpoints, but must not use that stance to inhibit our support for promoting tolerance of all citizens as part of the democratic project.

GENDER, SEXUALITY, AND THE SOCIAL STUDIES: AS IT SHOULD BE

This concluding section addresses several questions: What further evidence do we have about the state of civic education related to gender and sexuality in the social studies? What relationship does re-imagined citizenship education, the kind necessary for "strong democracy" (Barber, 1984), bear to issues of gender and sexuality? Could more inclusive forms of social studies education create civic competencies that lessen sexist and homophobic ideas that might transfer into more tolerant adult attitudes about what it means to be an American citizen? Next, I review evidence concerning civic education, consider what are generally taken to be the hallmarks of civic competence in this society, lay out the connections between civic education and civic competence; show why we need attention to these matters in social studies education, and argue that inclusion of gender and sexuality in the social studies curriculum is one way of enacting democratic citizenship education in the social studies classroom.

Scholars who have examined tolerance in high school students and homophobia in adults offer sobering evidence concerning limitations in students' attitudes. Avery's (2002) research into political socialization forces recognition that the value of tolerance has not been well assimilated by many American students. In researching which groups were least liked by high school students, she found that gay and lesbian groups were named by 30%–35% of high school males. By contrast, only 10%–15% of females placed gay and lesbian groups into this category. Avery's findings are consistent with research indicating that "adult males often harbor more intense homophobic attitudes or feelings than females, are more concerned about male homosexuality than lesbianism, and are more disturbed by lesbianism than are heterosexual females" (Sears & Williams, 1997, p. 21). Not surprisingly, research also indicates that those with negative attitudes about homosexuality often hold "more conservative religious ideology, more traditional attitudes about gender roles, more negative sexual attitudes or sexual guilt, greater social prejudices, and more likely express authoritarian beliefs than those holding positive attitudes" (Sears & Williams, 1997, p. 21). When such data are combined with another finding by Avery—that only one in five students see tolerance as a duty of citizenship and one in four see no relationship at all between tolerance and citizenship—then the challenges to social studies educators seem apparent.

Reflecting Dewey's perspective, Parker (2001) notes that "the norms and ideals of a political community will require citizens suited to them, and the formation of these citizens is the goal of citizenship education" (p. 98; see also Neimi, Junn, & Stehlik-Barry, 1995). Parker believes a gap exists between multicultural education and citizenship education. But, if multiculturalism now forms part of the national narrative, then why hasn't it permeated more thoroughly into the social studies curriculum? Parker believes four reasons account for this gap: understanding democracy as an accomplishment rather than an aspiration, misunderstandings of democratic citizenship as cultural rather than political identity, ethnocentrism among educators, and the failure to look at the interdependence of diversity and unity in sustaining and enriching the American experiment. These problems suggest the difficulties that will confront anyone committed to introducing gender and sexuality alongside race and ethnicity in a truly multicultural form of citizenship education.

Many social studies educators agree with Parker that this gap is "miseducative" (p. 98; see also Feinberg, 1998). The silencing of stories and privileging of a small number of American voices in the social studies curriculum, as commonly conceived and practiced in this country (Santora, 2001), undercuts the ability of students/citizens to engage directly with diverse peoples and experiences, thus poorly preparing them for the society they will encounter as adults. It is difficult to know how many social studies educators would include gender and sexuality alongside race and ethnicity as part of the multicultural platform. Many reasons for self-censorship by experienced teachers may exist. Although gender and sexuality are clearly connected (Crocco, 2001), explaining avoidance of these topics in the school curriculum may require some distinctions. Taken together, the reasons for ignoring gender and sexuality in the social studies curriculum might include the following: (a) the sense that gender has been "taken care of" because it was introduced as an issue in the 1970s and 1980s; (b) the belief that women's equality has been achieved in this country, so forms of "compensatory" education are not needed; (c) the unwillingness to tackle a subject that deals with "controversial issues," especially sexuality; (d) a sense that dealing with homosexuality intrudes on family values or religious beliefs; (e) sexism and homophobia among teachers. Whatever the reasons for the silence about gender and sexuality in the social studies curriculum, this misrepresentation of our national narrative and the false view it gives about who the American people are undercuts educators' ability to provide the knowledge, attitudes, and dispositions necessary for democratic schooling.

Besides problems with *what* we teach in civic education, Parker (2001) notes problems with *how* we teach, finding that "democracy is viewed and taught mainly as an accomplishment" (p. 109). In light of this, consider the insights of social learning theory, which holds that most of what we know comes to us through modeling—in other words, by watching others, forming an idea of behavior, and then applying it as a guide for action (Bandura, 1971). If democracy is seen only as an accomplishment, rather than an ongoing struggle, or if it is taught without modeling citizenship competencies such as deliberation, tolerance, inclusion of diverse pasts and perspectives, social awareness, and fairness, then the prospects for the "discourse of civility" in a "strong democracy" (Barber, 1984) (which Barber, 1999,) says are characterized by commonality, deliberation, inclusiveness, provisionality, listening, learning, lateral communication, imagination, empowerment) will be bleak (pp. 42–45).

Engaging in a discourse of civility requires citizenship competence, which has been taken to mean many things:

> Ever since Aristotle advised that democratic citizens must be capable of ruling and being ruled, the competence of citizens has been a subject for political theory and a worry for practicing democrats. The catalog of requisite cognitive and practical skills and moral dispositions is wide ranging. It includes the capacity of voters to judge character, attend to politically relevant information, and critically assess political claims. . . . Democratic competence entails more active participation, too. . . . And any list includes virtues such as tolerance, a sense of justice, willingness to provide collective goods and to accept sometimes painful policies, and the disposition to exercise one's rights and protect the rights of others. Of course, every one of these competences takes a backseat behind the capacity to exercise the necessary iota of self-restraint that keeps citizens from vicious public expressions of hatred and from violence. (Rosenblum, 1999, p. 67)

In a pluralistic and democratic mass society such as our own, citizenship competence must be enacted in everyday life as well as periodically at the ballot box. Rosenblum (1999) believes that two dispositions stand out as important in this regard: "treating others 'identically and with easy spontaneity'"—a phrase she borrows from Shklar—and "speaking out about ordinary injustice" (p. 68). One thinks of Avery's disturbing findings concerning the lack of acceptance among today's students of tolerance as a civic value:

> Moreover, citizens who are incapable of exhibiting these dispositions or who cannot expect to be treated with easy spontaneity are the truly excluded; indeed this lack of public standing is as serious, if not as evident, as exclusion from political rights. Viewed sociologically, small daily slights, arbitrariness, and public shows of deference or bullying are a form of ritual contempt or profanation. Viewed politically, they declare their objects second-class citizens. (Rosenblum, 1999, p. 68)

Historically, opponents of democracy have rested their case on what they took to be pervasive evidence of citizens' incompetence. Today, more faith seems to exist in democracy than was the case in the 18th century. Nevertheless, evidence like Avery's certainly gives one pause. As social studies educators, we must bear some responsibility for failures to promote the centrality of tolerance to a democratic society. Moreover, many thoughtful people have expressed concerns over the overall health of the civic polity. Questions have arisen about the adequacy of citizens' preparation for civic life, their declining participation in voting and community building, and the array of competencies demanded within a truly pluralistic democracy (see, e.g., Putnam, 2000; Sandel, 1998; Skocpol & Fiorina, 1999).

Many writers prescribe educational remedies, at least in part, to these problems. Niemi, Junn, and Stehlik-Barry (1996) talk about education as a means of creating "democratic enlightenment" and suggest the dimensions critical to this end. The common features across the varied programs of civic education they review, what might be considered the *sine qua non* of civic education, include teaching for this set of goals: elevated social awareness, sensitivity to difference, respect for basic norms of universal justice, capacity for democratic deliberation, readiness to become involved in civil society, and advocacy for one's positions (Steiner, 1999, p. 231).

How much of current social studies education embodies these features? Clearly, not as much as is necessary, especially if we wish to inculcate civic competencies necessary for strong democracy, including treating others equitably and speaking out about ordinary injustice. A further question should be posed: Does research show that civic education makes any difference at all? The good news is that social scientists have consistently shown a positive relationship between years of schooling and citizenship knowledge, attitudes, and behavior (Parker, 2000, p. 100; see also Niemi & Junn, 1998). Many analysts would agree with Nie and Hillygus (2001), whose data "clearly suggest that creating a more vibrant and attractive social science curriculum to attract more students will create a more participatory, engaged, and public-regarding citizenry (at least among young college graduates)" (p. 51).

Social studies educators can make a difference. Of note, the field has begun to address gender and sexuality in its publications. A recent issue of *Theory and Research in Social Education* deals with the topic of homophobia and provides a range of reflections, teaching strategies, and resources on gender and sexuality in the social studies (e.g., Levstik & Groth, 2002; Marchman, 2002, Oesterreich, 2002). A sense of urgency pervades the contributions to that issue, because it is clear that attention to this subject is long overdue within the field. As we critique the past and present and face the future, educators committed to democracy in a society that takes multiculturalism as its hallmark must use their energies, intellects, and imaginations to model democracy in the pages of research journals, at conferences, and throughout the public spaces of schooling. Our future as a democratic nation depends on it.

REFERENCES

Anderson, B. (1983). *Imagined communities: Reflections on the origin and spread of nationalism.* London: Verso.

Avery, P. (2002). Political socialization, tolerance, and sexual identity. *Theory and Research in Social Education, 30,* 190–198.

Bandura, A. (1971). *A social learning theory.* Mornshown, NJ: General Learning Press.

Barber, B. (1999). The discourse of civility. In S. Elkin and K. E. Soltan (Eds.), *Citizen competence and democratic institutions* (pp.39-49). State College, PA: Pennsylvania State University Press.

Barber, B. (1984). *Strong democracy.* Berkeley: University of California Press.

Bickmore, K. (2002). How might social education resist heterosexism? Facing the impact of gender and sexual identity ideology on citizenship. *Theory and Research in Social Education, 30,* 198–217.

Boydston, J. (Ed.). (1987). *John Dewey: The later years, 1925.* Carbondale: Southern Illinois University Press.

Cornbleth, C. (2001). Climates of constraint/restraint of teachers and teaching. In W. B. Stanley (Ed.), *Critical issues in social studies research for the 21st century* (pp. 73–95). Greenwich, CT: Information Age Publishers.

Crocco, M. (2002). Homophobic hallways: Is anyone listening? *Theory and Research in Social Education, 30,* 217–232.

Crocco, M. (2001). The missing discourse about gender and sexuality in the social studies. *Theory into Practice, 40,* 65–71.

Crocco, M. (2000). Women, citizenship, and the social studies. *The Educational Forum, 65,* 52–62.

Dewey, J. (1916). *Democracy and education.* New York: Macmillan.

Feinberg, W. (1998). *Common schools; uncommon identities.* New Haven, CT: Yale University Press.

Foner, E. (1998). *The story of American freedom.* New York: Norton.

Franck, K. (2002). Rethinking homophobia: Interrogating heteronormativity in an urban school. *Theory and Research in Social Education, 30,* 274–287.

Glazer, N. (1997). *We are all multiculturalists now.* Cambridge, MA: Harvard University Press.

Kerber, L. (1998). *No constitutional right to be ladies: Women and the obligations of citizenship.* New York: Hill & Wang.

Kessler-Harris, A. (2001). *In pursuit of equity: Women, Men and the Quest for Economic Citizenship in 20th century America.* New York: Oxford University Press.

Keyssar, A. (2000). *The right to vote: The contested history of democracy in the United States*. New York: Basic Books.

Levstik, L. & Groth, J. (2002). Scary thing, being an eighth grader: Exploring gender and sexuality in a middle school U.S. History unit. *Theory and Research in Social Education, 30,* 233–255.

Marchman, B. (2002). Teaching about homophobia in a high school civics course. *Theory and Research in Social Education, 30,* 302–306.

Mitchell, K. (2001). Education for democratic citizenship: Transnationalism, multiculturalism, and the limits of liberalism. *Harvard Educational Review, 71,* 51–79.

Nie, H., & Hillygus, D. (2001). Education and democratic citizenship. In D. Ravitch & J. Viteritti (Eds.), *Making good citizens: Education and civil society* (pp. 30-58). New Haven, CT: Yale University Press.

Niemi, R., & Junn, J. (1998). *Civic education: What makes students learn.* New York: Yale University Press.

Niemi, R., Junn, J., & Stehlik-Barry, K. (1996). *Education and democratic citizenship in America. Chicago: University of Chicago Press.*

Oesterreich, H. (2002). "Outing" social justice: Transforming civic education within the challenges of heteronormativity, heterosexism, and homophobia. *Theory and Research in Social Education, 30,* 287–302.

Okihiro, G. (2001). *Common ground: Reimagining American history.* Princeton, NJ: Princeton University Press.

Parker, W. (2001). Toward enlightened political engagement. In W. B. Stanley (Ed.), *Critical issues in social studies research for the 21st century* (pp. 97–119). Greenwich, CT: Information Age Publishers.

Parker, W. (1996). "Advanced" ideas about democracy: Toward a pluralist conception of citizenship education. *Teachers College Record, 98,* 101–126.

Putnam, R. (2000). *Bowling alone: The collapse and revival of American community.* New York: Simon & Schuster.

Rosenblum, N. (1999). Navigating pluralism: The democracy of everyday life (and where it is learned). In S. Elkin & K. E. Soltan (Eds.), *Citizen competence and democratic institutions* (pp. 67-88). State College, PA: Pennsylvania State University Press.

Roy, P. (1997). Language in the classroom: Opening conversations about lesbian and gay issues in senior high English. In J. T. Sears & W. L. Williams, (Eds.), *Overcoming heterosexism and homophobia: Strategies that work* (pp. 209-218). New York: Columbia University Press.

Sandel, M. (1998). *Democracy's discontent.* Cambridge, MA: Belknap Press.

Santora, E. (2001). Interrogating privilege, plurality and possibilities in a multicultural society. In W. B. Stanley (Ed.), *Critical issues in social studies research for the 21st century* (pp. 149-177). Greenwich, CT: Information Age Publishers.

Sears, J., & Williams, W. (Eds.). (1997). *Overcoming heterosexism and homophobia: Strategies that work.* New York: Columbia University Press.

Shklar, J. (1991). *American citizenship: The quest for inclusion. Cambridge,* MA: Harvard University Press.

Skocpol, T., & Fiorina, M. (Eds.). (1999). *Civic engagement and American democracy.* Washington, DC: Brookings Institution Press.

Smith, R. (2001). Citizenship and the politics of people building. *Citizenship Studies, 5,* 73–96.

Smith, R. (1997). *Civic ideals: Conflicting visions of citizenship in U.S. history.* New Haven, CT: Yale University Press.

Steiner, D. (1999). Searching for education coherence. In S. Elkin & K. Soltan (Eds.), *Civic competence and democratic institutions* (pp. 225–259). State College, PA: Pennsylvania State University Press.

Thornton, S. (2002). Does everybody count as human? *Theory and Research in Social Education 30,* 178–189.

Trouillot, M-R. (1995). *Silencing the past: Power and the production of history.* Boston: Beacon Press.

Chapter 3

Service Learning as a Strategy to Promote Citizenship Education and Civic Engagement in an Urban Elementary Charter School

Bernadette Chi and Tim Howeth

With the assistance of Tara Kintz, Cathleen Micheaels, Richard Lodish, Joanna Lennon
East Bay Conservation Corps
Oakland, California

On September 5, 2001, school began much like it did in thousands of schools across the country. A diverse group of children arrived on the opening day of the East Bay Conservation Corps (EBCC) Charter School with various degrees of excitement, anxiety, and anticipation. The Head of Elementary School and Dean of Students warmly greeted new students and their parents at the front gates. Some children, spanning grades K–4, stood uneasily around the asphalt play yard and warily sized each other up, whereas others were eager to make new friends and explore their new school.

We had no idea that a week later the September 11th attacks would create a new sense of urgency for us to realize the belief stated in our mission "that public schools must prepare children for the challenges, opportunities and responsibilities of life in a democratic, pluralistic society".

In its opening year, the elementary level of the EBCC Charter School faced many challenges that went beyond fostering student civic engagement. Some of the challenges and opportunities included the selection of core academic curricula; the evolution of music, visual arts, and physical education programs; the creation of a discipline policy; and the development of a strong parent association. However, as indicated in the mission of the school, building civic skills, competencies, and dispositions remained central to the work of every teacher

and staff member. Service learning was one of the primary strategies for fostering student civic engagement, but as is discussed further later, it was only one of
many strategies used by the school staff to support civic education and to promote civic engagement among elementary school students.

This chapter serves both to document the work of the teachers and school
during this year, as well as to articulate questions and issues that need to be addressed for improvement. Because it was the initial year of the school and the
first time a few of the teachers attempted service-learning projects in their classroom, the focus of the chapter is primarily on why and how service learning is
being used as a strategy for civic education from the perspective of the school's
faculty and administration.

LITERATURE REVIEW

There is evidence of youth civic disengagement even if it is somewhat contradictory (Battistoni, 2002; Galston, 2001; Gibson, 2001; National Association of
Secretaries of State, 1999). In addition, Putnam (2000) reports overall decreases
on a variety of indicators of social capital that he defines as the "connections
among individuals—social networks and the norms of reciprocity and trustwor-
thiness that arise from them" (p. 19).

In addition, it appears that schools have lost focus on their civic mission to
prepare youth to be engaged, responsible citizens (Conover & Searing, 2000;
Oakes, Hunter Quartz, Ryan, & Lipton, 2000; Reich, 2002). This chapter describes an urban elementary school that specifically has chosen to use service
learning as its primary strategy to promote youth civic engagement and civic
development. The findings of this case study address several gaps in the literature on civic education.

First, this study focuses on the civic engagement and service-learning experiences of elementary school students. Much of the discussion and research on
youth civic engagement focuses on high school-age youth, college students and
young adults (e.g., Melchior, 1999; Eyler & Giles, 1999; Morgan & Streb, 2001;
Perry & Katula 2001; Weiler et al., 1998; Walt Whitman Center for the Culture
and Politics of Democracy, 1998). This case study focuses on the ways in which
elementary-age students and the educators with whom they work engage in civic
education. It considers what kinds of knowledge, skills, attitudes, and behaviors
can and should be fostered in the K–4 grades to provide a foundation for future
civic engagement.

Second, by focusing on service learning as the primary strategy, our case
study addresses proposed reforms in civic education that go beyond teaching
content to also fostering skills and attitudes for active participation (National

Council of the Social Studies [NCSS], 2001). This study contributes to civic education literature in several ways: by focusing beyond social studies to examine how civic outcomes can be taught through other disciplines, and by examining project-based, issue-based and student-centered practices (Cuban, 1991) to teach academic and civic knowledge, skills, and attitudes in integrated, authentic way.

Research Questions

These limitations in the literature and our own needs to assess the development and progress of students in achieving our school literacies led the teachers and staff of the EBCC to examine the following research questions:

- Civic Engagement at the Elementary Level: What does civic engagement and citizenship preparation look like in the K–5 grade levels? What are appropriate measures to document student progress in their civic development?

- Program Theory: Why do we believe that service learning is a promising strategy to prepare students for civic engagement/citizenship? (i.e., What is our "program theory" for desirable activities and outcomes?) How can service-learning experiences help prepare students for citizenship in an increasingly connected, global society?

- Benefits and Limitations of Service Learning: What aspects of civic engagement/citizenship does service learning help to promote? What are the limitations of service-learning? What other activities (classroom and school) foster students' civic engagement? What are the challenges of implementing service learning?

Methods

Data is drawn primarily from individual teacher interviews, classroom observations of service-learning projects, school documents, teacher biweekly newsletters to parents, student records, and staff meeting notes throughout the school year. The data was collected and analyzed by EBCC staff and drafts of the findings were circulated to school administrators and two lead teachers at the EBCC Charter School whose perspectives were incorporated. Although we would like to describe each of the classrooms in detail, we highlight the story of the fourth-grade class and teacher to illustrate the challenges and accomplishments in greater detail.

BACKGROUND OF THE EBCC CHARTER SCHOOL

The elementary level of the EBCC Charter School was created as part of a natural evolution of the education programs and services already offered by the East Bay Conservation Corps. Since 1983, the EBCC has provided leadership in serving low-income urban youth and in developing active learning strategies that imbue young people with a sense of their role in the community. The EBCC Charter School emerged out of the organization's 19-year history in pioneering programs that promote the civic engagement of children and youth within the context of improving public education and strengthening the larger community. The curriculum framework and overall design for the school was created through a 3-year planning process by a national team of educators representing all grade levels and from various fields of expertise, including civic education, spiritual development, research and evaluation, and educational policy.

The EBCC Charter School includes two divisions: the corpsmember high school, which opened in September 1996 and is focused on meeting the immediate educational and employment needs of students between age 18 and 24; and the elementary school, which opened in September 2001 and serves students in grades K–4 (expanding to include Grade 5 in September 2002 and to include middle and high school grades in consecutive years). There were 111 students enrolled in the elementary school during its first year and class size was limited to 20 students, creating a small school community with manageable class sizes.

The foundational beliefs that shaped the EBCC as a youth and community development organization were also the foundation for the guiding principles that shaped the elementary level of the EBCC Charter School. As the mission of the school expresses: "The EBCC Charter School was created out of the belief that public schools must prepare children for the challenges, opportunities and responsibilities of life in a democratic, pluralistic society. Through service-learning, the curriculum and culture of the school integrates service, spiritual development and creative expression across a full range of academic subjects."

To achieve this mission, the EBCC Charter School strives to instill in students two kinds of literacy:

Academic and Artistic Literacy. The ability to read, write, speak, calculate, and reason with clarity and precision and to creatively express oneself through the arts.

Civic Literacy. The ability to "let your life speak" by participating thoughtfully, responsibly, and passionately in the life of the community with concern for the common good.

Ultimately, by engaging students in meaningful service as part of the school's routine and in the larger community, we are preparing them to become enlightened citizens and stewards of the community and environment.

THE PEOPLE AT THE EBCC CHARTER SCHOOL: TEACHERS, STUDENTS, AND FAMILIES

The EBCC Charter School brings together diverse populations of teaching staff, students, and families in common work and vision to achieve students' academic, artistic, and civic literacy. Although the life experiences of the people may vary widely, the commitment to the school's mission creates a common bond from which to work.

An Extraordinary Staff

After receiving over 200 applications for teaching positions at the school, we hired nine incredibly dedicated staff members: six classroom teachers, a half-time art teacher, and full-time music and support teachers. Eight of the nine teachers were credentialed with a range of teaching experience from 1 year to 15 years; many also hold advanced degrees and special certifications. In addition, many teachers have extensive knowledge and demonstrated leadership in various areas critical to the school, including service learning, technology, arts, and curriculum development.

Based on the 70 interviews for teacher candidates, the mission of the school and the opportunity to step in with a start-up of a school drew many of the applicants to the school, seeking to "educate the whole child" and not allow state testing systems to drive a singular focus on academic achievement. In fact, the focus on personal, civic, and spiritual development of children in the context of an environment with high expectations for academic learning was noted by almost every teacher we interviewed.

To prepare for the school year, the teachers participated in a 2-week Summer Teacher Institute in August, which was designed to allow them to create policies and practices that supported the school's culture and mission, to plan classroom activities, and to prepare their curriculum. Teachers also found this time to be invaluable in creating a network of strong relationships and community that would comfort and challenge them—both personally and professionally—throughout the first year.

Students with Diverse Needs and Strengths

One of the guiding principles stated in our charter specifies values, ethics, and spiritual development necessary to thoughtful citizenship in a pluralistic, democratic society. Looking out at the play yard that first day, it was evident that our school would represent a "pluralistic society." There were kids of many ethnicities and socioeconomic levels tentatively beginning to talk and play together. As it would turn out, 85% of the school population consists of students of color and the students are predominantly African American (52%). Also, 22% of the students marked "other" on their applications, suggesting a significant number of multiracial children. Two thirds of the students live in single-parent families. The students came with a range of academic abilities, although many had not been successful in their previous schools. For example, through summer assessments administered by the teacher, the fourth-grade class had a range of reading levels from preliterate to the 6th-grade level. In addition, students came from a variety of academic settings, ranging from charter schools, local public schools, independent schools, and home schooling cooperatives.

Overall, the EBCC Charter School is an urban school in an urban area with its corresponding problems and issues. Yet, we also drew a population of students who had strong skills and had been previously successful in school. This diversity of students was essential to the success within classrooms and schools and became the training ground for tolerance and patience as students learned from each other. As a result, whether we would be able to promote the values, ethics, and spiritual development necessary for democracy and thoughtful citizenship were open questions that we would struggle with those first few weeks and throughout our first year.

The following students' stories provide a snapshot of the student population and the challenges faced by the school in its first year.[1] We return to them at the end of the chapter to report on their development and pathways through the school year.

Derek was one such student who had struggled in previous schools. He was smaller than most of his classmates and had been held back once already. He'd been suspended twice in third grade for fighting and scored at the frustration level on the Qualitative Reading Inventory II. Apparently, his former teacher had allowed him to spend a lot of time under his desk withdrawn from classroom life and had attempted to have him assessed for possible special education services. She had told his mother that Derek was probably retarded, which offended his mother and brought back painful memories of her own school experiences. She refused to allow him to be tested. Through the urging of a "caring adult," a woman who had tutored Derek after school, his mother decided to enroll Derek at the EBCC Charter School. Derek was involved in a physical confrontation that first morning.

The incident involved two other boys who also had a history of violent behavior. Justin was a little out of control and was chasing a basketball. He acci-

---

[1] Students' true names are not used.

dentally knocked down a fourth-grade girl, then grabbed her arm in an attempt to help her up. This offended her cousin, Thomas, who became completely enraged and started hitting and kicking Justin. Derek jumped in to help and a teacher had to physically separate the three boys. So it was with this context of aggression and hostility in which we began the work of building our classroom learning community. It would turn out that throughout the school those first few weeks, there were many incidents of students acting out in defiance and hostility.

Because of this environment of uncertainty and aggression, all of the teachers found ways to create a sense of community at the school, to collectively create a safe and nurturing school culture that would become the foundation of teaching students about civic engagement. The fourth-grade teacher explained how he attempted to build community in his classroom:

> We eventually sat down to our first class meeting. I asked the students to reflect on their school last year. Many expressed experiencing feelings of fear and anxiety: fear of bullies, fear of failure and fear of not being accepted. I explained that we had a chance to create a new, better school. We talked about how we would like to be treated. We agreed on things like fairness, respect and kindness. Together we developed a set of agreements and we all signed them. Our agreements were based on mutual respect. Some of the kids quickly bought into these agreements. Other students such as Justin and Thomas would challenge our agreements.

Although there were also incidents of emotional integrity and intelligence demonstrated by students who modeled the behavior we were seeking to cultivate, it would take time for trust, mutual respect, and a sense of responsibility to develop. The "glue" that would make our community strong would be positive relationships.

CREATING A CULTURE OF CIVIC ENGAGEMENT

Defining What "Civic Engagement" Looks Like

Based on a review of the literature and curriculum, the school's development team was aware of the need to create age-appropriate resources to promote civic engagement at the elementary level as much of the research and available curriculum focused on the middle and high school levels. As a result, we had to discuss and work out in practice with the classroom teachers what civic engagement looked like in Grades K through 4, including civic skills, attitudes, behaviors, and knowledge.

Based on interviews with the teachers, these skills, attitudes, behaviors, and knowledge ranged from communication, sharing, resolving problems, and listening skills that "form the foundation in kindergarten because social, emotional and personal development are key to a healthy academic student" (kindergarten teacher). The other kindergarten teacher added "awareness of others (e.g., if you bump into others, you apologize), awareness of self in a group (if you stand up talking in the circle, you're affecting other people around you), taking turns, raising your hand, using positive words and problem-solving" to his list of "foundational skills and behaviors" necessary to prepare students to be civically engaged.

In contrast, the fourth-grade teacher sought to foster similar but more abstract skills and concepts, such as nurturing individuals who show respect for differences, support each other's growth and learning, feel a responsibility toward others, demonstrate active listening skills, empathize or take someone else's point of view, and ultimately participate or contribute to group efforts. Most importantly, he hoped to nurture kind and caring people. According this teacher, "service-learning has proven to be a powerful strategy to foster skills and attitudes for active participation in the life our community." Although the main strategy to foster civic engagement was service learning, other classroom- and school-based strategies are also described.

Value of Service Learning

Our theory to support service learning as an integral strategy for civic education is based on over 15 years of program experience in managing service-learning programs for K–12 youth in Oakland Unified School District (OUSD) classrooms. Ultimately, we believe that when students participate in service-learning projects, they gain important opportunities to practice what it means to be a citizen. For example,

- Students become knowledgeable about issues in their community because they are asked to identify issues that they observe or care about.
- Students feel empowered to contribute and to make a difference because they have the opportunity to actually do so.
- Students are exposed to opportunity to practice groupwork skills, communication skills, diversity of perspectives among other skills and attitudes that are significant for civic engagement.

- Students are exposed to broader policy issues that provide context for many issues in our communities.

- Students are encouraged to give and to share their skills/talents to help/benefit others: As observed by one of the teachers, "service-learning provides students an opportunity to apply what they are learning—it's really motivating because students get excited about doing something that is real and helping other people."

- Ultimately, students practice what it means to be an active citizen and community member: "[Service-learning is] such a really human thing. A lot of times what we do in the classroom is so abstract—with service-learning, it is so immediate." (classroom teacher)

In every classroom, students were engaged in a variety of service-learning projects based on broad themes selected by teachers to organize their curriculum. We offer a brief description of each of the projects across the school and then focus on the fourth-grade class to illustrate in more detail the rich and complex opportunities for civic engagement provided through service-learning experiences. For example, one of the kindergarten classes partnered with the nearby OUSD Child Development Center (CDC) to become reading buddies with the preschool students at the CDC while the other kindergarten class focused on ways to support the school, including lunch clean up and collecting attendance to fulfill the class theme of *Nurturing and Growing*. These activities fostered literacy development, as well as "foundational skills" for civic engagement.

As part of their class theme, *Helping Hands*, the first-grade class constructed window planter boxes for every classroom, tying together their study of plants, literature, and measurement. The second-grade class learned about murals in Oakland and San Francisco and focused on school beautification by designing graphics based on the life practices of the school and painting the main benches at the school to enliven their class theme, *Neighborhoods*. The second/third-grade class participated in an intergenerational project connecting interviewing skills, math activities, musical performances, and a quilting project with elders at the nearby senior center as part of their class theme, *Branching Out*.

The fourth-grade theme was *Circle of Life*, because each class member would be considered an integral part of the whole. The initial focus was to develop community within the classroom because before we could challenge students academically, artistically or civically, we needed to create a safe place to talk about and to prepare them to be ready to give in a sincere way. In addition to developing class agreements, community was built through a variety of classroom practices. For example, our theme was practiced daily as we sat in our community circle. The importance of each person's voice was stressed as we developed listening skills. A Native American *Talking Stick* was passed around to ensure that there would be one speaker at a time. Yoga, deep relaxation, and creative visualization classes helped kids learn to center and focus. Many cooperative learning activities were planned for team building, class building, and trust building during the first weeks. Instruction was differentiated, especially in reading, word study, and math, so students worked at their instructional levels and quickly began to experience academic success.

After fostering classroom community, the class focused on the school community and how they could participate in the life of the school. Early in the semester, the fourth-grade class partnered up with a kindergarten class for budding reading. This was one of the most successful service-learning projects because of the affectionate and caring relationships that developed. Success was experienced by both sets of students. Different levels of literacy development occurred for the fourth graders as well as the kindergartners. Students read to each other, wrote partner stories and poems, did art projects together, and co-wrote a manual on how to be a good buddy what the kindergarten class read to their preschool buddies. This project was so successful that all of the classes began to engage in buddy reading throughout the remainder of the school year.

The students then expanded their focus of concern to the larger community. During walking field trips, the fourth graders completed a community needs assessment. Many were concerned with homeless people in our community and wondered how they would get enough to eat. This was the beginning of the first service-learning project and their first cooperative group of four students began what would become weekly trips to serve at a local soup kitchen.

The teacher found opportunities to connect the projects to the California state standards for fourth grade as he was able to address students' concerns, community needs, and the fourth-grade curriculum by customizing the service-learning projects. The students began a study of nutrition with an exploration of the food pyramid and enjoyed examples of healthy snacks. They developed math skills working with statistics about food provided from the Alameda County Food Bank. They wrote different forms of poetry throughout the year on the different aspects of their projects.

This service was followed by written and artistic reflection. Students reported feeling very positive and enthusiastic about helping, making a difference, and feeling satisfied about doing something "good." Parents wrote notes of gratitude. One parent wrote that her daughter, who happened to have a learning disability, was thrilled at having the opportunity to serve at the soup kitchen and was feeling very positive and successful about school for the first time. The class also packed food at the food bank. By this time, the class was really starting to gel into a cohesive community. They worked together at the food bank with enthusiasm and at one point spontaneously began singing our school song

("I am free, I let go, I let my spirit be my guide, My heart is open wide, It's the practice of my life. Peace is my purpose, It's the practice of my life.").

A Schoolwide Culture Of Civic Engagement: Other Classroom- and School-Based Strategies

Whereas service learning was our primary strategy for promoting student civic engagement and development, it was not the only strategy used at the school. Service learning existed within a school culture that supported civic engagement and education on a variety of levels, as illustrated by the following aspects of the school:

Schoolwide Meetings. Schoolwide meetings provided an opportunity for students and adults to come together as a school community. Every Monday morning all of the students and teachers sat in silence in a large circle in our music room. Out of the quiet, children and adults were invited to share their reflections and thoughts with the entire school. On Fridays, all students participated in an assembly where the school song was sung. There was also time set aside for students and teachers to honor or praise one another. During our first "honoring," a second grader stood up in front of everyone and proudly said, "I want to thank all the people who volunteered their time to clean and build our great school."

Life Practices. To translate the school's mission into concrete expectations, we developed clear "life practices" about how to participate in the life of our school, which are boldly posted in our school's entryway and in all our classrooms:

> Be honest to yourself and others;
> Be a thoughtful listener;
> Speak from your heart;
> Be respectful of the differences we share;
> Be open to challenges and opportunities to grow;
> Be alive with purpose and practice thanks; and
> Find your part and work together.

Although present in every classroom and throughout the school, these practices were brought to life especially through the music and arts programs.

Art and Music Classes. Both the music and art teachers provided many opportunities for students to reflect and to learn about themselves and about others in a communal way. According to the music teacher, music was used to support "communication and self-discovery." The music teacher contributed significantly to the school community by composing the school song and other original music in student productions that exemplified the school's mission and life practices and that related to what they were reading or learning in the classroom. The art teacher also made a special effort to connect students' work to the life practices, assisting students in creating designs for school benches and large medallions that have beautified the school.

Discipline Policy. As in many urban schools, the persistent disruptive behavior of a number of children throughout the school presented us with serious obstacles to student learning, as exemplified by the second-grade teacher's note to parents:

> One of the areas where I have been most challenged thus far is in classroom behavior. I realized a little too late that this class needs a little more structure than I had originally thought. Now I am backtracking just a little bit and pulling the reins more tightly. Structured procedures and high expectations are necessary in maintaining a classroom environment that fosters both interactive and independent learning. I ask that parents support me in this by discussing with your children the importance of listening, following directions, and working toward collective goals in the classroom.

The head of the elementary school took leadership in addressing this issue with parents. For example, at our first parent back-to-school night (which 80% of our parents attended), he stressed the need to balance firmness, structure, and clear disciplinary policies with lots of gentleness, love, and academic challenge, a balance that would help create a cooperative school environment. On the second Monday of school, after our initial period of silence, he stood in front of the students and sounded a lot like Sidney Poitier in *To Sir With Love,* telling the students in no uncertain terms: "You will respect each other, you will listen to your class mates and your teachers, you will not hit or fight in OUR school, we need to be a comfortable and safe place where everyone can learn the best they can."

Teachers also took leadership to create a new discipline policy with yellow and red cards to document increasingly serious infractions of school rules. In addition, the policy also rewarded students by filling out green cards that documented students' positive contributions to the school, or "gotcha for being good."

Peer Mediation and Playground Monitors. Students have also taken a great deal of responsibility for many aspects of the day-to-day life of the school, fostering a feeling that this school belonged to us. Third and fourth graders have volunteered to monitor the playground, giving up play time to be trained as peer mediators. In addition, each class takes responsibility to do a maintenance job around the school, such as cleaning the cafeteria tables or cleaning the halls.

After 9 months, there were many noticeable changes that indicate a developing culture of civic engagement. For one thing, the hallways became much quieter. Students were kinder to each other and much more willing and able to settle disputes with words and negotiation instead of violence. There were signs of respect, kind smiles, polite words, and handshakes. The entire school was able to sit in utter silence for up to 10 minutes of communal reflection during our Monday meetings and students stood up in front of the entire school to express gratitude and to honor classmates, teachers, and staff. As we celebrated these indicators of our success in creating a caring and challenging school culture at the end of our first year, we were faced with many challenges along the way.

STUDENT OUTCOMES

> Service learning has proven to be an ideal instructional strategy in which to promote positive relationships, the development of positive self concept, and student learning. In addition, academics are not sacrificed by service-learning as evidenced by my end of year reading assessments and I am finding that all of the students made significant progress in their reading. (Classroom Teacher)

As indicated by this statement, service-learning experiences fostered powerful student outcomes, although not all were easily assessed. To help us assess student "civic engagement", an external evaluation consultant interviewed each teacher and identified at least 10 criteria that represented what "civic engagement" and "civic literacy" looked like in each grade level. These criteria were compiled as teacher observation checklists of student attitudes and behaviors that were used as documentation of student progress for the quarterly report cards. After the first round of piloting in the middle of the first year, the evaluator revised the checklists to contain five of the most desired criteria across all of the grades for the school.

Teachers administered the checklists for each student at the end of the school year and these lists represent evidence for the teachers to grade their students in service learning and civic engagement on their end-of-year report cards.

We will continue to use the civic engagement checklists at the beginning and end of each school year to document student civic development along age-appropriate indicators. We plan to revise the checklists for the 2002–2003 school year to remain grade specific, but they will also include a few schoolwide indicators.

The five indicators included the following:

1. This student takes the perspective of others to understand why they do what they do.
2. This student shows an appreciation for the contributions of other team members by finding appropriate times and ways to take turns.
3. This student demonstrates problem solving and communication skills, such as "ask three before me."
4. This student does not require constant reinforcement; is able to self-regulate and self-reinforce for positive behavior as well as reduce and check negative impulses and behavior.
5. This student is respectful and courteous.

Students were rated by their teachers along a 1 ("emerging") to 5 ("secure") scale. A rating of 3 was considered "developing." A rating of "not observed" was also available to teachers to assess students. An analysis of all of the check-lists (N = 98) showed that of the five indicators, the most number of students (60% with score of 4 or 5) were assessed as close to secure or secure in the indi-cator of students' demonstrating "respectful and courteous" behaviors (school average score 3.66). Overall, the teacher ratings illustrated that the greatest need for the school is to improve the first indicator, helping students "take the per-spective of others to understand why they do what they do" (school average score 2.89) as only 35% of the students received a score of 4 or 5.

Unfortunately, because the checklists were not developed at the beginning of the school year, we were not able to track growth in individual student behav-iors. But the following teacher comments on the checklists suggest the wide-scale changes that occurred for many students as the school developed its culture and high expectations for student civic behaviors:

> (The student) will see things that need to be done around the classroom and do them. She helps other students when they are working on math. She has made great improvements in her ability to listen to others and understand their perspectives. She can verbally solve more problems than at the beginning of the year. She can use various resources to problem solve and has begun to take initiative in helping herself and

others. She still needs a lot of positive reinforcement and regulation for negative behaviors. She can be respectful and courteous.

(The student) has begun to figure out how to do things on his own—asks his neighbors (at his table) before asking the teachers. He has made great progress in all areas of his behavior this year. He still can continue to work in specific areas, but he has worked hard. He is able to listen to others' perspectives at times, but still frequently argues his own perspective at the correct one. He is able to take turns and work with others in a group. When he has difficulties with his behavior such as shouting, not following instructions and arguing, he is able to change his behavior and return to the group more quietly than in previous months. He can be respectful and courteous but on "off" days, he says very inappropriate comments to his teachers and peers.

Not all students began the school year with challenging behaviors. One teacher wrote that a student in her class "demonstrates a high level of civic engagement. He is the student to pull an ice pack out of his lunch for an injured student, he is the one to clean out the turtle bowl or give up his turn/seat/share to give to another. He does many acts selflessly and to not gain recognition."

So what kind of changes took place in the three students mentioned at the beginning of this chapter? Thomas unfortunately continued to exhibit severely aggressive, hostile, and antisocial behavior. Apparently, he had the same problems at his former school and was to be assessed for a possible emotional disability. His mother withdrew him from the EBCC Charter School in mid-January after several suspensions.

Derek was not involved in any further violent behavior after that first day. In fact, he has become a very affectionate, cooperative, and helpful student. In addition, he has made over 3 years progress this year in reading, even though he is still reading at the third-grade level. His success has resulted in much greater confidence and greater self-esteem. His mother has been very positive about his progress at this school and has agreed to give permission for him to be assessed for special education.

Finally, Justin has also shown significant progress. His reading level has gone from the first-grade to fourth-grade level. He still needs a lot of support due to impulsive and emotional behavior; however, he is having his most successful school year yet. He is a very enthusiastic participant in service-learning projects. He is a very caring and patient buddy to his kindergarten partner and expressed feelings of pride in his accomplishments. He developed many positive relationships with peers and adults alike this past year.

To address the other areas of student achievement and development, academic assessments include many forms of teacher-developed methods of assessment and teachers used other assessments to document student academic progress. For example, the fourth-grade teacher focused on student reading abilities and reported the following findings:

As noted earlier, Table 2.1 shows a wide range in students' reading abilities at the beginning of the school year, as students scored between PrePrimer Frustration level to Grade Level 6. The classroom average shows students scoring slightly below Grade Level 4. By the end of the school year, students' reading scores averaged 5.5 and with the exception of one student, all students were reading at or above grade level (score of 4 or higher). The one student who scored below grade level gained at least three grade levels by the end of the year, making tremendous academic progress. In short, students did not appear to sacrifice academic learning because of their extensive involvement in service learning.

TABLE 2.1: Fourth-Grade Language Arts Assessments 2001–2002

	Qualitative Reading Inventory II Levels[a]		
	Fall 2001	Spring 2002	Grade Change
Student 1	3	5	2
Student 2	4	5	1
Student 3	PrePrimer	3	3
Student 4	4	5	1
Student 5	1	5	4
Student 6	5	6	1
Student 7	4	6	2
Student 8	5	Junior High	2
Student 9	3	5	2
Student 10	5	6	1
Student 11	5	6	1
Student 12	3	5	2
Student 13	5	6	1
Student 14	5	Junior High	2
Student 15	6	Junior High	1
Student 16	2	4	2
Student 17	4	5.5	1.5
Classroom Average	*3.76*	*5.5*	*1.74*

[a] For the purposes of analyzing changes in grade levels, "PrePrimer" was scored as "0" and "Junior High" was scored as "7."

CHALLENGES OF SERVICE LEARNING AND CIVIC EDUCATION

As discussed earlier, behavior issues with some of the students presented a serious challenge this first year as a new school with new students. As one teacher observed, "With my students, they don't have any problems with their academics. With my class, it's all about the civic education the behavior issues." Beyond behavior issues, every teacher was challenged by their students with highly diverse needs, from students who had been home schooled and were several grades ahead of their peers academically to other students who had struggled with school from the very beginning and were several grades behind.

The challenges of meeting the needs of diverse learners was in the context of teachers also implementing new curriculum, working with new colleagues, and coming to terms with new expectations for their work. As one teacher explained, "I am very motivated but sometimes feel very challenged—I have all the freedom I was asking for last year and yet I am not certain how to get my arms around all of this. I don't want to just return to what's comfortable."

There were requests for designated time for teachers to plan with each other; to develop, refine, and provide staff development; and to create a master plan with integration of the various curricular and service-learning projects across grade-level themes. Staff faced the logistical challenges of implementing meaningful service learning projects for their students, reinforcing the need for a service-learning project coordinator to help make contacts in the community and organize project logistics.

New forms of assessment were also needed to help document students' progress along dimensions unfamiliar to most public schools. For example, there was the need to think through the developmental outcomes of civic engagement at each grade level. In coordination with an educational evaluator, we developed teacher observation "checklists" of student aptitudes that related to the development of civic engagement for each grade level. In addition, descriptions of service-learning projects were developed that pay particular attention to how service-learning experiences helped to foster civic outcomes and enhanced academic and artistic learning.

With the observed power of service-learning activities in fostering many desired outcomes, including civic engagement, there were also potential limits as to what service-learning experiences may teach students.

Potential Limits of Service Learning

A few teachers observed that the relationship between direct service projects and the "next steps" for civic participation were not automatic. That is, students did not automatically take the "next step" of asking what else can be done beyond the service activity to address a particular social issue or need. Unless they are prompted or facilitated by teachers or adults, students may not understand that issues such as homelessness or hunger may also be addressed through other activities such as writing letters to political leaders to raise awareness of the issue, working with other organizations who address the issue in other ways, or questioning if there are other more effective ways to deal with hunger beyond going to a soup kitchen.

There was also some disagreement about whether service learning can teach all content: Service-learning experiences can certainly support or reinforce learning across many subject areas, but they did not replace direction instruction about some content or skills. Also a few teachers felt that students would get bored if the same content was stressed over and over again. So service-learning experiences required teachers to balance their need to teach content and skills with the need to follow students' interests and needs.

IMPLICATIONS

Service learning is a powerful civic educator that reaches many domains of student development—including civic, social, personal, and academic—because it enables students with diverse learning styles and personal needs to thrive. Service learning, however, cannot exist in a vacuum. Projects need to be supported by school culture and classroom practices that value active contributions from students. This environment is very different from what is currently occurring in many public schools and classrooms that focus on academic content learning driven by high-stakes testing.

Service learning also has potential limitations as a civic educator. Service learning experiences may be positive for developing efficacy as individuals and exposing students to issues in the community and it reinforces academic content and skills. However, there needs to be teacher intentionality in bridging service-learning activities with "next steps" that address larger issues of social justice (ways that students can be effective using other strategies to address social issues beyond direct service). This process does not happen automatically and teachers need assistance to think through how to make this happen in age-appropriate ways. This will help us create a form of civic education that does not simply promote volunteerism but motivates students to question why there are social ills in the first place and to address them in ways beyond direct service.

To close, we suggest that parents represent significant stakeholders in the success of the school and as evaluators of what we do. Many parents have written their teachers and the school administration with their assessments of the school. A parent of a third grader wrote the following, which represents the hope of the school in nurturing motivated learners who are caring contributors to the community:

> I am extremely impressed with the way the school has evolved in such a short duration of time. My daughter is absolutely thriving. When I pick her up after school she is bubbling over with information about her day. At night, she is excited and diligent about her homework. Her reading has improved immensely in just these four months and she is writing stories and poems that aren't even assigned! At home, she paints pictures and sings songs that are peaceful and kind. [All this] has infused a simple sense of spirituality in her that she carries throughout her daily life.

REFERENCES

Battistoni, R. (2002). *Civic engagement across the curriculum: A resource book for service-learning faculty in all disciplines.* Providence, RI: Campus Compact.

Conover, P. J., & Searing, D. S. (2000). A political socialization perspective. In L. M. McDonnell, P. M. Timpane, & R. Benjamin (Eds.), *Rediscovering the democratic purposes of education.* Lawrence: University of Kansas Press.

Cuban, L. (1991). History of teaching in social studies. In J. Shaver (Ed.), *Handbook of research on social studies teaching and learning* (pp. 197–210). New York: Macmillan.

Galston, W. (2001, November 16). Can patriotism be turned into civic engagement? *Chronicle of Higher Education, B16.*

Gibson, G. (2001, November 16). *From inspiration to participation: A review of perspectives on youth civic engagement.* Berkeley, CA: BTW Consultants/Grantmaker Forum on Community and National Service.

Morgan, W., & Streb, M. (2001). Building citizenship: How student voice in service learning develops civic values. *Social Science Quarterly, 8(1),* 154–169.

National Association of Secretaries of State. (1999). *New Millennium Project—Phase I: A nationwide study of 15–24 year old youth.* Washington, DC: National Association of Secretaries of State.

National Council of the Social Studies. (2001). NCSS position statement: Creating effective citizens. *Social Education, 65(5),* 319.

Oakes, J., Hunter Quartz, K., Ryan, S., & Lipton, M. (2000). *Civic virtue and the reform mill. Education Week, 19(24),* 43, 68.

Perry, J. L., & Katula, M. C. (2001). Does service affect citizenship? *Administration and Society, 33(3),* 330-365.

Putnam, R. (2000). *Bowling alone: The collapse and revival of American community.* New York: Simon & Schuster.

Reich, R. (2002). *Bridging liberalism and multiculturalism in American education.* Chicago: University of Chicago Press.

Chapter 4

Gender and Civic Education

Carole L. Hahn
Emory University

How might we better prepare all young people to be engaged citizens in a multicultural democracy in an integrated global society? That is the central question facing social studies educators in the United States today. In addressing that question, I believe we ought to give particular attention to one variable that is often overlooked in discussions about civic education—gender. Social studies educators, like young people today, make the assumption that the women's liberation movement of the 1960s and 1970s was successful in achieving gender equity and gender issues are no longer problematic. Although I would agree that citizens of the 21st century face new challenges, I do not agree that gender issues are irrelevant. Indeed, I believe gender issues require attention as much now as ever. Social studies teachers need to effectively prepare female and male students to be active, participating citizens. Social studies curriculum and instruction for all students should include information about female and male leaders and active citizens. Social studies classes should include opportunities for all students to investigate gender-related issues. Only with such preparation will citizens be prepared to resolve public policy issues in the future.

This chapter discusses findings from research conducted in the United States on gender differences in civic learning and gender and the social studies curriculum. Additionally, I discuss implications of feminist theory and recent research for needed changes in classroom practice and social studies research. I have argued elsewhere that "despite the centrality of citizenship education to social studies and of gender to human experience, almost no research on gender and political learning has been reported in the social studies literature" (Hahn, 1996, p. 8). That situation has improved slightly in recent years. However, teachers, curriculum developers, and teacher educators still pay too little attention to the implications of the new scholarship for social studies practice. Furthermore, there remains much that we do not know, which requires future researchers' attention.

GENDER DIFFERENCES IN CIVIC LEARNING

For years researchers reported that U.S. students learned at an early age that politics is a man's world. From the time they were quite young, boys seemed to know more than girls about politics and government and to show greater interest than girls in the political arena. Those gender differences were found throughout the elementary and high school years—until the late 1980s. In a series of recent studies, however, researchers and others have declared the gender gap closed with respect to students' civic and political knowledge. In addition, recent researchers find that gender differences persist in attitudes and experiences in ways that are more subtle and complex than were first thought. New scholarship reveals themes that need to be explored in greater depth if social studies teachers are to be effective in helping students connect new knowledge to their prior beliefs, attitudes, and experiences.

Civic Knowledge

Since the 1960s, researchers have been interested in whether or not there are gender differences in students' civic knowledge. The differences that were found by early researchers seem to have disappeared in recent years.

Past Research. Early political socialization researchers concluded that male students in the United States tended to be more knowledgeable about politics, civics, and government than female students (Easton & Dennis, 1969; Greenstein, 1965; Hess & Torney, 1967). For example, in the classic study of New Haven elementary school students, Greenstein (1965) reported that boys were more likely than girls to recognize the names of political leaders and attend to political news.

Similarly, researchers who analyzed data obtained from large-scale nationally representative samples of students in the 1970s and 1980s concluded that 8th- and 12th-grade males were more knowledgeable about political life than females. Their conclusions were based on student responses to items measuring knowledge of government, law, and international issues used in the National

Assessment of Educational Progress (NAEP) (Anderson, et al., 1990; Applebee, Langer, & Mullis, 1987; Education Commission, 1971, 1973, 1974).[1]

In 1971, the International Association for the Evaluation of Educational Achievement (IEA) conducted the first Civic Education Study. IEA researchers assessed nationally representative samples of 14-year-old students in nine countries for civic knowledge, as well as attitudes and experiences. In that study, researchers found that males scored substantially higher than females in half of the countries, including the United States, on items measuring civic knowledge (Torney-Purta, 1991).

Some researchers gained interesting insights by looking at the content of the multiple-choice items to which males and females responded differently. For example, researchers found the largest gender differences in NAEP results in the 1970s and early 1980s occurred in response to items dealing with World War II, territorial expansion, foreign policy, maps, and chronology (Applebee et al., 1987). Items requiring knowledge of social and economic history yielded smaller gender differences. These findings suggested to researchers that gender differences in student interest were influencing the results.

In 1988, NAEP the gender gap for 12th graders was small. Over all the 150 multiple-choice items, males scored 67% correct, as compared to 64% correct for females—a difference of only three percentage points (Niemi & Junn, 1998). Females did as well as males, and in some cases better, on items about citizen rights, criminal and civil justice, and the United Nations. Males did better than females on items about war, foreign affairs, political parties, elections, lobbying, and protest activities. Similar results were obtained from a statewide assessment in California; males scored higher than females on questions about structure of government, wars, and geography (Kneedler, 1988). Females, on the other hand, performed better than males on items related to democratic processes, rights, and responsibilities, and that focused on female subjects.[2]

---

[1] The NAEP assessments are administered to nationally representative samples of students in the 4th, 8th, and 12th grades. They measure student knowledge in a variety of subjects and the results are reported as "The Nation's Report Card."

[2] A similar phenomena may be occurring when researchers claim that male adults are more politically knowledgeable than females based on asking the respondents to name officials who are predominantly male (DelliCarpini & Keeter, 1996). However, when respondents are living in states that had a female senator, governor, or lieutenant governor, no gender differences were found in knowledge. Furthermore, females are more likely than males to be able to name the head of the local school system (DelliCarpini & Keeter, 1996).

Recent Findings. In contrast to previous researchers, contemporary researchers studying nationally representative samples of students in the United States have found either no gender difference in civic knowledge or on some tasks females exhibit higher levels of achievement than males (Baldi, Perie, Skidmore, Greenberg, & Hahn, 2001; Lutkus, Weiss, Campbell, Mazzeo, & Lazer, 1999; Torney-Purta, Lehmann, Oswald, & Schulz, 2001). In the 1988 NAEP assessment, whereas males were more likely than females to reach the higher levels of proficiency, females scored higher than males on items requiring students to read and interpret text material (Niemi & Junn, 1998). Similarly, in the recent NAEP assessment in civics and government, females in grades 8 and 12 had higher overall average scores than males (Lutkus et al., 1999).

Similar trends were found for the U.S. sample of the IEA Civic Education Study conducted in 1999 (Baldi et al., 2001; Torney-Purta et al., 2001).[3] No gender differences were found in civic knowledge overall or in the subscale measuring knowledge of civic content. Further, on the subscale measuring civic skills, females did significantly better than males (Baldi et al., 2001). That subscale contained items in which students were asked to distinguish fact from opinion, interpret political cartoons, and comprehend information from a fictitious political leaflet. The finding of females' higher achievement on the civic skills scale appears, therefore, to be consistent with the results of the 1988 NAEP in which females did better than males in interpreting text material. It is possible that this is related to other research indicating that females tend do better than males on reading comprehension tasks.

It is clear that today female students are no less knowledgeable than their male peers about civic and political life. Indeed, in some ways, females may be more proficient than males. Gender differences, however, continue to exist in civic attitudes and behaviors, as is apparent in the next two sections.

Attitudes

Political socialization and social studies researchers, primarily using samples of convenience, often have investigated gender differences in student attitudes, such as political interest, efficacy, and trust. Although some researchers operationalized political interest by asking if students followed politics in the media and discussed politics with others, I address those indicators in a later section on

---

[3] IEA studies are administered to nationally representative samples of students. In 1999, surveys were administered to samples in 28 countries. The U.S. sample contained 2,811 ninth graders from 124 public and private schools. The questionnaires were administered in October, near the beginning of the school year (see Baldi et al., 2001, for details).

political experiences. This section focuses on studies of political interest and other attitudes that are measured by attitude surveys and interviews.

Political Interest, Trust, and Efficacy. Typically, survey researchers measure political interest with items such as "I am interested in political matters," or "I would enjoy having lessons where politics and government are discussed." Political trust is usually measured by items such as "people in government can be trusted to do what is right for the country," "most people in government are honest," and "people in government care a lot about what all of us think." Using such measures, I found no gender differences in political interest or political trust among students in the ninth-grade civics classes I studied for one case study (Hahn, 1996).[4] Similarly, as part of another study conducted in selected schools in five Western democracies, I found little or no gender difference on political interest and political trust scales for the samples from the United States in both 1986 and 1994 (Hahn, 1998).[5]

In the recent IEA Civic Education Study, researchers did not measure political trust in terms of trust in politicians or people in government, as in previous studies. Rather, the IEA questionnaire asked students if they trusted a variety of political and government institutions, such as political parties, the local council, national government, the police, Congress/Parliament, or the courts (Torney-Purta et al., 2001). Interestingly, using this new measure, female ninth graders in the United States responded with higher levels of trust in government-related institutions than did males (Baldi et al., 2001).[6]

The findings with respect to political interest are less conclusive. Responses to only one item were reported in the international report and the authors con-

---

[4] In the case study of ninth-grade civics classes, I observed two classes in one school in the southeastern United States over a semester. I interviewed the two teachers of the classes and students in both classes, as well as administered questionnaires to all ninth-grade students in civics classes in the school (see Hahn, 1996).

[5] In 1985–1986 and 1993–1994 I administered questionnaires to purposefully selected samples of students in schools in Denmark, England, Germany, the Netherlands, and the United States. Additionally from 1985–1995, I made observations in the equivalent of social studies classes and interviewed teachers and students (see Hahn, 1998).

[6] That finding is similar to the results reported in the international report for Belgium (French), Denmark, and Switzerland. However, in Cyprus and Portugal, males reported more trust in government institutions than females, and in the other 22 countries, no gender differences were found (Torney et al., 2001).

cluded that there were no gender differences for the U.S. sample (Torney-Purta et al., 2001). However, in a secondary analysis of the U.S. data, my colleagues and I found that males were slightly more likely than females to agree with the statement: "I am interested in politics."[7]

A third political attitude that has been examined for gender differences over the years is political efficacy — the belief that citizens can "make a difference" in influencing government policies. Most researchers who used nonrepresentative samples of students concluded that there were no gender differences in political efficacy (Blankenship, 1990; Jennings & Niemi, 1974; Lyons, 1970; Owen & Dennis, 1988); one early researcher, however, found males to have higher efficacy than females (Vaillancourt, 1972). In my own work, I found no differences in political efficacy among ninth graders in civics classes in the one school I used for the case study (Hahn, 1996). However, for the U.S. sample in the five nation study, females reported slightly higher levels of efficacy than did males (Hahn, 1998). It is unfortunate that we do not have recent data on this variable from large representative samples, but NAEP assessments do not measure student attitudes and the IEA researchers did not measure political efficacy in terms of belief that citizens can influence local or national government. They did, however, look at efficacy in terms of whether students thought that they could influence school policies. On that variable, female ninth-graders in the United States were more likely than their male counterparts to report confidence that participation in school activities can be effective (Torney-Purta et al., 2001).

The IEA Civic Education Study moved beyond the traditional practice of measuring only political interest, trust, and efficacy. IEA researchers also measured students' attitudes toward citizenship, government, and a number of social issues. With only a few exceptions, males and females in the United States tended to respond to the attitude scales differently.[8]

---

[7] Using weighted responses, 63% of females disagreed that they were interested in politics and 37% said they agreed. In comparison, 59% of males disagreed and 42% agreed with the statement. The difference between male and female responses were significant at the .001 level.

[8] Unlike previous research, the 1999 IEA study contained scales to measure student perceptions of practices that could be considered good for democracy or bad for democracy. Higher percentages of females than males expressed opinions about practices they perceived to be either good or bad for democracy (Baldi et al., 2001). On the scale containing items describing practices that students might perceive as "good for democracy," percentage responses for females were consistently higher than for males. Ninety percent of females, as compared to 85% of males, agreed that having the right to elect political leaders was good for democracy. Similarly, 89% of females agreed, as compared to 83% of males,

Attitudes Toward Citizenship and Government. The IEA questionnaire asked students what behaviors they associated with being a good citizen. The researchers factor analyzed the responses, and labeled the two constructs that emerged "conventional citizenship" and "social-movement related citizenship" (Torney-Purta et al., 2001). No significant gender differences were apparent for U.S. ninth graders on the Conventional Citizenship scale. Similarly, no gender differences were found on this scale for students in 25 of the 28 countries that participated in the study. That is, when looking at the scale as a whole, females and males were equally likely to associate a number of conventional activities with being a good citizen. The conventional activities they considered were: voting in every election, showing respect for government leaders, knowing about the country's history, following political issues in the media, engaging in political discussion, and joining a political party.

In contrast, gender differences were found in response to the Social-Movement Related Citizenship scale. Female ninth graders were more likely than their male counterparts in the United States to say that it is important for a good adult citizen to participate in social movement activities. The activities listed on this scale were helping the community, promoting human rights, and protecting the environment.[9] In responding to items on another scale, U.S. fe-

---

that having many different organizations to join was good for democracy. Females were also more likely than males to agree that policies supporting gender equality were good for democracy. Eighty-eight percent of females, (as compared to 80% of males) agreed that political parties having laws to support women becoming political leaders is good for democracy. Similarly, 78% of females, as compared to 66% of males, agreed that changing laws women claim are unfair to them is good for democracy.

On the scale listing practices students might consider "bad for democracy," females were also more likely than males to agree that particular practices were bad. For example, 79% of females, as compared to 69% of males, said that it was bad for democracy when all television stations present the same opinion. Similarly, 81% of females, as compared to 75% of males said it was bad for democracy when one company owns all the newspapers. And according to 85% of females and 76% of males, it is bad for democracy when wealthy business people have more influence on government. It is not clear why gender differences would appear in responses to this scale. The international report did not include comparative results by gender for other 27 countries on the good–bad for democracy and no other researchers had previously examined this phenomena.

[9] Although no gender differences were found in social movement citizenship in 19 countries, the United States was not alone in finding that females were more

males were also more likely than males to say that the government should be responsible for society-related services (e.g., education, peace and order, health care, standard of living for the elderly, control pollution, promote honesty, and ensure equal political opportunities for women).[10]

National Autonomy. On another attitude scale used in the IEA study, students were asked the degree to which they agreed with items designed to measure attitudes toward national autonomy. In response to such items, male ninth graders were more likely than females to say that the United States should try to prevent countries from influencing political decisions (71% of males agreed, 65% of females agreed). Males were also more likely to say citizens should buy products made in the United States (62% of males, 53% of females) and that we should stop outsiders from trying to influence U.S. traditions and culture (50% of males, 35% of females, Baldi et al., 2001).[11]

Rights for Women. International and national documents, such as the Universal Declaration of Human Rights and many national constitutions written after World War II, assert the importance of women as well as men taking part in governments, yet women remain a minority of political leaders everywhere.[12] Whether or not that discrepancy continues in the future may in part rest with

---

likely than males to associate social movement activities with good citizenship. Similar findings were obtained in Denmark, Finland, Germany, Greece, Italy, Norway, Sweden, and Switzerland. In no countries were males more likely than females to associate good citizenship with social movement activities (Torney-Purta, 2001).

[10] Similarly, in Belgium (French), England, Finland, Greece, Italy, Portugal, and Slovenia, females were more likely than males to attribute society-related activities to government. There were no gender differences on this scale for the other 20 countries.

[11] No gender differences were reported in the international report on this scale.

[12] Among the countries participating in the IEA study, Sweden, with 42.7%, had the largest proportion of women in the national legislature (Torney-Purta et al., 2001). Women held close to one third of the seats in the national legislatures of Denmark, Finland, Germany, and Norway. Six of the countries had fewer than 10% of the seats in their national legislature filled by women. As of January 2003, women held 13.6% of the seats in the U.S. Congress and 22.3% of the seats in state legislatures, according to the Center for American Women and Politics (http://www.cawp.rutgers.edu/gacts/cawpfs.html, accessed February 20, 2003).

attitudes that young people acquire in their youth. For that reason, researchers have been interested in assessing students' attitudes toward women as political leaders.

In the first IEA study, which was conducted in nine nations, U.S. students were the least supportive of women in politics. In all of the countries studied, females were more supportive of women's rights than were males (Torney, Oppenheim, & Farnen, 1975; Torney-Purta, 1991). My case study of ninth-grade civics classes and my study of samples of secondary school students in five nations found that U. S. students tended to be more supportive of women's rights than were their counterparts in the earlier IEA study. However, U.S. males were still less supportive than females of rights for women (Hahn, 1996, 1998). Furthermore, both studies found that males and females alike were more supportive of females holding local positions, such as being on the city council, than in holding national positions like being the President or a member of Congress (Hahn, 1996, 1998). In another study of U.S. students, Richardson (2001) similarly found that females were more supportive than males of women in politics. In addition, as I had earlier, she found that males and females were more supportive of women holding local level rather than national level positions.

The recent IEA study yielded results that were similar to earlier findings. U. S. females, like those in the other 27 participating countries, were more likely than their male counterparts to support rights for women (Torney-Purta et al, 2001). Indeed, the largest gender differences of any reported for both the U. S. sample and the total international sample appeared in response to the scale measuring attitudes toward rights for women (Baldi et al., 2001; Torney-Purta et al., 2001). Ninety percent of U. S. ninth graders agreed that: women should run for public office and take part in the government just as much as men do, they should have the same rights as men in every way, and men and women should get equal pay when they are in the same jobs. Still, almost 10% of students disagreed with those statements and said that women should stay out of politics, and 17% said that men are better qualified to be political leaders than women (Baldi et al., 2001).

Rights for Immigrants. In several studies, researchers have reported that females tend to be more tolerant than males. For example, on the 1976 NAEP, females were found to be more "tolerant" in terms of supporting rights for women and minorities (Jones, 1980). Conflicting results were obtained when "tolerance" was measured in terms of a willingness to extend rights to one's most disliked group. One study using such a measure found females to be more tolerant than males (Avery, 1988), but another revealed no gender differences (Avery, Bird, Johnstone, Sullivan, & Thalhammer, 1992).

In the recent IEA study, it was not possible to ask students about rights for particular racial and ethnic minorities because the salient minority groups in a country differed from one country to the next. Rather, students were asked about their attitudes toward rights for one group that existed everywhere—immigrants. Students were asked questions concerning whether or not they thought immigrant children should have the same opportunities for an education as other children and whether or not immigrants should have the right to vote in elections. On this scale, U.S. ninth-grade females indicated greater support for rights for immigrants than did male ninth graders (Baldi et al., 2001). A similar finding was obtained in 22 of the other 27 countries participating in the IEA study (Torney-Purta et al., 2001).

In summary, for the most part recent researchers have uncovered no consistent gender differences in political interest or efficacy. In a few cases, males were found to be slightly more interested and efficacious than females; in other cases, females were found to be more efficacious than males. Researchers have found no gender differences in attitudes toward conventional citizenship, such as voting or showing respect for leaders. However, studies have shown that females are more likely than males to say that it is important for a citizen to participate in social movement activities and that government should be responsible for society-related services. This is consistent with research indicating that young females tend to be interested in a broad array of social issues (Hahn, 1996).

Additionally, young females tend to be more supportive than males of rights for women and immigrants. We do not yet know why this occurs. It is possible that females are more likely than males to be socialized to give the socially acceptable response, such as a good citizen is tolerant and supports rights for all. Alternatively, females who are knowledgeable about past discrimination against women may identify with others who have experienced or might experience discrimination. A third possibility is that young males may be worried about entering the labor market and facing what they perceive as competition from females and immigrants.[13] Females are also less likely than males to be concerned about protecting the nation's autonomy from a variety of possible threats.

Moving from attitudes to behaviors, the next section examines whether gender differences are found in students' civic and political experiences. I look at research on students' anticipated experiences, as well as on experiences that students may have already had.

---

[13] These hypotheses are adapted from ones suggested by Amadeo, Torney-Purta, Lehmann, Husfelt and Roumiana (2003) in explaining similar findings among a 16-nation sample of upper secondary school students (not including the United States).

Experiences

Long before they reach voting age, young people begin to develop images of themselves as adult citizens. For that reason, researchers are interested in how students imagine themselves participating (or not) in a variety of civic and political activities. Furthermore, many young people participate in civic and quasi-political activities during their school years. Some students run for positions on the student council; some petition the school administration and/or volunteer in the local community. Additionally, youth are acting "politically" when they do—or do not—follow news and discuss political events with adults and peers around them. This section examines research on gender and civic-political experiences.

Expected Participation. Although adult citizens do not necessarily act as they thought they would when they were younger, young people's stated intentions can provide some indication of their initial orientation toward political participation. In the IEA study, female ninth graders in the United States were more likely than males to anticipate being politically active adults. For example, 89% of female ninth graders said they expected to vote in national elections, as compared to 80% of males (Torney-Purta et al., 2001). Sixty-nine percent of females, as compared to 49% of males, anticipated that they would collect money for a charity and 56% of females, as compared to 44% of males, thought they would collect signatures for a petition (Torney-Purta et al., 2001).[14]

Additionally, the IEA survey asked students if they would participate in a number of activities that are usually undertaken by only the most politically active members of society. Female ninth graders were more likely than their male peers to anticipate joining a political party, writing letters to newspapers about social or political concerns, and becoming a candidate for local political office (Baldi et al., 2001). In contrast, male students in the United States were more likely than females to say they expected to engage in a number of protest activities. Close to 20% of males and 10% of females said they probably or definitely would protest by spray painting slogans on walls, blocking traffic, or occupying buildings (Torney-Purta et al., 2001).

Media Consumption. Early political socialization researchers reported that males were more likely than females to say they followed political news (Green-

---

[14] In 24 of the 28 countries, females were more likely than males to say they thought they would be likely to collect money for a charity as an adult and in 16 of the countries females were more likely than males to say they expected to vote in national elections.

stein, 1965; Owen & Dennis, 1988). Recent researchers have obtained conflicting information about possible gender differences in media consumption.

For example, examining data from the National Household Education Survey, Niemi and Chapman (1999) found that male high school students were more likely than females (45% vs. 36%) to say they read news once a week or more. Males were also more likely to report viewing television news at least once a week (43% vs. 36%). However, for the U.S. sample in the IEA study, there were no significant gender differences in ninth graders reporting that they obtain news from television or newspapers (Baldi et al., 2001; Torney-Purta et al., 2001). Males, however, were less likely than females to report getting news from the radio.

Political Discussion. In earlier studies, males reported more political discussion than did females (Torney et al., 1975; Torney-Purta 1991). In the recent IEA study, males in the United States were more likely than females to say that they discussed international political issues with people their own age. However, the frequencies were low for both groups; 21% of males, as compared to 15% of females, reported such discussions (Baldi et al., 2001). There were no gender differences in reported discussions of political news with teachers or other adults.

Community Service. In recent years, researchers have broadened their view of civic-political behaviors and no longer focus only on behaviors such as voting and joining political parties. Recognizing that participation in community organizations is an indication of engagement with civil society, contemporary researchers are giving increased attention to young people's, as well as adults', participation in community service activities. The recent IEA study revealed that U.S. ninth graders were more likely than their counterparts in 27 countries to have participated in a group conducting activities to help the community (Torney-Purta et al. 2001). Fifty percent of students from the United States said that they participated in such a group.

Other researchers have concluded that females tend to engage in community service activities more than males and that there are differences in the groups joined by males and females from different ethnic groups. Chapin (2001) found gender differences in community service when she examined data from the National Education Longitudinal Study (NELS) of students. In 1988, a nationally representative sample of 25,000 eighth graders was interviewed. Researchers interviewed the sample students again in 1990, 1992, and 1994 when they were 10th and 12th graders (or dropouts) and young adults. Chapin found that 44% of the high school seniors reported having participated in community work. Females were more likely to have participated than males (50% vs. 39%). The most popular types of activities young people joined were church-related groups and the least popular were political groups. Young women participated more in all categories except youth groups, such as coaching Little League or helping with Scouts. Furthermore, race/ethnicity was related to the type of group students were most likely to join. African American females were the most likely to participate in political groups. Asian females were most likely to participate in hospital groups. White females were most likely to participate in environmental groups and White males participated most in youth groups (Chapin, 2001).

Another nationally representative survey conducted in the 1990s provides further information about students' participation in community service (NCES, 1997, cited in Chapin, 2001). The National Household Education Survey (NHES) asked students in grades 6 through 12 about their community service activities. Overall, 49% of students reported participating in community service in the 1995–1996 year, which was similar to the rate reported in the 1999 IEA study. As in the 1992 NELS study, females were more likely to report having participated than males (53% vs. 45%).

The NELS study is one of only a few studies that provides some information on participation in community service after students graduate from high school. In 1994, 2 years after graduating, 35% of respondents reported volunteering in the previous year—a 10% drop from their reported participation as high school seniors (Chapin, 2001). Interestingly, as young adults, females were no more likely than males to participate—in contrast to earlier periods. However, gender differences in the kinds of volunteer work they did continued. Females were more likely than males to report participation in church-related organizations (25% of females, as compared to 18% of males), organized volunteer work such as in a hospital (22% of females, as compared to 16% of males), and educational organizations (12% of females, as compared to 8% of males). Males reported they participated more in youth organizations such as being a Little League coach or Scout leader (18% of males, as compared to 13% of females) and they participated more in sports teams or sports clubs (17% of males, as compared to 7% of females).

In another longitudinal study, researchers linked participation in high school extracurricular activities with women's later civic participation. Damico, Damico, and Conway (1998) examined data obtained by the National Center for Education Statistics (NCES) on the high school senior class of 1972, who were surveyed in 1972, 1974, 1976, 1979, and 1986. The researchers found that women who had been active in high school activities were the most likely to be members of and leaders in community organizations as adults in 1976 and 1986—up to 14 years after finishing high school. Being a leader in high school, such as a student council officer or newspaper editor, increased the likelihood of later civic activism. Furthermore, activist students were more likely to value democratic processes—to indicate that democracy mattered to them—in ways that it did not for those who failed to participate. The researchers cautioned that young women enrolled in higher academic tracks and from higher socioeco-nomic backgrounds tended to participate more in high school activities than did students in lower academic tracks and from lower socioeconomic backgrounds. Thus, social inequalities were mirrored in young women's civic participation in high school and seemed to have long-term effects on their civic and political life as adults.

Voting. In recent years, there has been widespread concern about declining levels of voting, the traditional measure of civic and political engagement. In the 1996 presidential election, only 49% of Americans voted, and in the 1998 mid-term election, the percentage was down to 26% for all potential voters (Chapin, 2001). The percentages of voter turnout were somewhat higher for those who registered—36% in 1998. Although there appear to be no gender differences in registering and voting among the youngest age group, the low rates for both males and females are troubling. For the sample that was followed from the eighth grade in 1988 until they were 2 years beyond high school in 1994, 45% of males and 45% of females reported they voted in the 1992 presidential election. The percentages were lower in the 1994 midterm elections, but again, there were no significant gender differences. Thirty-one percent of both males and females reported that they had voted. Furthermore, there were no gender differences be-tween White males and females in registering or actual voting in either the 1992 or 1994 election. Similarly, there were no gender differences between African American males and females on either measure for both elections. However, Asian American males reported that they registered to vote more than did Asian American females. Also, Hispanic females reported voting more than did His-panic males in the 1992 presidential election (Chapin, 2001).

In summarizing the research on political experiences and behaviors, several gender differences emerge. At age 14, females expect to be more politically ac-tive as adults than do their male peers, regardless of whether expected political activity is measured in relation to anticipated voting, running for office, or pass-ing petitions and collecting money for a cause. The overall voting rate for fe-males has been higher than that for males in recent years. But, in the studies of the youngest cohort of voters, there appear to be no gender differences in regis-tering to vote or voting overall. However, for some ethnic groups, gender differ-ences have been found.

When following news in the media and engaging in political discussion are examined, previously identified gender differences may be disappearing. Past studies found males reported following the news and discussing politics more than did females; these differences, however, for the most part were not found in the recent IEA study. Male and female ninth graders were equally likely, or not likely, to report obtaining political news from newspapers and television. This is consistent with research on adults, which finds no gender difference in watching television news or reading newspapers (Delli Carpini & Keeter, 1996). For the ninth graders, there were also no gender differences in discussing national news with adults (family members and teachers). Males, however, were more likely than females to say that they discussed international news with their peers. The latter finding could be similar to the finding that adult males are more likely than their female counterparts to report discussing news daily and enjoying political discussions (Delli Carpini & Keeter, 1996). More research is needed to explore these subtle differences in reported discussions.

Today, civic engagement is studied not only in terms of traditional political behaviors, but also in terms of participation in civil society. Females tend to exhibit more participation than do males in this arena. Furthermore, the kinds of activities that young people select for their community service varies by gender and ethnicity.

Summary

This section has reviewed research on gender differences in students' knowledge, attitudes, and experiences. It is clear that male and female students of today are equally knowledgeable about civic and political content. At last, we can put to rest the old idea that young females are less interested in and knowledgeable about political life than their male peers. Moreover, male and female ninth graders are equally likely to associate "good citizenship" with conventional political behaviors such as voting. Both genders are equally likely, or not likely, to obtain political news from television and newspapers and to discuss news with adults. Males, however, still report that they are more likely to discuss international news with their peers than do females—but the numbers of students of either gender who engage in such discussions is very small indeed.

Females, as compared to males of the same age, are more likely to be able to exercise civic skills, such as interpreting political material. Females are also more likely than their male peers to indicate trust in government institutions and to support rights for both immigrants and women. Female ninth graders are also more likely than males to believe that the government should be responsible for providing society-related services, such as health care, education, and an adequate standard of living for the elderly. Furthermore, females tend to associate "good citizenship" with participation in social movement activities such as taking part in a group to help the community. And, finally, females are more likely to anticipate being politically active than males and they are more likely than males to have participated in community service activities during their school years. The irony, however, is that this new view of politically active female citizens is not reflected in the social studies curriculum, as is evident in the next section.

Gender and Social Studies Curriculum and Instruction

Young people's constructions of civic knowledge and attitudes are influenced by a variety of sources—the family, peer group, school, extracurricular and out-of-school activities, the media, and the micro- and macrocultures of which children and youth are a part. Social studies researchers have a particular interest in the role that social studies curriculum and instruction can play in that process. A few researchers have conducted studies that provide insights into how gender-related topics are addressed in social studies curriculum and instruction.

Curriculum

Prior to assessing representative samples of students, the IEA Civic Education Study researchers developed case studies of civic education in the participating countries (Torney-Purta, Schwille, & Amadeo, 1999). In order to develop the case study for the United States, my colleagues and I sent a survey to the 50 state social studies coordinators or their equivalents. We also conducted focus groups with 14- to 15-year-old students and eighth- and ninth-grade social studies teachers in several states (Hahn, 1999; Hahn, Dilworth, Hughes, & Sen, 1998). Additionally, Avery and Simmons (2001) contributed to the case study by analyzing civics and U.S. history textbooks. Some information obtained from these multiple sources is useful for understanding how gender issues are or are not included in the social studies curriculum.

Courses. Despite the presence of women's studies or feminist studies departments and programs at universities since the 1970s and the creation of women's studies courses for high school students in the 1980s, apparently few such courses exist in schools today (Hahn, 1985; Hahn et al., 1998). Only a few of the state social studies coordinators reported in 1995 that school districts in their state offered separate courses in women's studies. Rather, the coordinators thought that content on women and gender was infused into courses like U.S. history. That assumption, however, is not supported if textbooks are any indication of the curricular content that is delivered to students.

Textbooks. Researchers have repeatedly concluded that textbooks play a dominant role in social studies instruction (Niemi & Junn, 1998; Shaver, Helburn, & Davis, 1979). Indeed, in the IEA study, 89% of ninth graders said they read from the textbook when studying social studies (Baldi et al., 2001). Similarly, on the recent NAEP, 95% of eighth graders reported using a social studies textbook at least weekly—66% said they used one daily (Lutkus et al., 1999). Earlier researchers concluded that textbooks for civics and government, U.S.

history, economics, and world history courses contained few women, presented women in stereotypic roles, and gave little attention to gender-related issues (Commeyras & Alvermann, 1996; Hahn & Blankenship, 1983; McLeod & Silverman, 1973; Tetreault, 1984). By the late 1990s, educators assumed that publisher's nonsexist guidelines had "taken care of the problem." Such a conclusion was premature, however.

Avery and Simmons (2001) examined three widely used civics textbooks and three widely used U.S. history textbooks for Grades 7 through 9. Using a rubric they developed to systematically address the questions that were the focus for the IEA case study, Avery and Simmons did a content analysis of the books. They found that with only a few exceptions, such as Martin Luther King, Jr., the people most frequently mentioned in the books were European American male office holders. Women received significantly less coverage than men in both the civics and history books.

In the civics textbooks, women were mentioned 258 times, as compared to 1899 for men; in the history textbooks, women were mentioned 691 times as compared to 11,762 for males (Avery & Simmons, 2001, pp. 122–123). Although women were mentioned more in the history than the civics texts, their presence in comparison to men was still small indeed. Furthermore, several women who were mentioned, such as Abigail Adams and Eleanor Roosevelt, were wives of presidents, and few women of color were mentioned in either the history or civics books. The civics books, in particular, rarely highlighted women as political or governmental role models. Only one of the three civics texts examined directly discussed the disparity between men and women in the political realm; the authors drew attention to a chart showing the underrepresentation of women in Congress.

An earlier case study of civics classes in one school examined the textbook in use and came to conclusions similar to those of Avery and Simmons. Male "founding fathers," presidents, vice presidents, and chief justices of the Supreme Court were mentioned far more frequently than women political leaders (Hahn, 1996). The textbook authors, however, had apparently tried to portray women as activist citizens through photographs and anecdotes. Additionally, they included women in some of the special features titled Applying Skills, Solving Problems, and Citizens in Action. For example, the text suggested that students write a research paper on women in politics. Other special features included a story about a group's exclusion of women and a biography of Sandra Day O' Conner.

However, neither one of the two teachers whose classes I observed over a semester drew attention to the special sections or to the women pictured in textbook photographs. Neither mentioned the few sentences in the textbook discussing women's suffrage, the increased numbers of women in the workforce, and the Democratic party's nomination of a female candidate for vice president. The textbook contained chapters on state and local government, which could have been used to highlight increasing numbers of women running for and winning state and local offices. However, both teachers chose to skip those chapters because they assumed students studied state and local government the previous year in their state history course. Further, neither teacher drew attention to the textbook authors' use of the League of Women Voters and the National Organization of Women as examples of groups concerned with citizen participation. Similarly, neither teacher mentioned the textbook discussion of support for the Equal Rights Amendment as an example of a party platform. In essence, even when the textbook contained the potential to explore gender-related issues, the teachers in the classrooms studied did not pick up on those opportunities, and they did not supplement the textbook with information on gender-related issues. Moreover, despite the textbook's avoidance of male pronouns, the teachers were not as careful. Given this context, it was not surprising that when students talked about political leaders, they only mentioned males. I saw nothing in their civics class to lead them to any conclusion but that politics is a male field (Hahn, 1996). Unfortunately, we do not have other case studies or surveys to shed light on how "typical" these civics classes were.

Curriculum Standards. In recent years, national curriculum standards were developed in various content areas. Such standards could serve as models for the development of state and local guidelines, textbooks, and classroom instruction. The *Curriculum Standards for Social Studies* (National Council for the Social Studies, 1994), *Standards for Civics and Government* (Center for Civic Education, 1994), and *National Standards for History* (National Center for History in the Schools, 1996) are relevant to an exploration of gender and civic education. The *Curriculum Standards for Social Studies* developed by the National Council for the Social Studies (NCSS) and the *National History Standards* both point to how gender-related issues might be included in the curriculum. The *National Standards for Civics and Government*, however, only mentions gender twice, on pages 95 and 111, when it suggests that women's suffrage and discrimination against women, along with similar topics related to race and ethnicity, can be used to demonstrate how citizen participation has expanded over time.

Additionally, in a content analysis of the quotations used as graphics in the margins of the civics and government standards, researchers concluded that 90% were from males (Gonzales, Riedel, Avery, & Sullivan, 2001). Sixty-four (83%) of the quotations that appeared in the civics and government standards were attributed to European American men. Of the remaining 13 quotations, 7 were by European American females, 5 by African American men, and 1 by a Native American man. The researchers noted that quotes by African American females were "conspicuously absent," as were quotes by Latino and Asians of either gender (Gonzales et al., 2001). This was particularly surprising to the researchers in light of the fact that most of the quotes were from the 20th century. The

researchers pointed out that the ratio of "quotables" did not reflect the proportion of females and males in different ethnic groups that make up the U.S. population as a whole or elected officials locally and in Congress.

Apparently, the women's suffrage movement, which is mentioned in all of
the curriculum standards and the textbooks, is the one gender-related topic that
students are likely to study. In the focus groups for the IEA case study in the
United States, both teachers and students said that in their social studies classes
they had talked about the suffragists, as well as about women in colonial America. A few students also mentioned learning about Rosa Parks and Eleanor Roosevelt (Hahn, 1999). This is inadequate if social studies educators are to convey
that all citizens should participate in the workings of a democratic society.

Classroom Climate

Social studies students learn about citizen participation not only from the content of their textbooks and topics that are explored in lessons, but also by the
practices that are modeled in the classroom. Only one study conducted in the
1970s looked at classroom interaction patterns by gender in a social studies class
(Hedrick & Chance, 1977). They found that males had more verbal interactions
with the teacher than did females. I have not been able to locate any recent studies that have pursued that line of inquiry.

More frequently, studies look at students' perceptions of their social studies
classroom climate in terms of openness to discussion of controversial issues. In
a series of studies, colleagues and I have examined student responses to a Classroom Climate scale by gender (Hahn, 1998; Hahn & Tocci, 1990; Harwood &
Hahn, 1992). The Classroom Climate scale used in these studies contains items
that ask if students feel they are encouraged to express their views and explore
controversial social, economic, and political issues in their social studies classes.
The scale also asks if students think that their teacher presents more than one
side of an issue, and if students feel comfortable expressing their views in the
class even when their views differ from that of the teacher or other students. In
my case study of civics classes and in another by Harwood conducted in the
same metropolitan area, female ninth graders reported a more open classroom
climate than did males (Harwood & Hahn, 1992). Similarly, in the U.S. sample
that I used for my five-nation study of civic education, females were more likely
than males to report an open classroom climate. However, the effect size was
small (Hahn, 1998).

The two IEA studies are the only ones in which the Classroom Climate
scale was administered to nationally representative samples of students. In the
recent study, female ninth graders in the United States were more likely than
males to report that their classes had an open climate for discussion. As with the
earlier studies, the difference in perceptions by gender was statistically signifi-

cant, but it was not large (Baldi et al., 2001). Furthermore, in 23 of the 28 countries participating in the IEA study, females perceived their classroom climates to be more open than did males (Torney-Purta et al., 2001).

All of the research reported in this section relied on student reports of classroom climate. We do not know whether the gender differences reflect the fact that males are using a different mental metric to judge if the climate in their class is open or if males in the same class are encouraged to express their views less than are females in the same class. This phenomena needs to be explored further using qualitative methods to observe classes and interview students.

Summary

Although the evidence on what students learn about women and gender in their formal civic education is quite sparse, it does all point in one direction. Gender-related topics are rarely addressed and female civic-political action is rarely portrayed. Given such a situation, it is not surprising that females are less likely than males to say that government is their favorite subject or they enjoy civics more than other classes (Niemi & Junn, 1998). Even though young women may feel they are encouraged to express their views and explore issues, they may not be engaged with content that excludes people like them.

NEW SCHOLARSHIP

For over 25 years, some social studies scholars have been calling for changes in social studies textbooks and curriculum to more accurately reflect women's contributions to society and to address gender-related issues (Bernard-Powers, 1996; Grambs, 1976; Hahn, 1978, 1980; Hahn & Bernard-Powers, 1985; Tetreault, 1987). Recent feminist scholars in social studies and other fields have called for two changes in particular—the use of broader conceptions of "citizenship" and "politics" than have been used in the past and attention to the diverse experiences of women by class, race, ethnicity, and sexual orientation.[15] First, in calling for the use of more encompassing definitions, scholars emphasize that the traditional concepts that focused narrowly on the public realm of voting and

---

[15] See Stone (1996) for a discussion of the history of political theory. In particular, she describes how the association of males with the public political space and women with domestic and private space came to be. She also describes how the diversity of feminisms in the 1990s has varied meanings for citizenship today.

holding office overlooked important participation in civil society and the many ways that citizens take action to influence public policies (Bernard-Powers, 1996; Noddings, 1992a, 1992b; Woyshner, 2002). Second, scholars today emphasize that because lived experiences of women (and men) vary by class and race or ethnicity, gender issues need to be viewed in more subtle and complex ways than they have been in the past (Ladson-Billings, 1996a, 1996b). These two points have implications for social studies practice and research, as I illustrate later.

A number of authors have emphasized the need to move beyond traditional views of what counts as "civic" or "political" content. Noddings (1992a) challenged educators to rethink the concept of citizenship that was based on male experience in the public domain. Noddings asked educators to contemplate an ideal of "citizenship" rooted in women's culture. She suggested, for example, that one might think of good citizens as individuals who demonstrate neighborliness and refrain from harmful acts, not merely because they want to act legally, but because they do not want to hurt their neighbors. Discussions of decent, responsible behavior in personal and family relationships would be as important as discussions of traditionally conceived ideas of civic/political behavior. If women's culture were taken seriously, according to Noddings, then students would study about social issues and reformers, such as those who worked for child labor laws and better living conditions for immigrants. Her point was not the usual one of needing to add women to textbooks, but rather, to argue that when one uses a broader lens, the issues that have concerned women for centuries move to the forefront of curricular content. Consistent with such a view, pacifists, peace movements, and topics such as domestic violence would receive as much attention in social studies classes as military leaders, wars, and presidents do now (Noddings, 1992a, 1992b).

Demonstrating the advantages of using a broader view of citizenship and political life, Woyshner (2002) showed why the social studies curriculum should include the history of women's activism in social movements and voluntary associations. Prior to the passage of the 19th Amendment to the U.S. Constitution, members of African American and White women's clubs were active citizens. They organized, petitioned, and wrote letters to get legislation passed. They lobbied for compulsory school attendance, child labor laws, school taxes, and women's participation in school boards (Woyshner, 2002). Similarly, Bernard-Powers (1996) showed how women's actions during the Progressive Era illustrate the absurdity of trying to separate the political–public and social–private domains. She discussed how both middle-class Anglo European and African American women of the Progressive Era expanded the role of the "citizen" by redefining relationships among family, society, and the state. They worked for families, health, the environment, the needs of the elderly, and the special needs of children (Bernard-Powers, 1996). History and civics books that overlook such citizen action misrepresent civic and political life of the past and fail to suggest important avenues for future citizen participation.

A second theme that runs through much of the new scholarship is the need to represent the diversity of experiences among women by race/ethnicity, class, and sexual orientation. Ladson-Billings (1996a, 1996b) pointed to several ways that social studies educators can address this need.

Ladson-Billings (1996a) argued for the inclusion of a "womanist" or Black feminist perspective. Race, class, and gender simultaneously inform such a per-spective and have implications for theory and research in social education, as well as curriculum development. Ladson Billings (1996a) described how social studies teachers can use the lives of four individuals to illustrate the ways in which African American women have had to continuously confront the dual oppressions of race and gender as they exercised the role of citizen. Sojourner Truth confronted both racism and sexism and refused to be silenced or defined by either Black men or White women. Ida B. Wells, Septima Clark, and Fannie Lou Hamer epitomize citizen activists. As a journalist, Wells was instrumental in exposing the truth about lynching; she was also a "prime mover" in the estab-lishment of the NAACP. Clark was a founder of the Highlander Folk School and the Citizenship Schools, which prepared many of the leaders of the civil rights movement. Hamer, one of the graduates of a Citizenship School, testified about what African American women and men suffered when they tried to exercise their right to register and vote. Ladson-Billings' point, like that of Noddings, is not to merely add women and women's issues to the social studies, although that is important. Rather, Ladson Billings argues that to accurately understand his-toric and contemporary issues, citizens of both genders need to understand the ways that gender, race/ethnicity, and class have interacted to influence peoples' lived experiences and their differing perspectives on issues.[16]

Further, Ladson-Billings (1996b) emphasizes that students should learn to question the way things are or have been. In her chapter in the *Handbook of Is-sues—Centered Social Studies,* she explained how students might learn to ques-tion the "knowledge" presented to them and consider the implications of class and race/ethnicity, as well as gender, when they examine historic and contempo-rary social issues. Ladson-Billings suggested, for example, that students look at

---

[16] An African American womanist tradition, however, is not limited to including biographies of previously overlooked citizen activists. Santora (2001, p. 153) explains that this tradition privileges wisdom gained from lived experience, em-phasizes dialogue as a means to assessing knowledge claims, and grants primacy to an ethic of caring. Santora (2001) discusses other new feminist theoretical positions as well. However, she does not uncover research in social studies classes that reflects these varied theoretical positions.

the distribution of males and females in different jobs and ask: Why does society pay less to the jobs women are more likely to do? Or after examining textbooks, students might ask: Why are women's voices absent or muted in history books? Further, Ladson-Billings emphasized that issues of gender, race/ethnicity, and class provide opportunities for students to ask: How do we know what we know? What is the evidence? Whose point of view or perspective is presented? How else could it be considered? What difference does it make? Ladson-Billings (1996b) further recommended that students observe and discuss how race, class, and gender affect them on a personal level and consider the multiple effects of those factors as they read biographies and fiction.

Overall, much of the work in civic education today reflects a broader view of citizenship than was prevalent in the past. However, it still does not directly address the arguments made by feminist and womanist scholars. Civic education practitioners' and researchers' increased attention to community service and engagement in the civil society has the potential to more fully capture the lived experiences of women and girls (as well as the majority of men and boys who never seek political office) than did previous work. However, the recent studies of textbooks and curriculum standards indicate that social studies educators will need to undertake deliberate proactive actions to supplement the official curriculum and change the way it is delivered in the nation's classrooms.

Needed Changes in Practice

Social studies methods courses and professional development programs should include discussion of gender and citizenship. Both beginning and experienced teachers need to be shown why and how they can make a deliberate effort to highlight women as active in the civic and political arena. Teachers will need to consciously draw attention to activist women citizens and supplement the material presented in textbooks, national standards, and local or state curriculum guidelines. It is important that curriculum and instruction feature women's participation in civic and political life. It is equally important that citizens-in-training have opportunities to investigate some of the many gender-related social issues they will face as adults.

U.S. history teachers can draw attention to women's activism in antilynching societies and the long struggle for civil rights. They can also highlight women's activism in obtaining Progressive Era reforms, and in peace movements prior to the U.S. entry into the two world wars and during the Vietnam war (see Bernard-Powers, 1996; Ladson-Billings, 1996; Noddings, 1996b; Woyshner, 2002). Students should learn about more than just the first wave feminist movement and the suffrage movement of the 19th century. They should also know about the work required to pass the Equal Rights Amendment, the second wave feminist movement, including the importance of publications such as *Ms* magazine and Friedan's *Feminine Mystique*, as well as the founding of the National Organization of Women. Students should learn about the social changes brought about as a result of the passage of Title IX of the Higher Education Acts and the extension of the Equal Employment Opportunity Act to cover gender discrimination. Older students might investigate questions posed by third wave feminists, who since the 1970s have been asking whether there are enough commonalities of women across race and class to consider women as a category affecting citizenship. Students might consider whether or not using multiple feminisms that recognize the particular perspectives of, for example, Black feminists, lesbian feminists, and socialist feminists might more accurately reflect reality or diffuse potential political power. Clearly, there is much that history teachers can do to better prepare their students to be citizens of a multicultural democracy by attending to issues of gender.

Civics and government teachers also have many opportunities to include women's experiences and gender issues in their classes. The most frequently taught topics in such courses—the Constitution and the three branches of government—have traditionally focused on men and depicted national politics as being for men only. It is time for this to change.

In discussing the judicial branch, teachers can deliberately include Supreme Court opinions written by Sandra Day O'Conner and Ruth Bader Ginsburg and they can illustrate judicial processes with case studies of challenges to Title IX and affirmative action. Similarly, civics and government teachers can draw attention to women in the executive branch and to policies that concern women. Madeleine Albright, Condoleeza Rice, and other women who have held cabinet level positions can be shown in relation to a variety of policies. Instead of focusing primarily on the President's role as commander in chief, teachers can point out how the President and cabinet departments address health, education, and environmental issues.

In discussions of the legislative branch, as well as discussions of electoral politics, teachers can feature women in Congress and the issues they have championed. Importantly, students should investigate why, despite recent gains, women are still less likely to be elected to national office than men. Students can compare the experience in the United States with that of Scandinavian and other countries, where women's percentage of the national legislature has increased to one third as a result of changes in policies and public attitudes. Students might consider how the winner-take-all policies followed in the United States and the United Kingdom have hindered women's participation, as compared to that in countries with proportional representation.[17] Students should have the opportunity to talk with women who have been active in state and local politics, both as elected leaders and as activists working in organizations trying to influence public policies.

When students work in communities on service-learning projects, teachers can ask them to consider how men and women and boys and girls of various racial/ethnic, and class backgrounds are affected. Teachers should encourage students to learn about groups that are working to address the issue and about alternative policies that have been proposed. Teachers can help students see the potential connections between gender, citizen action, and public policies.

Needed Research

The recent studies using nationally representative samples of students reveal substantial gender differences in civic and political attitudes and experiences (but not knowledge). We need further research to determine whether the trends found are occurring similarly with students in other age groups and at other points in time (i.e., whether these are cohort or developmental effects). Most importantly, we need qualitative studies to determine how young males and females construct meaning about social and political issues and what in the socialization process might contribute to the differences in attitudes and experiences that are occurring. For example, we need to understand why young men tend to perceive the classroom climate for discussion to be less open than do females and why males tend to be less supportive of rights for women and immigrants than are their female peers.

Furthermore, the recent NAEP and IEA studies, studies of the NCES and NELS longitudinal data sets, and studies that used smaller and less representative samples all point to important differences in student political knowledge, attitudes, and experiences by race/ethnicity and socioeconomic background. Unfortunately, we do not yet have sufficient numbers of studies that look at the interaction of those factors with gender. For example, we do not yet know if African American female students from middle income families have similar or different political attitudes from African American males from middle income families, nor do we know how they compare to Hispanic, Asian American, or White middle income females. Importantly, as increasing numbers of immi-

---

[17] For a discussion of how proportional representation and winner-take-all policies affect female representation, see Webster (2000). This article also provides useful information the effects of geographic distribution on women's political representation in state legislatures, in Congress, and in the ratification of the 19th Amendment, and the lack of ratification of the Equal Rights Amendment.

grants to the United States come from Asian and Latin American nations, we do not know if civic-political socialization processes differ for males and females from particular cultural and political backgrounds. There are no data sets that use large enough representative samples to make valid comparisons. Until they are available, replications of small studies that use nonrepresentative samples and qualitative studies using purposefully selected samples could shed much-needed light on the interaction of gender with other variables that affect civic learning.

Finally, most of the research reviewed here focuses on the role of school in preparing young people to be citizens of a multicultural democracy. We know less about how young people construct political and civic meaning from the media, families, pop culture, and wider national and international events. Researchers from different social science disciplines and scholars with an expertise in cultural studies can bring fresh viewpoints to help social studies and civic educators and researchers understand how young people come to think of themselves as civic political beings.

REFERENCES

Amadeo, J. A., Torney-Purta, J., Lehmann, R., Husfeldt, V., & Nikolova, R. (2002). *Civic knowledge and engagement: An IEA study of upper secondary students in sixteen countries.* Amsterdam: International Association for the Evaluation of Educational Achievement.

Anderson, L., Jenkins, L., Leming, J., MacDonald, W., Mullis, I., & Turner, M. J. (1990). *The civic report card.* Washington, DC: U.S. Department of Education.

Applebee, A. N., Langer, J. A., & Mullis, I. (1987). *Literature and U.S. history: The instructional experience and factual knowledge of high school juniors* (Rep. No. 17-HL-01). Princeton, NJ: Educational Testing Service.

Avery, P. G. (1988). Political tolerance among adolescents. *Theory and Research in Social Education, 16,* 183–201.

Avery, P. G., Bird, K., Johnstone, S., Sullivan, J. L., & Thalhammer, K. (1992). Exploring political tolerance with adolescents: Do all of the people have all of the rights all of the time? *Theory and Research in Social Education, 20,* 386–420.

Avery, P. G., & Simmons, A. M. (2001). Civic life as conveyed in U.S. civics and history textbooks. *International Journal of Social Education, 15,* 105–130.

Baldi, S., Perie, M., Skidmore, D., Greenberg, E., & Hahn, C. (2001). *What democracy means to ninth-graders: U.S. results from the international IEA civic education study.* Washington, DC: National Center for Education Statistics, U.S. Department of Education. Retrieved 10. 6. 2003 from http://nces.ed.gov/surveys/cived. (Order from U.S. Department of Education, ED Pubs, P. O. Box 1398, Jessup MD 20794-1398, or call 1-877-4ED-Pubs.)

Bernard-Powers, J. (1996). The "woman question" in citizenship education. In W. C. Parker (Ed.), *Educating the democratic mind* (pp. 287–308). New York: SUNY Press.

Blankenship, G. (1990). Classroom climate, global knowledge, global attitudes, political attitudes. *Theory and Research in Social Education, 18,* 363–386.

Center for Civic Education. (1994). *National standards for civics and government.* Calabasas, CA: Author.

Chapin, J. R. (2001). From eighth grade social studies to young adulthood voting and community service: National education longitudinal study of 1988 eighth graders. *The International Social Studies Forum,1,* 33–44.

Commeyras, M., & Alverman, D. E. (1996). Reading about women in world history textbooks from one feminist perspective. *Gender and Education, 8*, 31–48.

Damico, A., Damico, S., & Conway, M. (1998). The democratic education of women: High school and beyond. *Women in Politics, 19*, 1–31.

Delli Carpini, M. X., & Keeter, S. (1996). *What Americans know about politics and why it matters*. New Haven, CT: Yale University Press.

Easton, D., & Dennis, J. (1969). *Children in a political system: Origins of political legitimacy*. New York: McGraw-Hill.

Education Commission of the States. (1971). *Citizenship: Group results for sex, region, and size of community* (National Assessment of Educational Progress Rep. No. 16). Washington, DC: Government Printing Office.

Education Commission of the States. (1973). *Political knowledge and attitudes.* [National Assessment of Educational Progress Report No. 16]. Washington, DC: U.S. Government Printing Office.

Education Commission of the States. (1974). *The first social studies assessment: An overview* (National Assessment of Educational Progress Rep. No. 16). Washington, DC: U.S. Government Printing Office.

Gonzales, M. H., Riedel, E., Avery, P. G., & Sullivan, J. L. (2001). Rights and obligations in civic education: A content analysis of the national standards for civics and government. *Theory and Research in Social Education, 29*, 109–128.

Grambs, J. D. (Ed.). (1976). *Teaching about women in the social studies: Concepts, curriculum, and strategies*. Washington, DC: National Council for the Social Studies.

Greenstein, F. I. (1965). *Children and politics*. New Haven, CT: Yale University Press.

Hahn, C. L. (1978). Review of research on sex roles: Implications for social studies research. *Theory and Research in Social Education, 6*(1), 73–99.

Hahn, C. L. (1980). Social studies with equality and justice for all: Toward the elimination of sexism. *Journal of Research and Development in Education, 13*(2), 103–112.

Hahn, C. L. (1985). The status of the social studies in the public schools of the United States: Another look. *Social Education, 49*, 220–223.

Hahn, C. L. (1996). Gender and political learning. *Theory and Research in Social Education, 24*, 8–35.

Hahn, C. L. (1998). *Becoming political: Comparative perspectives on citizenship education*. Albany: State University New York Press.

Hahn, C. L. (1999). Challenges to civic education in the United States. In J. Torney-Purta, J. Schwille, & J. A. Amadeo (Eds.), *Civic education across countries: Twenty four national case studies from the IEA civic education project* (pp. 583-607). Amsterdam: The International Association for the Evaluation of Educational Achievement. (ERIC Document Reproduction Service No. ED431705)

Hahn, C. L., & Bernard-Powers, J. (1985). Sex equity in social studies. In S. Klein (Ed.), *Handbook for achieving sex equity through education* (pp. 280–297). Baltimore, MD: Johns Hopkins University.

Hahn, C. L., & Blankenship, G. (1983). Women and economics textbooks. *Theory and Research in Social Education, 11*, 67–76.

Hahn, C. L., Dilworth, P.P., Hughes, M., & Sen, T. (1998). *IEA civic education project phase I: The United States—Responses to the four core international framing questions.* (Vol. 3). Unpublished manuscript. (ERIC Document Reproduction Service ED444887)

Hahn, C. L., & Tocci, C. (1990). Classroom climate and controversial issues discussions: A five nation study. *Theory and Research in Social Education, 18,* 344–362.

Harwood, A. M., & Hahn, C. L. (1992, April). *Gender and civics learning.* Paper presented at the annual meeting of the American Educational Research Association, San Francisco, CA.

Hedrick, T. E., & Chance, J. E. (1977). Sex differences in assertive achievement patterns. *Sex Roles, 3*, 129–139.

Hess, R., & Torney, J.V. (1967). *The development of political attitudes in children.* Chicago: Aldine.

Kneedler, P. E. (1988). Differences between boys and girls on California's new statewide assessments in history/social science. *Social Studies Review, 27*(3), 96–124.

Jennings, M. K., & Niemi, R. G. (1974). *The political character of adolescence.* Princeton, NJ: Princeton University.

Jones, R. S. (1980). Democratic values and pre adult virtues. *Youth and Society, 12,* 189–220.

Ladson-Billings, G. (1996a). Lifting as we climb: The womanist tradition in multicultural education. In. J. A. Banks (Ed.) *Multicultural education, transformative knowledge and action* (pp. 179-200). New York: Teachers College Press.

Ladson-Billings, G. (1996b). Multicultural issues in the classroom: Race, class, and gender. In R. W. Evans & D. W. Saxe (Ed.), *Handbook of issues—centered social studies* (pp. 104–110). Washington, DC: National Council for the Social Studies.

Lutkus, A. D., Weiss, A. R., Campbell, J. R., Mazzeo, J., & Lazer, S. (1999). *NAEP 1998 civics report card for the nation.* Washington, DC: National Center for Education Statistics, U. S. Department of Education. IERIC Document Reproduction Service No. ED 435 583)

Lyons, S. L. (1970). The political socialization of ghetto children: Efficacy and cynicism. *Journal of Politics, 32*, 288–304.

McLeod, J. S., & Silverman, S. T. (1973). *You won't do: What textbooks on U. S. government teach high school girls.* Pittsburgh, PA: Know, Inc.

National Center for History in the Schools. (1996). *National standards for history: Basic edition.* Los Angeles: University of California, Author.

National Council for the Social Studies. (1994). *Curriculum standards for social studies.* Washington, DC: Author.

Niemi, R. G., & Chapman, C. (1999). *The civic development of 9th through 12th grade students in the United States.* Washington, DC: U. S. Department of Education.

Niemi, R., & Junn, J. (1998). *Civic education: What makes students learn.* New Haven, CT: Yale University Press.

Noddings, N. (1992a). The gender issue. *Educational Leadership, 49*(4), 65–70.

Noddings, N. (1992b). Social studies and feminism. *Theory and Research in Social Education, 20*, 230–241.

Owen, D., & Dennis, J. (1988). Gender differences in the politicization of American children. *Women and Politics, 8*(2), 23–43.

Richardson, W. K. (2001, February). *Adolescent attitudes towards women in politics.* Paper presented at the Dogwood Conference, Emory University, Atlanta, GA.

Santora, E. (2001). Interrogating privilege, plurality, and possibilities in a multicultural society. In W. B. Stanley (Ed.), *Critical issues in social studies research for the 21st century* (pp. 149–178). Greenwich, CT: Information Age Publishing.

Shaver, J., P., Helburn, S., & Davis, O. L. (1979). The status of social studies education: Impressions from three NSF studies. *Social Education, 43*, 150–153.

Stone, L. (1996). Feminist political theory: Contributions to a conception of citizenship. *Theory and Research in Social Education, 24*, 36–53.

Tetreault, M. K. (1984). Notable American women: The case of U.S. history textbooks. *Social Education, 48*, 546–550.

Tetreault, M. K. (1987). Rethinking women, gender, and the social studies. *Social Education, 51*, 170–178.

Torney, J., Oppenheim, A., & Farnen, R. (1975). *Civic education in ten countries.* New York: Wiley. (ERIC Document Reproduction service No. ED 132 059)

Torney-Purta, J. (1991). Cross national research in social studies. In J. P. Shaver (Ed.), *Handbook on social studies teaching and learning* (pp. 591–601). New York: Macmillan.

Torney-Purta, J., Lehmann, R., Oswald, H., & Schulz, W. (2001). *Citizenship and education in twenty eight countries: Civic knowledge and engage-*

ment at age fourteen. Amsterdam: The International Association for the Evaluation of Educational Achievement.

Torney-Purta, J., Schwille, J., & Amadeo, J.A. (1999). *Civic education across countries: Twenty-four national case studies from the IEA Civic Education Project.* Amsterdam: International Association for the Evaluation of Educational Achievement.

Vaillencourt, P.M. (1972). *The political socialization of young people: A panel survey of youngsters in the San Francisco Bay Area.* Unpublished doctoral dissertation, University of California, Berkeley.

Webster, G. R. (2000). Women, politics, elections, and citizenship. *Journal of Geography, 99,* 1–10.

Woyshner, C. (2002). Political history as women's history: Toward a more inclusive curriculum. *Theory and Research in Social Education, 30,* 354–380.

PART II

RETHINKING CIVICS AND CITIZENSHIP IN A GLOBAL CONTEXT

Connections between Concepts of Democracy, Citizen Engagement, and Schooling for 14-Year-Olds across Six Countries

Wendy Klandl Richardson and Judith Torney-Purta
University of Maryland, College Park

Political theorists have spent considerable effort defining democracy and citizenship and delineating related knowledge, attitudes, and skills (reviewed in Fratczak-Rudnicka & Torney-Purta, 2003). Although such efforts have failed to produce fully satisfying conceptualizations of either term, this discourse has established certain domains around which various models of democracy are detailed, with corresponding characteristics of good citizenship. One example of a domain would be the distinction between rights and responsibilities. A "rule of law" model is associated with citizens' support and practice of responsibilities, and rights defined by law. In participatory models of democracy, good citizens would be expected to take a more active role in supporting rights and might also seek to expand those rights.

If an understanding of democratic concepts and concepts of good citizenship is essential for strong democracies and the development of good citizens, then understanding the current conceptualizations of democracy and good citizenship held by citizens and how such concepts develop is important for educators. Taking this one step further, if models of democracy and citizenship are related in theory, then it would be beneficial to determine empirically whether holding such concepts in fact influences citizens to engage in the key behaviors outlined in the models. In other words, once concepts of democracy and citizenship are established (in a nascent or more elaborated form), how do such concepts impact civic engagement? This chapter explores the connections between concepts of democracy and good citizenship and civic engagement for adolescents and the implications for civic educators.

Civic educators, political scientists, and policymakers have made some effort to assess what adolescents know about democracies. However, much of this research has emphasized measuring adolescent knowledge of either specifics about U.S. government (e.g., in the National Assessment of Educational Progress) or key principles and institutions of democracies (e.g., in the IEA Civic Education Study 38-item civic knowledge test). Less is known about how students integrate this specific knowledge into broader conceptual understandings about democracy. The recent International Association for the Evaluation of Educational Achievement (IEA) Civic Education Study provides empirical data to investigate these broader concepts. The IEA Civic Education Study is a large cross-national study that surveyed nearly ninety thousand 14-year-olds in 28 countries (see Torney-Purta, Lehmann, Oswald, & Schulz, 2001, and Amadeo, Torney-Purta, Lehmann, Husfeldt, & Nikolova, 2002, for findings). In addition to a test of civic knowledge, the IEA civic education instrument also included an attempt to assess student understanding about concepts of democracy by measuring attributes that students believed strengthen or weaken democracy. Conceptual models about democracy developed by political science theorists provided the framework for selecting attributes for inclusion in the instrument.

An initial analysis of the average student response in each country from the IEA study found that there is considerable consensus across countries about some attributes that students believe strengthen democracies. Fourteen-year-olds across countries agree that it is good for democracy when citizens have the right to elect political leaders freely or have many different organizations available for participation. They also agree that it is good for democracy when courts and judges are influenced by politicians and when wealthy business people have more influence on the government than others. However, there are other attributes of democracies that students in some countries believe will strengthen democracy, whereas students in other countries believe they will weaken democracy. For example, across countries students varied in their opinions about whether having political parties with different opinions was good or bad for democracy. This could indicate that some students do not understand the implications of certain democratic principles.

The IEA study also assessed students' conceptualization of an adult who is a good citizen. The study found that although students agree that obeying the law and voting are important, they were more likely to endorse social movement-related qualities, such as taking part in activities to benefit the community, as important characteristics of a good citizen than conventional activities, such as joining a political party.

This chapter further explores these findings by presenting an analysis of the IEA data connecting 14-year-olds' concepts of democracy and good citizenship with their anticipated future political participation in the areas of voting, political party membership, and activities to benefit the community. This analysis also investigates the relationship between opportunities for learning such concepts (especially in school), students' current participation, and their future intended engagement. The cross-national sample offers the opportunity to investigate to what degree concepts of democracy are common across these democratic countries and to what degree they are influenced by varying cultural and academic contexts.

QUESTIONS TO BE ADDRESSED USING THE IEA CIVIC EDUCATION STUDY DATA

The following are some questions to consider:

1. Are adolescents who hold concepts of democracy and good citizenship that are consistent with a particular activity more likely to believe they will engage in that activity in the future?

2. Are adolescents who report learning about particular forms of political engagement in school more likely to believe they will engage in such activities in the future?

3. To what extent do an adolescents' level of civic knowledge, trust in government institutions, interest in politics, confidence about participation in school, and current participation in organizations influence their perceived likelihood of adult participation?

4. Does engagement in activities that are closely associated with future adult activities make adolescents more likely to believe they will engage in those activities as adults than engagement in less related activities (e.g., Does involvement in a youth organization associated with a political party lead to stronger likelihood of joining a political party as an adult than participation on a sports team)?

RESEARCH BACKGROUND

Concepts of Democracy

Research about concepts of democracy frequently takes the approach of comparing adult concepts of democracy to characteristics of theoretical models outlined by political scientists. Although there are a number of highly differentiated models of democracy (Dahl, 1998; Fuchs, 1999; Held, 1996), theories of representative democracy and participatory democracy are among the most widely recognized. Moodie, Markova, and Plichtova (1995) found that adults in Scotland and Slovenia identified individual freedoms and rights and justice as aspects of ideal democratic societies. Rose, Mishler, and Haerpfer (1998) added nondemocratic attributes such as a military takeover of government and found that few adults endorsed these attributes. Students at the college level may also have differentiated understandings of democracy. The Walt Whitman Center at Rutgers University (1997) found that university students endorsed several models of democracy, including individual participation and group participation, rather than making clear differentiations. Multiple models of democracy have also been identified by civic teachers. Teachers in the Czech Republic identified forms of government and the rights of citizens to be important aspects of democracy, whereas Czech curriculum writers and U.S. teachers identified tolerance and decision making as important components of their conceptualization of democracy (Bishop & Hamot, 2001).

It appears that adolescents hold concepts of democracy that are similar in nature to those of adults or college students. Menezes and Campos (1997), Sigel and Hoskin (1981), and Sinatra, Beck, and McKeown (1992) noted that individual freedoms and elections were readily identified as important aspects of democracy. However, they also noted that students did not often move beyond these more basic ideas and were less familiar with functions of institutions. In interviews with adolescents from Budapest and Pécs, Hungary, in the early 1990s, Van Hoorn, Komlósi, Suchar, and Samelson (2000) found that freedom of speech and equality were the most common characteristics of democracy identified. A second wave of interviews from this study showed that a larger portion of students mentioned freedom of press, pluralism, and free elections. Students in Gdańsk, Poland, appeared to have more difficulty defining democracy and its key features, suggesting that conceptual understanding may vary across countries. This group of students showed a noticeable decline in support for democratic systems over the two interview periods, perhaps reflecting a similar skepticism among adults in their society.

Concepts of Good Citizenship

Research on adult conceptualizations of good citizenship has not identified one particular model. Rather, there appear to be multiple models of good citizens. For example, Janoski (1998) identified models of adult citizenship that relate to several different models of democracy, including a liberal democracy model. Theiss-Morse (1993) identified four distinct concepts of adult citizens. An emphasis on freedom and rights and a responsibility to vote are among the more common features.

Some research about teachers' concepts of citizenship has found that they are more likely to endorse models of citizenship that include an emphasis on social concerns and being an informed, questioning citizen (Anderson, Avery, Pederson, Smith, & Sullivan, 1997; Davies, Gregory, & Riley, 1999; Lee, 1999; Prior, 1999). Teachers in the IEA Civic Education Study were asked to select qualities of good citizenship that they believed important for students to learn (from a list of 15 qualities). Across countries, they identified "knowing about the country's national history" and "obedience to the law" as two of the most important. Protecting the environment and human rights were other qualities that were considered important (Torney-Purta et al., 2001). The teachers also noted that although current civic education curriculum stresses knowledge, most teachers would prefer that the curriculum emphasize critical thinking, values, and participation (Torney-Purta & Richardson, 2002). Their ideal curriculum objectives are more in line with models of citizenship identified in previous research about teachers' attitudes toward citizenship.

Multiple models of good citizenship have also been identified as relevant for adolescents. Westheimer and Kahne (2004) identify three different concepts of good citizenship: a personal responsibility model, a participatory model, and a justice-oriented model. Through an empirical analysis of two high school programs supporting civic participation, they ascertained that student concepts of good citizenship varied depending on which model of a good citizen formed the foundation of the program's curriculum and the experiences that students had through their participation in community activities.

Some research has found that adolescents' concepts of citizenship do not appear to be as fully developed as they are in adults. Conover and Searing (2000) found that students had a more highly developed sense about rights than responsibilities. Ichilov and Nave (1981) noted that Israeli youth in the late 1970s limited their concepts of citizenship to the political sphere, rather than to the wider community. Van Hoorn et al. (2000) found that adolescents from Hungary and Poland identified obeying laws and completing work as important qualities of a good citizen.

Concept Development

Other research about concepts of democracy and good citizenship in children and adolescents has focused on the development of such concepts. Early research in this area stressed the cognitive developmental stages of Piaget as an explanation for the more sophisticated conceptual understanding of older students. This approach argued that because the older students have reached formal operations, they are more able to comprehend abstract principles of democracy (Connell, 1971). However, the focus of research has moved beyond an emphasis on stage development to include explanations of more specific social influences, such as family interactions and school curriculum, because some research indicated that younger children can possess nascent abstract concepts (Helwig, 1998). The theories of domain-specific knowledge suggest that the development of political concepts is due to the interaction of children's naïve theories about democracy with their exposure to certain types of information, to different modes of organization, and that is scaffolded in different ways (Torney-Purta, 1991). To give just one example, according to a study by Berti and Andriolo (2001), Italian children who received direct instruction in school about political concepts (e.g., law and the state) performed significantly better on tests of such concepts, both 1 month and 10 months later.

Howard and Gill (2000) used the theories of Piaget and Vygotsky to argue that concepts of politics are developed through lived experiences that are mediated through social interaction. In an investigation of perspectives of young people (ages 5–12) from Australia on issues of power and politics, they found that older students possess a more complex understanding of power than younger students. The experiences of the older students allowed them to construct an understanding of power that moved beyond attributing power to a simple age hierarchy, where older adults have more power. These older students were able to recognize that those in power also have responsibilities and rights associated with the position, which are not solely related to age.

The influence of social context on concept development has also been emphasized in other research. In a secondary analysis of U.S. NAEP data, Niemi and Junn (1998) found that students knew more about topics to which they had more exposure. One example of this was that students knew more information about courts and the law than could be accounted for by learning in school. Niemi and Junn hypothesized that this may be because the students had the opportunity to learn about these topics from programs on television. Flanagan, Bowes, Jonsson, Csapo, and Sheblanova (1998) indicated that across seven countries and for both genders, a family ethic of social responsibility had the greatest impact on adolescents' civic commitment. A democratic school climate and student's engagement in volunteering were also related, although the influence of these factors varied across country and by gender.

Van Hoorn et al. (2000) explained that adolescents in Hungary and Poland frequently had less to say about concepts of democracy and good citizenship than they did about more personal issues such as their career plans or their family's financial status following political changes in their country. However, they seemed to develop less ideal, more complex conceptualizations of democracy and good citizenship as they got older. This increase in complexity was concurrent with an increased stabilization of democratization in their countries and therefore may not be strictly an age-related effect. Additionally, this apparent increase in cognitively complex understanding of institutions occurred at a time when the participants noted a decrease in their interest in and attention to politics. It is unclear if this declining interest was due to increased preoccupation with specialized college programs, or a shift in trust or distain for the government, perhaps related to the failed promise of the initial democratic reforms in their country. The authors concluded that the split between politics (which students limited in its scope to national and international issues) and everyday life was "a barrier to students' further development of knowledge" (p. 275).

Concepts of Democracy and Good Citizenship in the IEA Civic Education Study

One feature of citizenship education that was identified in many countries during the phase 1 case study of the IEA Civic Education Study was that young people should develop an understanding of important concepts of democracy, citizenship, and government (Torney-Purta, Schwille, & Amadeo, 1999). This agreement led to the creation of a content framework for the study based on three domains: democracy, democratic institutions, and citizenship; national identity and international relations; and social cohesion and diversity. Two types of items were developed for a knowledge test designed to measure these concepts of democracy. One type of item emphasized conceptual content knowledge, whereas the other measured student skill at interpreting political communication. Despite the high correlation between the two subscale scores constructed from these items, there were still different patterns of performance across countries. For example, the U.S. performed above the international mean on the skills scale score and at the mean for the content scale score, whereas the Czech Republic students performed above the mean on the content scale score and at the mean on the interpretative skills scale score (Torney-Purta et al., 2001). Interestingly, only the content knowledge scale score was significantly related to the students' intent to vote, when the countries were used as the unit of analysis (Torney-Purta & Richardson, 2003).

Although some of the ideas about concepts of democracy were successfully incorporated into the knowledge test, many other questions could not be formulated into questions with right or wrong answers, and consequently formed items in the survey. Using characteristics from a variety of models of democracy, such as a rule of law model, a participation model, and a communitarian model, items were developed asking respondents if they believed a particular situation would be good or bad for democracy. Thirty-nine such items were used in a pilot test and 25 were included in the final version of the survey. A section was also included that asked respondents which characteristics an adult good citizen should demonstrate.

Across countries, the average student's model for democracy is the closest to exemplifying a rule of law model of democracy (e.g., endorsing items like the right to elect leaders freely as good for democracy). Results also suggested that, in some countries, students believe in a model of democracy that emphasizes participation. This was especially the case for upper secondary students who showed more differentiated beliefs about democracies (Amadeo et al., 2002). The analysis for the IEA report identified 7 items for which there was a high level of consensus across countries. There were also 8 items for which there was a moderate level of consensus and another 10 items for which there was a low level of consensus, meaning that the average student in some countries thought an attribute was good for democracy, whereas the average student in other countries thought it was bad for democracy.

In the case of concepts of good citizenship, the items suggested that there are at least two underlying modes of good citizenship: more conventional citizenship, such as obeying the laws; and social movement-related citizenship, including items about acting to improve a community or the environment. In many countries, including the United States, students were more likely to endorse characteristics of good citizenship relating to social movement-related citizenship than conventional citizenship.

In summary, much of the previous research on adolescents' concepts of democracy and good citizenship has focused on describing characteristics that they endorse as part of their understanding. Fewer studies have tried to link conceptual understanding to participation (Flanagan et al., 1998; Westheimer & Kahne, 2004). The analysis in this chapter attempts to connect concepts with participation by analyzing the impact of conceptual understanding across different modes of participation, using nationally representative samples from six countries. Additionally, it considers the relationship between concepts and participation in the context of both current participation and opportunities for learning in school.

METHODS

Sample

The main focus of this chapter is to analyze the impact of students' concepts of democracy and good citizenship in depth. The nationally representative samples and carefully constructed instrument of the IEA Civic Education Study provides an excellent resource for investigating these issues. However, trying to grasp these connections in all 28 countries participating in the IEA study is unmanageable and so the sample was narrowed to 6 countries in the following way. First, given the intended audience for this conference and resulting book, the United States was included. Next, it was important to identify students who expressed a point of view on the concepts of democracy and good citizenship. Therefore, as a first cut, countries were selected for analysis if the country sample had less than 16% of its responses categorized as "missing" on the items used in this analysis to measure students' concepts of democracy and good citizenship. Missing data includes "don't know" responses, as well as those left out or not administered. From the countries remaining after this reduction, one country was selected from the regions of Latin America, Scandinavia, Southern Europe, Eastern Europe, and Western Europe, where the percentage of missing data was closest to the percent for students in the United States on the greatest number of the concept items. The countries analyzed were Chile, Estonia, Finland, Greece, Switzerland, and the United States. Data from nationally representative samples was collected in each country in 1999. Specific sample sizes for this analysis are presented in Tables 1–4 (see also Torney-Purta et al., 2001).

Analysis

In order to explore the connections between concepts of democracy, concepts of good citizenship, opportunities for learning such concepts, and civic engagement, items were selected from the IEA study that could be linked across these four areas. Taking guidance from previous analysis of the IEA data (Torney-Purta & Richardson, 2004) and the research literature more generally (as summarized in Carnegie Corporation & CIRCLE, 2003), we chose three types of civic engagement and identified sets of linked factors for each type of engagement (see Table 4.1 or the appendix for full descriptions). The first set of linked factors is in the area of informed voting. The intention to be an informed voter is a composite measure of two items, one asking students about how likely it is that they will vote in the future and the second about whether or not they are likely to gather information before voting. The items in this area include one concept of democracy item about the right to elect leaders, one concept of a good citizen item about if it is important for adults to vote, an item about the perceived opportunity to learn about voting in school, and whether or not students were currently a member of a school council and therefore likely to have some direct experience with voting in such a group.

The second set of factors is in the area of joining a political party. There are two conceptual items about democracy in this set; political parties have different opinions and people join parties to influence the government. The concept of good citizenship item asked how important it is for an adult who is a good citizen to join a political party. Although there is no item specifically asking students if they learn about political parties in school, an item was selected that asked students to what degree their teacher encourages them to discuss political and social issues about which people have different opinions. The final item asked students if they currently belonged to an organization affiliated with a political party.

TABLE 4.1: Related and General Factors
Influencing Multiple Modes of Civic Engagement

Factors	Mode of Civic Engagement		
	Intent to Be an Informed Voter	Intention to Join a Political Party	Intention to Volunteer
Related Factors			
Democratic concept	Citizens have the right to elect political leaders freely	Political parties have different opinions on important issues People participate in political parties to influence government	Young people have an obligation to participate in activities to benefit the community
Good citizen concept	A good adult citizen votes in every election	A good adult citizen joins a political party	A good adult citizen participates in activities to benefit the community
Related organizational participation	School council/parliament	Youth organization affiliated with a political party	Group conducting activities to help the community
Learning in school	Learned about importance of voting in national elections	Teacher encourages discussion of issues about which people have different opinions	Learned to contribute to solving problems in the community
General Factors			
	Civic knowledge	Civic knowledge	Civic knowledge
	Trust in government	Trust in government	Trust in government
	Interest in politics	Interest in politics	Interest in politics
	Confidence in participation at school	Confidence in participation at school	Confidence in participation at school
	General organizational participation	General organizational participation	General organizational participation

The final set of factors is on the topic of engagement through volunteering in the community. The concept of democracy item asked whether or not young people should have the obligation to participate in activities to benefit the community. The good citizen concept item asked if adults should be involved in activities to benefit people in the community. The final two items were about the degree to which adolescents learned about the importance of solving problems in the community in school and whether or not they currently were members of a group conducting activities to benefit the community.

For each of the three types of engagement, the potential impact of a set of general factors was also considered. These factors included whether or not adolescents are more likely to believe they will engage in future activities if they have higher levels of civic knowledge, trust in government institutions, interest in politics, confidence that student participation in school matters, and participation in a number of general activities such as an environmental organization or sports team (see the appendix). Civic knowledge was measured using a 38-item test, scored with correct and incorrect responses. This knowledge scale has a Cronbach's alpha of .88. Trust in government and confidence in participation at school are scales constructed and validated across all 28 countries, with Cronbach's alpha's of .78 and .69, respectively. Current participation in organizations is the adolescent's summed participation in 12 activities. One final item asked adolescents to rate their interest in politics. Because the emphasis of this analysis was on the connections between concepts and engagement, consideration of other individual factors, such as gender or socioeconomic status, were left for future analysis.

Three simultaneous regression analyses were conducted to explore the impact of concepts of democracy and good citizenship, current activities, learning in school, and other personal factors on three different types of civic engagement. The personal factors and a measure of general organizational participation were held constant across each form of engagement. Concepts of democracy and good citizenship, one related activity, and learning in school varied across each regression to be specifically aligned with the type of engagement.

RESULTS

This section presents findings about the connections between concepts of democracy, concepts of good citizenship, organizational participation, and schooling specifically selected as related to three different modes of civic engagement: the intent to be an informed voter, the intent to join a political party, and the intent to volunteer. The associations between the three modes of engagement and more general factors, such as civic knowledge or interest in politics, are also presented. Comparisons are made across the six countries to offer additional insight about the nature of the connections between concepts, engagement, and schooling.

Informed Voting

The factors used in this model to account for variance in students' anticipated involvement in an informed voting process explained more than 22% of the variance in all six countries and as much as 35% in the United States (see Table 4.2).

TABLE 4.2: Simultaneous Regression Analysis
for Predictors of the Intent to Be an Informed Voter

	Chile	Estonia	Finland	Greece	Switzer-land	United State
Democratic Concept[a]	NS	.048**	NS	.075***	.069***	.109***
Good Citizen Concept[b]	.144***	.125***	.239***	.192***	.127***	.229***
School Parliament	NS	NS	NS	NS	NS	NS
General org. Participation	NS	.069***	.108***	NS	.085***	.133***
Learned in School	.226***	.182***	.148***	.089***	.111***	.106***
Knowledge	.184***	.235***	.157***	.206***	.224***	.216***
Trust	.102***	.148***	.154***	.125***	.103***	.080***
Confidence	.041**	.107***	.141***	.166***	.065***	.130***
Interest	.209***	.142***	.151***	.098***	.191***	.146***
Adj. R sq.	.261	.262	.326	.228	.227	.354
N	3662	2387	1945	2828	2110	1929

**$p \leq .01$ ***$p \leq .001$ (Standardized beta coefficients reported)

[a] When citizens have the right to elect political leaders freely that is . . . good/bad . . . for democracy.

[b] An adult who is a good citizen votes in every selection.

Although trust in government institutions and confidence about participation in school have some impact across countries, knowledge was the largest predictor in three out of six countries and a strong predictor in the other three. The concept of democracy (value of having the right to elect leaders) had a small or insignificant effect on informed voting across countries, with the largest (but still only modest) effect in the United States. The belief that an adult who is a good citizen should vote was a moderate predictor in all the countries, and was the largest of all the predictors in Finland and the United States. Interest in politics was a moderate predictor in every country except Greece, where the effect was smaller but still significant. Learning about the importance of voting in school was significant in every country and was the largest of all predictors in Chile. Current participation in a school council or parliament did not predict beliefs about future voting. General organizational participation was moderately significant in four countries, including the United States.

Joining a Political Party

The factors used in this model to predict likelihood of joining a political party showed the most similar pattern across all six countries (see Table 4.3).

Interest in politics and the belief that an adult who is a good citizen should join a political party were the largest predictors in each country. Concepts of democracy were not significant predictors, suggesting that students have not consistently learned about these principles. Nearly 30% of adolescents (in the six countries analyzed here) thought that when political parties have different opinions this is somewhat bad for democracy. However, nearly 30% of adolescents felt that this was somewhat good for democracy.

Civic knowledge was a moderate predictor in Finland and the United States, and a small predictor in Switzerland. Receiving encouragement from teachers to discuss political and social issues was a significant, although small, predictor in Chile, Estonia, and Switzerland, but it was not a significant predictor in Finland, Greece, or the United States. The impact of current participation in organizations, specifically related to political parties or more generally, was not very strong across countries, with both forms of participation significant only in Finland. Trust in government institutions has only a small impact on joining a political party. Confidence in participation at school is not significant in most of the countries and has only a small, negative effect in Greece and Switzerland. Adolescents with higher levels of confidence about student participation in school in those two countries are less likely to join a political party.

TABLE 4.3: Simultaneous Regression Analysis
for Predictors of the Intention to Join a Political Party

	Chile	Estonia	Finland	Greece	Switzer-land	United States
Democratic Concept A[a]	NS	NS	NS	NS	.068**	NS
Democratic Concept B[b]	NS	NS	NS	NS	NS	NS
Good Citizen Concept[c]	.167***	.146***	.305***	.172***	.214***	.280***
Pol. Party Org.	.049**	NS	.087***	.104***	.105***	NS
General Org Participation	NS	NS	.071***	NS	NS	.070**
Learned in School	.057***	.068***	NS	NS	.071***	NS
Knowledge	NS	NS	.105***	NS	.057**	.192***
Trust	.072***	.065**	.089***	.056**	.086***	NS
Confidence	NS	NS	NS	.063***	-.072***	NS
Interest	.318***	.297***	.250***	.342***	.312***	.305***
Adj. R sq.	.195	.150	.255	.201	.230	.295
N	3158	2055	1701	2522	1915	1644

**$p \le .01$ ***$p \le .001$ (standardized beta coefficients reported).

[a] When political parties have different opinions on important issues, that is . . . good/bad . . . for democracy.

[b] When people participate parties in order to influence governement, that is . . . good/bad . . . for democracy.

[c] An adult who is a good citizen joins a political party.

Volunteering in the Community

Across all six countries, adolescents who held the belief that a good adult citizen participates in activities to benefit the community were more likely to think they themselves would engage in such activities in the future (see Table 4.4). Learning in school about how to contribute to solving problems in the community and confidence that student participation in school made a difference were significant factors in five out of the six countries in predicting anticipated future involvement. In contrast to its relationship with other modes of civic engagement, civic knowledge was a negative predictor of student likelihood of volunteering in the community in Chile, Estonia, Greece, and Switzerland, and not significant in Finland and the United States. Interest in politics was not a significant predictor of the intent to volunteer in five out of the six countries. The concept of democracy linked to this form of engagement was a significant predictor only in Estonia and Finland. Current participation in a volunteer organization was a significant predictor in Chile, Greece, and the United States. General organizational participation was a significant predictor in Finland, Switzerland, and the United States.

TABLE 4.4: Simultaneous Regression Analysis for Predictors of the Intention to Volunteer

	Chile	Estonia	Finland	Greece	Switzer-land	United States
Democratic Concept[a]	NS	.083***	.092***	NS	NS	NS
Good Citizen Concept[b]	.078***	.101***	.236***	.135***	.180***	.283***
Volunteer Org	.106***	NS	NS	.075***	NS	.162***
General Org. Participation	NS	NS	.136***	NS	.094***	.110***
Learned in School	.139***	NS	.123***	.146***	.070**	.107***
Knowledge	.185***	.170***	NS	.108***	.123***	NS
Trust	NS	.102***	NS	NS	.064**	NS
Confidence	.130***	.075***	NS	.154***	.132***	.085***
Interest	NS	.096***	NS	NS	NS	NS
Adj. R sq.	.105	.077	.155	.110	.108	.254
N	3557	2181	1664	2703	1930	1811

**p≤ .01 ***p ≤ .001 (Standardized beta coefficients reported)

[a] When young people have an obligation to participate in activities to benefit the community, that is . . . good/bad . . . for democracy.

[b] An adult who is a good citizen participates in activities to benefit people in the community.

Overall, the factors used here to explain variation in student responses about their intention to participate in three different forms of civic activity provide more information about students in the United States than in other countries. The models had the largest R-squared values for the United States. Comparatively, the analysis undertaken here suggests fewer firm conclusions about the connections between conceptual understanding, schooling, and engagement for students in Estonia, where the models explained as little as 7% of the variance in student responses.

IMPLICATIONS FOR CIVIC EDUCATION AND SOCIAL STUDIES EDUCATORS

Our comments regarding implications for further research, policy action, and practice are formulated with several audiences in mind, including people from *nongovernmental organizations* (many of them with a background in service learning, some with a more general focus on youth development, and some in law-related-education), *professional educators and their organizations* (e.g., the National Council for the Social Studies and the Association for Supervision and Curriculum Development), those participating in *federal initiatives* in history teaching (sometimes framed to have a civic purpose) or service learning (through the Corporation for National Service) and *foundation-funded efforts* (e.g., initiatives supported by the Center for Information and Research on Civic Learning and Engagement funded by the Pew Charitable Trusts), participants in *university-level initiatives* (e.g., those in the Carnegie Foundation network and programs at universities like Rutgers University, the University of Maryland, and the University of Minnesota), *state and local government outreach organizations, and researchers* (especially in social studies, but also in political science, communications, developmental psychology, literacy education, and evaluation).

Let us look at the analysis reported in this chapter in relation to implications for these groups, beginning with understanding how students most effectively learn about democracy and citizenship and how this is linked to civic participation of various types. The finding that adolescents at age 14 who subscribe to abstract concepts of democracy are not necessarily more likely to say they intend to vote and get information about candidates, join a political party, or volunteer in the community, *but* that adolescents who understand concepts of good citizenship are more likely to do these things, suggests that teaching about democratic concepts in isolation may be too abstract. Additionally, the fact that some of these items have higher percentages of adolescents responding "don't know" might also indicate that democratic concepts are too abstract. The abstract or complex nature of these concepts may have attenuated their impact on participation.

Further, students who reported learning in school about the importance of voting and about solving problems in the community were more likely to believe that they will engage in such activities as adults. The link between learning in school about the importance of these types of engagement and the likelihood of future involvement highlights one role schools can play in civic education. This may be especially relevant for voting because this topic often receives more attention than other forms of participation in many civics textbooks (Murray, Strachan, & Hildreth, 2002; Riedel, Avery, Gonzales, Sullivan, & Williamson, 2001). Although similar percentages of teachers and students within each country agree that the importance of voting is learned by students in school, the proportion of teachers who believe that students learn about voting is higher than the proportion of students reporting such learning (Torney-Purta & Richardson, 2002, 2003). This discrepancy suggests that additional opportunities exist for teachers to make the importance of voting more explicit in the curriculum. The findings of this study substantiate an initial finding in the IEA Civic Education Study report, which indicates that learning about the importance of voting in school made a difference on likelihood to vote in the future (Torney-Purta, 2002; Torney-Purta et al., 2001). It should be noted that the lack of effect on the intent to join a political party for discussing political and social issues in school may be an indication that this item was more about a climate for discussion about issues where there are different opinions than learning specifically about political parties.

These findings suggest that it may be necessary to be very explicit about links to models of citizens' action. In other words, students may need assistance connecting abstract concepts about democratic principles with civic engagement. For example, when history teaching is the context in which civic education is taking place, studying about the history of elections or famous elected officials may not always communicate the explicit message that elections make differences in policy and that citizen's lives are influenced by these policies. Encouraging students to see voting as an important component of democratic citizenship could be augmented by more explicit links between the study of history or of the structure of political systems and how citizens might be involved or influenced by the political process.

Although a majority of adolescents see volunteering in activities that benefit the community as a characteristic of an adult who is a good citizen, such activities are apparently considered to be unconnected to the domain of politics by many adolescents. Furthermore, higher levels of civic knowledge were actually correlated with lower levels of anticipated participation in future volunteering in some countries (and not correlated at all in others). This suggests that the policy-related aspects of volunteering are not readily apparent and that guided reflection on political connections of such action is necessary in order for adolescents to see the two as related. This idea has been suggested in other studies about involvement in community service in the United States (Youniss & Yates, 1997). Or, it may be that the students perceive volunteering as intentionally NOT political, in effect acting as a form of opposition to conventional politics (Westheimer & Kahne, 2002). That interest in politics is not a significant predictor of future volunteering in most of the countries also supports the idea that volunteering in the community is not associated with "politics" in the minds of adolescents.

Schools and teachers who subscribe to civic education aims that include community participation may need to make special efforts to place those volunteer activities in the context of political issues (e.g., differences in views about the causes of poverty or environmental pollution) and to encourage the incorporation of service learning into the curriculum rather than just encouraging a certain number of hours of voluntary activity. Reviews of research also emphasize the importance of reflection on service-learning activities that encourage students to connect their activity to broader civic concepts (Billig, 2000; Torney-Purta, Hahn, & Amadeo, 2001).

Furthermore, although adolescents consider volunteering to be an important activity for adults, many suggest that an "obligation" to participate may run counter to other democratic principles of freedom and individual rights. In a survey of students enrolled in classes emphasizing the discussion of controversial public issues, Hess & Posselt (2001) found a similar attitude among U. S. adolescents regarding political discussion. Learning how to engage in political discussion was acknowledged as an important skill, yet students felt aggrieved when participation in class discussions was required (e.g., if such participation was computed into the grade).

Current participation in organizations does not seem to be living up to its potential in preparing students for future civic engagement. The influence of general participation on anticipated future engagement varied by country and was not a strong factor in any country in the analysis reported here. Participating in school councils did not appear to serve as preparation for voting among adolescents in these countries. It may be the case that knowledge and skills from such participation, although likely to include procedures relevant to elections, are not perceived as similar enough to voting in national or local elections. Like general participation, the impact of current participation in volunteering and political party organizations varied across country. For example, in the United States volunteering primed students for later voluntary participation, but participation in a political party organization did not have an impact on the likelihood of future involvement with a political party. This pattern was reversed in Switzerland. Helping students explicitly link the skills and knowledge gained from organizational experiences with future civic engagement may increase the likelihood that these activities will have an impact on future engagement. It should also be noted that differences between countries might be because the nature of the activities varies considerably across countries. For example, in this analysis, the United States is the country where current engagement in volunteering is most frequently reported by students and where it makes the biggest contribution to expressions of future willingness to volunteer.

Confidence that participation in schools makes a difference has a positive impact on informed voting in every country, and a positive impact on beliefs about future volunteering in most countries. Such confidence is not related to joining a political party except in Greece and Switzerland, where higher confidence relates to students' thinking it is less likely that they will join a political party in the future.

Clearly, students conceptualize each form of political participation in a slightly different way. Consequently, various experiences and types of knowledge have different impacts. Volunteering appears to be considered a nonpolitical activity. On the other hand, joining a political party may be considered the most political form of participation. Informed voting is most strongly influenced by political knowledge, suggesting that voting is associated with a need to be informed about specific principles.

In summary, educators and policymakers should note that there is evidence that the school can address attitudes and concepts that prime different kinds of participation (especially when they present concepts in a way that explicitly links citizenship to activities, such as voting and understanding community problems, and fosters a sense of confidence in the value of school participation). There is evidence for the value of dimensions such as these across countries, especially in the United States. It would be extremely shortsighted to discount the potential positive effects of schools in civic education reform (Carnegie Corporation & CIRCLE, 2003). In our opinion, some of the arguments against civic education in schools are based on narrow views of civic education, perhaps referring to a time in the past when civic education meant rote recitation of textbook facts, not on what a more optimal type of civic education in schools is or might be. Furthermore, dismissing the importance of schools based on research with college students or adults who have had extensive opportunities outside of school to develop political reasoning and skills in participation neglects the fact that these opportunities are not available to all students.

In short, civic education can be improved and is necessary, especially for young people who are not college bound. It is not realistic to think that youth organizations, media campaigns, or families will provide sufficient opportunities for all youth. Schools are the public arenas in which nearly all young people spend substantial amounts of time in the first two decades of their lives. Schools are sensitive to policy direction in a way that families and youth organizations are not. In addition to results from this analysis, there are findings replicated over three decades of research about the characteristics of multifaceted school programs (courses with civic content, a classroom climate for respectfully discussing issues, and a school climate empowering students) that are likely to be effective. However, we have inadequate information about how teachers view these efforts and how they envision being able to meet increasing demands in other subject areas at the same time becoming more conscious of potential contributions to civic education goals. It could also be argued that we have failed to develop the knowledge about implementation in the administrative climate of schools and in teacher preparation to carry these research findings into action. In our view, these are the leading issues in civic education that should receive further consideration.

APPENDIX: SELECTED ITEMS FROM THE IEA CIVIC EDUCATION STUDY

Dependent Variables

Intent to be an Informed Voter: When you are an adult, what do you expect that you will do?
  . . . vote in a national election and get information about candidates before voting in an election

Intention to Join a Political Party: When you are an adult, what do you expect that you will do?
  . . . join a political party.

Intention to Volunteer: When you are an adult, what do you expect that you will do?
  . . . volunteer time to help people in the community.

(Response: 1—*I will certainly not do this* to 4—*I will certainly do this*)

Independent Variables

General Factors (variables used in all three regressions)

General Organizational Participation: Composite variable of 12 organizational activities

Knowledge Scale (Knowledge)

Trust Scale (Trust)

Confidence in Participation at School (Confidence)

I am interested in politics. (1—*strongly disagree* to 4—*strongly agree*) (Interest)

Related Factors for the Intention to be an Informed Voter

Democratic Concept: When citizens have the right to elect political leaders freely that is . . . (1—*very bad for democracy* to 4—*very good for democracy*).

Good Citizen Concept: An adult who is a good citizen votes in every election. (1—*not important* to 4—*very important*)

School Parliament: A student council/government

Learned in School: In school I have learned about the importance of voting in national and local elections. (1—*strongly disagree* to 4—*strongly agree*)

Related Factors for the Intention to Join a Political Party

Democratic Concept A: When political parties have different opinions on important issues, that is . . . (1—*very bad for democracy* to 4—*very good for democracy*)

Democratic Concept B: When people participate in political parties in order to influence government, that is . . . (1—*very bad for democracy* to 4—*very good for democracy*)

Good Citizen Concept: An adult who is a good citizen joins a political party. (1— *not important* to 4—*very important*)

Pol. Party Org: A youth organization affiliated with a political party or union.

School: Teachers encourage us to discuss political or social issues about which people have different opinions . . . . (1—*never* to 4—*often*)

Related Factors for the Intention to Volunteer

Democratic Concept: When young people have an obligation to participate in activities to benefit the community, that is . . . (1—*very bad for democracy* to 4—*very good for democracy*)

Good Citizen Concept: An adult who is a good citizen participates in activities to benefit people in the community. (1—*not important* to 4—*very important*)

Volunteer Org.: A group conducting (voluntary) activities to help the community.

Learned in School: In school I have learned to contribute to solving problems in the community. (1—*strongly disagree* to 4—*strongly agree*)

REFERENCES

Amadeo, J., Torney-Purta, J., Lehmann, R., Husfeldt, V., & Nikolova, R. (2002). *Civic knowledge and engagement among upper secondary students in sixteen countries.* Amsterdam: IEA.

Anderson, C., Avery, P. G., Pederson, P. V., Smith, E. S., & Sullivan, J. L. (1997). Divergent perspectives on citizenship education: A Q-method study and survey of social studies teachers. *American Educational Research Journal, 34*(2), 333–364.

Berti, A. E., & Andriolo, A. (2001). Third graders' understanding of core political concepts (law, nation-state, government) before and after teaching. *Genetic, Social, and General Psychology Monographs, 127*(4), 346–377.

Billig, S.H. (2000, May). Research on K–12 school-based service learning: The evidence builds. *Phi Delta Kappan, 81,* 658–664.

Bishop, J. J., & Hamot, G.E. (2001). Democracy as a cross-cultural concept: Promises and problems. *Theory and Research in Social Education, 29*(3), 463–487.

Carnegie Corporation of New York & CIRCLE (2003). *The civic mission of schools.* New York: Carnegie Corporation of New York.

Connell, R.W. (1971). *The child's construction of politics.* Melbourne, Australia: Melbourne University Press.

Conover, P. J., & Searing, D. D. (2000). A political socialization perspective. In L. M. McDonnell, P. M. Timpane & R. Benjamin (Eds.), *Rediscovering the democratic purposes of education* (pp. 91–124). Lawrence: University Press of Kansas.

Dahl, R. (1998). *On democracy.* New Haven, CT: Yale University Press.

Davies, I., Gregory, I., & Riley, S. (1999). *Good citizenship and educational provision.* London: Falmer.

Flanagan, C. A., Bowes, J. M., Jonsson, B., Csapo, B., & Sheblanova, E. (1998). Ties that bind: Correlates of adolescents' civic commitments in seven countries. *Journal of Social Issues, 54* (3), 457–475.

Fratczak-Rudnicka, B., & Torney-Purta, J. (2003). *Competencies for civic and political life in democracy.* In D. S. Rychen and L. H. Salganik, Defiition and Selection of Key Competencies: Contributions to the Second Disco symposium. Nevchatel: Swiss Federal Statistical Office. Pp. 71–89.

Fuchs, D. (1999). The democratic culture of unified Germany. In P. Norris (Ed.) *Critical citizens: Global support for democratic government* (pp. 123–145). Oxford, England: Oxford University Press.

Held, D. (1996). *Models of democracy.* Palo Alto: Stanford University Press.

Helwig, C. (1998). Children's conceptions of fair government and freedom of speech. *Child Development, 69,* 518–531.

Hess, D., & Posselt, J. (2001, April). *How students experience and learn from discussing controversial public issues in secondary social studies.* Paper presented at the American Educational Research Association annual meeting, Seattle, WA.

Howard, S. & Gill, J. (2000). The pebble in the pond: Children's constructions of power, politics, and democratic citizenship. *Cambridge Journal of Education, 30* (3), 357–378.

Ichilov, O., & Nave, N. (1981). "The good citizen" as viewed by Israeli adolescents. *Comparative Politics, 13* (3), 361–376.

Janoski, T. (1998). *Citizenship and civil society: A framework of rights and obligations in liberal, traditional, and social democratic regimes.* Cambridge, England: Cambridge University Press.

Lee, W. O. (1999). A comparative study of teachers' perceptions of good citizenship in three Chinese cities: Guangzhou, Hangzhou, and Hong Kong. In J. Lu (Ed.), *Education of Chinese: The global prospect of national cultural tradition* (pp. 270–293). Nanjing, China: Nanjing Normal University Press.

Menezes, I., & Campos, B. (1997). The process of value-meaning construction: A cross section study. *European Journal of Social Psychology, 27,* 55–73.

Moodie, E., Markova, I., & Plichtova, J. (1995). Lay representations of democracy: A study in two cultures. *Culture and Psychology, 1,* 423–453.

Murray, L., Strachan, J. C., & Hildreth, A. (2002, August). *In search of effective civic education messages: A content analysis of high school government texts.* Paper presented at the American Political Science Association annual meeting, Boston.

Niemi, R., & Junn, J. (1998). *Civic education: What makes students learn?* New Haven, CT: Yale University Press.

Prior, W. (1999). What it means to be a "good citizen" in Australia: Perceptions of teachers, students, and parents. *Theory and Research in Social Education, 27* (2), 215–248.

Riedel, E., Avery, P., Gonzales, M., Sullivan, J., & Williamson, I. (2001, July). *Variations of citizenship education: A content analysis of rights, obligations, and participation in high school civic textbooks.* Paper presented at the International Society for Political Psychology meeting, Cuernavaca, Mexico.

Rose, R., Mishler, W., & Haerpfer, C. (1998). *Democracy and its alternatives: Understanding post-Communist society.* Baltimore: Johns Hopkins University Press.

Sigel, R., & Hoskin, M. (1981). *The political involvement of adolescents.* New Brunswick, NJ: Rutgers University Press.

Sinatra, G., Beck, I., & McKeown, M. (1992). A longitudinal characterization of young students' knowledge of their country's government. *American Education Research Journal, 29*, 633–661.

Theiss-Morse, E. (1993). Conceptualizations of good citizenship and political participation. *Political Behavior, 15* (4), 355–380.

Torney-Purta, J. (1991). Schema theory and cognitive psychology: Implications for social studies. *Theory and Research in Social Education 19* (2), 189-210.

Torney-Purta, J. (2002). The school's role in developing civic engagement: A study of adolescents in twenty-eight countries. *Applied Developmental Science, 6*, 202–211.

Torney-Purta, J., Hahn, C., & Amadeo, J. (2001). Principles of subject-specific instruction in education for citizenship. In J. Brophy (Ed.), *Subject-specific instructional methods and activities* (pp. 307–408). Greenwich, CT: JAI Press.

Torney-Purta, J., Lehmann, R., Oswald, H., & Schulz, W. (2001). *Citizenship and education in twenty-eight countries: Civic knowledge and engagement at age fourteen*. Amsterdam: IEA.

Torney-Purta, J. & Richardson, W.K. (2002). An assessment of what 14-year-olds know and believe about democracy in 28 countries. In W. Parker (Ed.), *Education for democracy: Contexts, curricula, assessments* (Vol. 2,) (pp. 185-209). Greenwich, CT: Information Age Publishing.

Torney-Purta, J., & Richardson, W. K. (2003). Teaching for the meaningful practice of democratic citizenship: Learning from the IEA Civic Education Study in 28 countries. In J. Patrick (Ed.), *Principles and practices of democracy in the education of social studies teachers (Vol. 2,)* (pp. 25-44). Bloomington, IN: ERIC Clearinghouse for Social Studies/Social Science Education.

Torney-Purta, J., Schwille, J., & Amadeo, J. (1999). *Civic education across countries: Twenty-four national case studies from the IEA Civic Education project*. Amsterdam: IEA.

Torney-Purta, J., & Richardson, W.K. (2004). Anticipated political engagement among adolescents in Australia, England, Norway and the United States. In J. Demaine (Ed.), *Citizenship and political education today*. pp. 41–58, London: Palgrave Publishers.

Van Hoorn, J. L., Komlósi, Á., Suchar., E. & Samelson, D. A. (2000). *Adolescent development and rapid social change: Perspectives from Eastern Europe*. Albany: State University of New York Press.

Walt Whitman Center for the Culture and Politics of Democracy (1997). *The measuring citizenship project: The final report*. New Brunswick, NJ: Rutgers University.

Westheimer, J., & Kahne, J. (2004). What kind of citizen? *The politics of educating for democracy, 41*(2), 237–269.

Westheimer, J., & Kahne, J. (2006). *The limits of efficacy: Educating citizens for a democratic society.* In B. Rubin and J. Giarelli (Eds.). *Civic education for diverse citizens in global times. Returning theory and practice.* Hillsdale, NJ: Lawrence Erlbaum.

Youniss, J., & Yates, M. (1997). *Community service and social responsibility in youth.* Chicago: The University of Chicago Press.

Chapter 6

A Primer on Democracy and Education in the Era of Globalization

William Cahill
Edison Township High School

In a passage with uncannily ironic resemblances to the rhetoric of globalization heard today, Dewey (1927) described the "Great Community" as one that would only be achieved by the thorough democratization of all human interests in society:

> The idea of democracy is a wider and fuller idea than can be exemplified in the state even at its best. To be realized it must affect all modes of human association, the family, the school, industry, religion. And even as far as political arrangements are concerned, governmental institutions are but a mechanism for securing to an idea channels of effective operation. (p. 143)

Dewey meant that democracy needed to structure all human social relations and perspectives, a process that would have to evolve by means of a long commitment, to be fully achieved in American life or anywhere. His writing in *The Public and its Problems* seems to deliberately avoid any restriction to the American scene or its history as grounding for democracy, as if to say that the democratic dispensation he imagined could suit any modern, developing society. Thus, his theory has a universalist implication, although it was rooted in the particulars of American experience in his time. Contemporary rhetoric concerning globalization and education, which draws frequently on the concept of democracy, urges a new formulation for the universal and the particular that would radically change the conception of democratic education that has been an important part of the modern history of education in the United States.

Dewey's writing on democracy and education came as a culmination of sorts in a longer history in which American education experimented with various forms for schooling and social growth that resonated in one way or another with the principles of democracy on which the country was founded. These might all be read as moments in a longer history of changing conceptions of a universal dispensation for modern living, which yielded up certain democratic ideals of education, along with other things that seemed to have little to do with such ideals.

Today, in the new era of "globalization," educators hear much about community, democracy, new valuations for schooling, and the spread of such things into countries and regions of the world where they were previously little known, a rhetoric of harmony and change that seems full of promise for a new humanity. Its ironic echoes with Dewey's vision of the "Great Community" are in its sense of extension, permeation, and unity, as well as in its advocacy for democracy and wider education, and its frank desire to make knowledge and learning practical. This new rhetoric seems to have usurped certain commonplaces about democracy and education from the American tradition to use in its own new ways, which have little resemblance to their former meanings as they are used in this radical new context.

Another hallmark of this new rhetoric of globalization is its disdainful reference to the liberal and the modern as dated and outmoded. Educators familiar with the tradition of democratic and modern thought in education will realize how many ideas from that legacy are embedded in teaching practice today as valued principles, but also how many others remain in the minds of some teachers and students of education as shining promises that remain only partially tested in academic experience. This view suggests that this modern tradition has not even reached its own fulfillment, let alone its obsolescence.

This chapter looks at democratic educational theory from this "modern" period through several perspectives. The first is the recent history (of the last 100 years or so) of educational thought in the United States in its awareness of international relations. The next is the contemporary field, from which several representative views are taken. The history and theoretical views described here have been selected to represent aspects of a legacy that contrast saliently and perhaps suggestively with the rhetoric of globalization being heard so stridently by educators today. The point in calling this chapter a "primer" is to pitch it primarily to teachers, who must make practical choices from among the many theoretical and political perspectives heard in the world of education today with regard to the nature of knowledge in the American school experience. This experience has become increasingly involved with the globalizing world, through, among other things, migrations of families bringing students from distant places to the American school, the internet, electronic communications, and worldwide consumerism fostering a new homogeneity among people, regardless of their origins, and so on. The pluralist ideal of liberal democratic society has been challenged recently by new multiculturalist criticisms, prompting new questions and possible adjustments in American schools and made more compelling by the experience of a new metropolitanism, new migrations, and new forms of cosmopolitanism. English remains the dominant language of our schools, but if this is a fulfillment of the ideal promoted by "Americanization" projects in Progressive Era schools then, it is an ironic one, because the English spoken in the American school is increasingly inflected not only with the accents of many lands but with the commercial values and the orientations of a new globalizing culture that makes the Anglo-Saxon inspiration of that older advocacy of English in American culture seem rather quaint.

Before proceeding to the history and the theoretical perspectives this chapter is mainly about, some description of globalization and its possible effects on education are given.

The rhetoric of globalization as a "new world order" promises many social benefits, including the spread of education and democracy in the world. Before proceeding further, perhaps a brief definition of globalization would be in order, with a few comments on its implications for education. Stromquist and Monkman (2000), and other writers in their book, define various phenomena and implications of globalization. These include, briefly, the following:

- Technological developments making possible the global unity of economic and communication processes and thus linking commerce and other human activities in many parts of the world in time and space.
- The expansion of free markets in large regions and potentially worldwide.
- Increasing valuation of knowledge insofar as it can become a marketable skill.
- The spread of English as a global language.
- Increased value for competitiveness.
- Privileged valuation of efficiency and administrative expertise.

Other phenomena associated with globalization include the rapid flow of financial capital and its preeminence in the economic realm (over production capital and natural resources); the formation of "global cities" functioning as nerve centers and magnets for financial capital, material resources, service resources, and migrations of peoples, often creating new social and infrastructure problems that regional governments and economies are at a loss to deal with; an expectation that national boundaries and authorities will lose all or much of their meaning; new expressions of metropolitanism and cosmopolitanism coming with new migrations of people in search of work in global cities; new solidarities formed of mutual ethnic, religious, and linguistic identities shared by migrant peoples living in diasporas within global cities far from their original homes; increased homogenization of culture (influenced by consumerism as a tool of global financial capital, making more of the world into customers for the same products); an economic shift making natural resources and industrial production less profitable than the sophisticated skills in their development and marketing; and so forth (Bamyeh, 2000; Sassen, 2001).

The effects of these and other phenomena of globalization on education would remodel schools to resemble the institutions winning the most power from such phenomena and give privileged valuation to the kinds of learning that serve them. This might, according to Giddens (cited by Stromquist & Monkman, 2000, pp. 11–12), result in knowledge becoming fragmented and treated only as positivistic "information" manageable by large institutions whose work specializes in the use of such information (a tautological and thus uncritical relation of knowledge to its use in the world). This, in turn, (again according to Giddens), might usher in a new period of "reflexivity" and "doubt" on a new order, as people outside these institutions seek to interpret and evaluate knowledge according to principles separate from their unifying perspectives. In other words, if these institutions (e.g., the World Bank, cited by Stromquist and Monkman as an example) devise a new paradigm for the valuation of knowledge, the older paradigms might dissolve and truth seekers on the periphery of those institutions would have to imagine new ones, thus making for much disparity and particularity in their perspectives.

Stromquist and Monkman further note that the new cult of "efficiency" and of "market values" for learning will lead to devaluing studies concerned with "the search for truth" in favor of a new esteem for administrators in education (a point posited by McLaren in 1988, cited in Stromquist & Monkman, 2000, pp. 12–13). Other effects these authors note include diminishing importance given to equality in favor of efficiency and marketability among knowledge-seekers; training in new kinds of knowledge leading to new migrations of people toward places that offer it; the revaluation of universities as "clients" or "customers" of transnational corporations encroaching on their research facilities; the draining away of researchers from universities to such corporations doing their own research; and the rise of private institutions of higher technical learning, which will lack research departments and humanistic faculty (Stromquist & Monkman, 2000, pp. 3–25). Effects on general education and primary education, in particular, noted by other authors in Stromquist and Monkman's book, include increased privatization and decentralization of authority among schools, new inducements for the spread of free primary education throughout the world, and increasing fees for higher education.

These latter changes would suit the economic needs of globalization for a literate workforce while appeasing its desires for decentralized governments assuming less responsibility for the growth and opportunities of individuals. These latter elements in the list of globalization's effects are not mere descriptors. Privatization, decentralization, and a new vocationalism for education, in particular, are hardly necessary results of globalization as a phenomenon of technology and new structures for financial capital, as are some of its other descriptors. Rather, these latter indicate a subtle shift from description of phenomena to the advocacy of measures that would support the powers reaping the most benefit from them. Privatization, decentralization, control by standards, personal financing for higher education and vocational training, and other public agendas for education all seem to suit the demands of the new globalized "economy," but they also serve to keep transnational corporations and other players in that economy profitable by reducing their responsibilities for training workforces, by limiting the resources and purviews of governments—and thus reducing governments' potential regulation of such businesses—and in general promoting a world order favoring "human capital" theorists over others (see Carnoy, in Stromquist & Monkman, 2000, pp. 43–61).

HISTORIC BACKGROUND OF INTERNATIONALISM IN AMERICAN EDUCATION

Spencer's influence on American education marked a disruption, as did the bureaucratic ideals brought to the American school by Harris, in the later periods of the 19th century. These sent the schools and their social visions on new paths that brought them into new encounters with social philosophy.

English philosopher and evolutionist Spencer's writings were popular in the United States in the latter 19th century for their instruction on how people might better utilize their individual gifts and manage their behaviors for a better life. Spencer argued that only evolution could advance certain human characteristics and thus that universal improvement could not be effected by human effort; but he argued, at the same time, that education could teach people what were the fittest and most desirable traits they might cultivate for happiness and success. Economic and material happiness were extensions of nature and education could show people how to enjoy them. Spencer advocated a careful educational attention to the needs of health, pleasure, and civic order as well. The schools, he asserted, could conserve and teach the best practices for happiness in these realms. Spencer's arguments coalesced with the interests in social progress through efficiency and scientific management that became hallmarks of progressive education in the United States during the latter part of the 19th and early 20th century. These interests asserted a new universalism rooted in a common, hermetic cultural self-consciousness that deeply influenced education and particularly the school curriculum.

American educational policy occasionally took an interest in international education in the American school. Among the first—or perhaps the first—

national publication on the subject was *the International Conference on Education held at Philadelphia in Connection With the International Exposition of 1876*, published by the U.S. Department of the Interior's Bureau of Education in 1877. Harris, who was superintendent of schools for St. Louis, Missouri, delivered the featured remarks given at this conference. Harris, here and in other writings, interpreted Hegelian idealism as a philosophy specially suited to Americans and incorporated key principles from this philosophy in his revisions of the American school curriculum, which have had a lasting effect. In the 1876 Centennial Exposition, Harris spoke with an international gathering of educators from Russia, Sweden, Great Britain, Hawaii, and Brazil, propounding his philosophy of mental discipline and curricula seen as manifestations of cultural ideals that would advance human society. Harris's educational thought was universalist with a modern difference, stressing the world in its becoming and valuing education as instrumental in this transcendent process. Identifying and standardizing school subjects as disciplines, Harris sought to help the ideal in its American unfolding by bringing the population, through schooling, closer to rationality and the structural principles of human achievement. His remarks to the 1876 conference seem extraordinarily confident and full of idealistic promise. The conference report does not transcribe any dialogue between Harris and the foreign educators who were present, although it does give their reports on education in their respective countries, with special emphasis on the uses of museums, school schedules, textbooks, preparation of teachers, and scientific apparatus. These latter were obviously of some interest, but Harris's philosophical pronouncements stood out as a coherent and universalizing program. Here we find an American educator seeking to inculcate his wisdom in foreigners but demonstrating little interest in cultural and educational borrowing from societies beyond the United States because the idealism he drew his insights from was presumed to be universal.

Whereas Harris's bureaucratic idealism sought to organize the schools as systems for the optimum unfolding of potential social development on a transcendent plan, John Dewey's instrumentalism, beginning in the 1890s, sought to make his "method of intelligence" the guiding intrinsic principle in a new education. Dewey's pedagogy, described in *The School and Society* (1899), sought to join youngsters in the experience of the new metropolitan world their migrant parents had come to inhabit as a scene that was implicitly instructive and could become explicitly educational in an innovative sense. Occupations youngsters might observe in their neighborhoods, brought into the school as subjects of study, could reveal to them the world in its many diverse purposes and at the same time challenge their understanding through studies in history, math, language and art, as they and their teachers worked to interpret the instrumental meanings of these human endeavors in the world. "All subjects are social studies," Dewey wrote. His statement meant that studies were inherently moral because they were all about society in some important way or another (Dewey,

1909/1975, p. 31). Intelligence must function socially and its "trained capacities" were intrinsically moral, according to Dewey (p. 43).

Dewey's pedagogic interest in occupations and socialization assumed their full form in his Laboratory School at the University of Chicago during the 1890s in a social scene of new immigration, migration, and metropolitanism that, he saw, challenged the parochial nature of the 19th-century American school. In this sense, Dewey's interests looked to the world in its metropolitan diversity and to people in the midst of unpredictable and unsettling changes thrust on them by large-scale economic patters they hardly understood. Dewey's instrumentalism imagined building improved social orders from such conditions, through an education that could create social structures of mutual moral interest. This would (as Dewey described in *Democracy and Education*, 1916) be an education through which people identified possibilities for social happiness collaboratively, democratically, using the resources of intelligence already given in custom, work, and academic interests. Dewey's "instrumentalism" gave new form to the Kantian inspiration, linking it with democracy and an unpredictable, although rational, development of social conditions in response to environmental change.

The foregoing history suggests certain problematic resemblances with current educational debates, particularly those touching on questions of globalization, multiculturalism, the reading of our present interests as a deconstruction of our own past, and other concerns. Teachers often bother rather little with the educational past, but they should perhaps be more aware of to what extent certain ideals of the past remain present and cogent—although changing in their expression, or "deconstructing" themselves and forming new texts whose expressions distort and obscure the meanings of the past.

Early on, education in the colleges held to the belief that classical studies were humanizing and that a canon of literary and philosophical works (including mathematics and some physical science) represented and incorporated the ideals of humanity for people with the ability to learn them and thus equip themselves as community leaders. In some senses, American education today remains wedded to this ideal, though it has mutated considerably through 19th-century versions of mental discipline and various trends of democratization of the academic curriculum.

This history has also pointed to the presence of Harris, a philosophic idealist, in one of American education's early ventures into the international scene, the 1876 International Exposition's conference on education. Harris's idealism—like certain idealist voices heard today with agendas that strangely imitate his—sought to bring Americans in line with the unfolding manifest of the ideal in the world through education (as Walt Whitman would through poetry), but Harris also bureaucratized the American school and gave it much of its stubbornly enduring organizational form, something that has become an icon for many teachers, parents, and politicians in this country, and that has reproduced itself to a certain extent in other countries. This bureaucratic form is so much a part of American educational consciousness that it seems natural, and in this illusion of naturalness it can become an obstacle to envisioning projects in education mutually with people living in or raised in cultures that know little of it.

Dewey's instrumentalism offered a different insight—though not unfamiliar with idealism—concerning development and educational innovation that became an influential though sometimes suspect legacy for the American school. Dewey's outward interest in occupations, metropolitanism, and the challenges of democracy in societies marked by sudden demographic change seem to capture a pattern that the present reenacts with a vague sense of familiarity.

Educators interested in the possibilities of global citizenship today might consider the (somewhat distorted, "deconstructed") resemblances their new conceptions of intercultural and international education bear to these histories. These histories might have some absorbing appeal for American educators because they are their history, seen perhaps as their legacy, but they might also, read in a certain light, represent lost ideals and a vocabulary of possibility rendered necessarily archaic because they belong to the past and are in some sense irrecoverable. Ironically, their interest resonates with the present, in some important ways, but at the same time it sounds discordant, as if its imagined harmonies must be irrevocably lost.

THE HISTORIC FOREGROUND: THE NEW INTERNATIONALISM IN 20TH-CENTURY AMERICAN EDUCATION

Other versions of universalist and internationalist interest appeared in American education in the 20th century in response to the world wars, the Cold War, and the quest to extend modernism further in the world through economic development that was fostered through American educational expertise.

This history is traced briefly and selectively through a review of selected national reports and yearbooks devoted to or significantly touching on international interests of American education published in the 20th century by the National Society for the Study of Education. It also includes a report issued in 1918 by the National Educational Association. These yearbooks (and other such national reports) represent the work of professional educators and scholars in education and are each the work of various authors. They are interesting, perhaps more than incidentally, for their representations of scholarly standards and methods in their times and for their ways of demarcating the limits of educational vision and interest in those times—although these were not among their stated purposes. (Thus, they might represent a fruitful area of study in the poetics of educational historiography, but such a study cannot be undertaken here.)

American educational policy assumed a new internationalist dimension in response to the U.S. entry into two world wars. An early national report, *A National Program for Education: A Statement Issued by the National Education Association Commission on the Emergency in Education and the Program for Readjustment During and After the War* (1918), contrasts Germany's use of education to promote imperialist, autocratic rule with the democratic traditions of England and France, which the United States should continue to emulate. Connecting such education with "universal welfare," the report calls for strengthening existing schools in America for "the highest possible level of collective intelligence" (p. 8), its phrasing reflecting the idealist temperament of the day. Another national report, *International Understanding Through the Public School Curriculum* (Kandel & Whipple, 1937), expresses similar concerns with the fear that a new war was imminent. This National Society for the Study of Education report advocated greater emulation of the British democratic model as the highest political standard and the use in American schools of reading materials from European cultures that showed a common culture shared by these countries. It sounds its universalizing theme, with strongly utopian associations, in advocating a "disarmament of the mind" (Kandel & Whipple, 1937, p. 13). The society published *American Education in the Postwar Period* (1945 yearbook), with a small section devoted to international interests of American education and calling for an international organization for educational policy that would study and disseminate knowledge of developments in education "in terms of their contribution to . . . better international understanding and good will" (Henry, 1945, p. 183).

As is well known, the period following the end of World War II witnessed a return to an isolationism reinforced by the fear of the Soviet Union and the spread of communism. McCarthyism was instrumental in not only suppressing communists and alleged communists, but dampening creativity in many intellectual fields, including education. The 1950s and early 1960s were not conducive to developing innovative pedagogies, but rather a defensive mode, protecting American values against the threat posed by the Soviet Union and its Eastern bloc allies. Progressive education fell into obscurity during this period. The Educational Policies Commission, an adjunct of the National Education Association, published numerous books and pamphlets on democracy, education, and international relations during this time, but these were intent on defining an already achieved democratic civic form to be strengthened by teaching it in civics lessons in the schools. They were often frankly propagandistic in the context of America's involvement in the Cold War.

The communist threat did stimulate important developments at the level of higher education. Many American universities developed area studies centers following the passage of the National Defense Education Act in 1958. These centers trained a new generation of scholars who became well-versed in the history, culture, and society of non-Western regions as well as the Soviet Union and Eastern bloc countries. The turmoil that embroiled American society during the mid- and late 1960s as a result of the civil rights movement and the Vietnam war led this new generation of area scholars to more critically examine the U.S. role in the world. This new critical approach may have annoyed some of these scholars' mentors, but it led to many publications and research projects that helped develop a deeper understanding of foreign cultures and societies. Whereas the collapse of the Soviet Union and the Eastern bloc in 1989 led once again to a false sense of security, the continuation of international turmoil in the form of intensified ethnic conflict in Africa, Latin America, and especially the Middle East, continued to stimulate a large number of educators to search for new paradigms through which to study America's relationship with foreign societies, especially those of the non-Western world.

Another element in American education's international interest in the period of the Cold War was "development education," described in the National Society for the Study of Education's 1969 yearbook, *The United States and International Education*, which dealt with the extension of American educational resources—in universities and governmental agencies—to the "developing" world, and also to an extent with international content in American curricula. Gutek (1992, p. 64) has criticized this form of "development education" as a "top-down" model for social improvement through education modeled on the Marshall Plan. One prominent author included in this yearbook devised a new scheme for classifying the American or Western (now called "northern" by some) educational interest in the rest of the world. Butts here describes certain types, evolving over time: the missionary, the proprietary, the plenipotentiary, the military, and finally the "educationary." The latter, Butts's visionary type, was characterized by professionalism and interest in bringing developed skills in education to others across national boundaries. The term Butts uses for this extension beyond the nation is "transcend" (Shane, 1969, pp. 28–33, 37). Gutek's criticism notwithstanding, the 1969 yearbook contains its own critical insights about the work of development education. For instance, Anderson writes with an awareness of insights from the new historiography of American education of the period, suggesting that culture as well as pedagogical structures must be studied if a true picture of a developing society is to be achieved. Arguing from this premise, Anderson advises that comparative studies of the cultures in which the new development education was applied under auspices of American expertise might be needed to determine their effectiveness (Shane, 1969, p. 78).

The term *development education* has been widely used in the literature since the time of the 1969 report and before, sometimes in ways that have more to do with grassroots movements and pedagogies in developing countries undertaken apart from American governmental, university, or foundation auspices. Development education continues to be an evolving academic specialty.

An interesting contrast to the top-down model of development education is UNESCO's "community education," initially advanced in the 1950s, which worked from the grassroots level to generate benefits through education for communities with minimal resources and expense. "Community education" directed local human resources toward solving immediate community problems, mostly in so-called developing countries, in ways that would lead to permanent improvement through new learning as well as through technical know-how. American teachers' involvements with community education, as UNESCO workers, necessarily forced many of them to confront their cultural biases and gave them a more realistic internationalist interest than did development education. Perhaps a quintessential example of the kind of education described in this yearbook is to be found in the work of Philippine educator Orata, who devised programs for people in his country around problems of hygiene, landscape, and animals kept for food. Orata encouraged people to fence their yards, keeping in the pigs they raised for food, and to build hygienic latrines as well. He linked these by teaching ecological principles in a basic way, showing people links between animal waste and pollution of local waters. Fish ponds replaced bush latrines, and fencing in pigs kept these ponds clean so that the fish raised in them could be used for food. Thus, hygienic, ecological, domestic, and aesthetic results were combined in a single project. Orata managed those who failed to follow the new rules by having them attend instruction in ecology and public health matters during which they would read (or have read to them) the new ordinances. In this way, literacy development became part of the community education scheme. In keeping with the principles of community education, this new pedagogy was inexpensive, multifaceted, and it involved people in development projects created within their communities rather than imposing them from beyond. The new education they promoted used technological and scientific knowledge familiar to the developed world, but through resources belonging to the community itself.

Community education projects under UNESCO made literacy through reading in indigenous cultural texts an important aspect of development, but this entailed a certain theoretical contradiction, pointed out by William S. Gray in the 1959 NSSE volume. Hindu texts, for instance, were used in teaching literacy in certain places in India; but literacy itself —its pedagogy—could be regarded as a Western technology, if it was taught with the values associated with it in the West. Gray advocated learning, on the part of literacy workers, as much as possible about the lives of those served in such programs, to make their culture and economic interests subjects for literacy. Without this, he argued, the programs might be less successful (Henry, 1959, p. 135). But Gray did not recommend that the learning be mutually transforming, that is, that it should involve as an important and necessary element the teacher's openness to cultural change through learning the lives of the people served in the literacy program. Such mutuality became part of Freire's *Pedagogy of the Oppressed* (1970), discussed later, which Freire would have us read as a postmodern version of community education (not under the auspices of UNESCO).

An interesting comparison between UNESCO's community education and the American educational scene is offered by the example of the settlement houses of American cities in the later 19th century. The settlement house movement, which began in urban English slums, became a catalyst for new experiments in multi-ethnic development of urban life in the United States through self-help and collaborative practical education. Led by educated sons and daughters of the prosperous classes, the settlement houses offered shelter, hygienic improvement, language instruction, and cultural activities to build dignity, practical and social skills for the new American environment in immigrant groups and the poor of the cities. The urban environment represented the opportunities and the ills of modern American life most graphically for these people and the settlement house goal was to help them learn how they might avail themselves of its opportunities, avoid its pitfalls and discriminations, develop and share their skills with others, and collaborate in mutually beneficial health programs. Settlement house programs addressed common social needs of urban life— harmonious integration of cultural differences, sanitation and hygiene problems, and the development of a skilled workforce. They differed from the "Americanization" programs of the same period in that they fostered independence through work and intelligent collaboration without requiring cultural sterilization or assimilation. Jane Addams's Hull House evolved from the same context and from some of the same insights as John Dewey's Laboratory School, its neighbor in late 19th century Chicago.

A more recent example of something approximating UNESCO's community education in America is the case of Horton (1998) and his Highlander Folk School, which also resembled and was influenced in its formation by the settlement house movement. Horton's work involved ordinary Americans in learning for themselves how they might address and resolve certain civic problems that reduced in their lives the full promise of American society. In the early years of Highlander, in the 1920s and 1930s, Horton's work provided leadership and facilitation for miners unionizing in Appalachia. In the 1950s, the time of UNESCO's community education, Highlander became an important scene for learning among America's civil rights leaders—most prominently Rosa Parks and Martin Luther King, Jr.

Horton's plans sought the development of local solutions by people involved directly in and suffering from the public problems they would address. Through community action (legal investigations, unionizing rallies, historical investigations, and protests) Highlander's "students" (all adults) would learn more about their problems and more of the skills needed to address them as they worked toward their solutions. Rosa Parks, Martin Luther King, Jr., and many of their colleagues participated in workshops at Highlander, which were rather like retreats, where they worked collaboratively to identify problems and resources for solving them. Horton insisted that his role was that of a facilitator providing the space and atmosphere to enable such collaborations, as well as a rich cultural environment of song and tradition (a pedagogic device learned from the Danish Folk schools) that would be conducive to creative thought. In his later years, Horton worked abroad and became involved in international education projects.

In more recent times, it can be argued that more diffuse forces have undermined the ability of American students, whether at the secondary school or university level, to develop understanding of particular cultures and societies that are not their own. The decline of "social Keynesianism," which resulted from the abandonment of many of the policies of the New Deal, has fostered a more individualistic and materialist culture. The enshrining of the market and productive efficiency have directed attention towards economic growth and wealth enhancement rather than toward community values. The "downsizing" of most major American corporations and the fear that many students, especially those at the university level, have of finding a secure career has made student approaches to education much more instrumental. Although the events of September 11, 2001, may have changed that perspective somewhat as many students returned to more "idealistic" pursuits, it remains to be seen whether, in the current atmosphere of fear and suspicion, a new pedagogical approach to international education (i.e., one that is truly effective) can be developed.

These passages in the educational history of internationalism show an interest in incorporating concerns for peace and later for development as concerns of education, but with certain limitations that could be labeled ethnocentric, as if educators clung in these periods to new versions of the old universalist motive that inspired classical education in the colonial period and later. The first reports (1918 and 1936) speak of an urgent concern for teaching democracy and world understanding in the schools, but they draw their texts from certain northern European cultures and from the political history of democracy in Great Britain. The outreach interests of "development education," as treated in the 1969 report of the National Society for the Study of Education, show a bias toward optimistic modernist faith in Western, particularly American, expertise as the means to improving life in any country. They also show a rather limited affiliation of internationalist educational projects with the American government and with American philanthropic foundations that were closely allied with government policies in that era.

The reports on "community education" show more internationalist interest in another sense, namely, an interest in what grassroots educators such as Pedro T. Orata were inventing for peoples in the developing world. These are just two salient landmarks to be noted in passing over this complex history. They represent two aspects of the legacy of this internationalism, namely, its interest in expertise as a legacy of modernism and a studied recognition of pedagogic innovation particular to educators who were not working for official American interests. The professionalism of American educators involved in the work of "development education" sponsored by the U.S. government and foundations—those who worked on loan from their universities—perhaps deserves mention as well. This was the period when the Peace Corps was created, as well, bringing its special brand of expert optimism and generosity from the imagination of the Kennedy administration to many parts of the developing world. In some of these projects, perhaps, we find the modernist themes of improvement through intelligence transformed from Harris's idealism and Dewey's instrumentalism to a self-assured, generous, and professional expertise interested in spreading its dispensation in far-flung parts of the world in response to the backwardness there perceived to be exacerbated by contrast with the modernization already achieved in America. This is perhaps a hasty characterization, but it points up the possible genealogy of change certain motives in our educational history have undergone in moving from the distant past toward the globalizing present. The autochthonous community development interests of settlement houses and Horton's Highlander, combining strong practical insights with utopian social vision, provide an interesting contrast, as does the instrumentalism of Dewey.

CONTEMPORARY THEORETICAL CHOICES

Contemporary theoretical choices are many, but this chapter focuses on several for their differences from one another and from the examples studied here from the past. These might be classed roughly as "utopian" and "liberal democratic," for convenience. Others might be found that are either more radically utopian or less liberally democratic, but those offered here should serve to mark out rough, general coordinates in the terrain.

These views represent American educational theory's attempt to address questions of universalization and inclusion in new ways that bear the wisdom of learning from the immediate past. Particularly, they constitute an important part of its responses to the multiculturalism's challenge to the democratic model of education and to the utopian ideal of "global citizenship" as an emerging new interest. The utopian schemes discussed here represent a kind of pedagogy for global citizenship, rather frankly. Those concerned with democracy and education might seem at first exclusively interested in American education; but their affirmations of the general modern philosophy that inspires democracy draw from some of the same wellsprings that inspire global citizenship, and thus they are linked historically. These formulations for democratic education can be read as implying a universal form for autonomous people in inclusive societies to educate themselves and their children in ways that would reproduce their public mode of living. The democratic theories for education selected for review here represent the American educational legacy (although they are not the only theories that do this), and thus they should be regarded as substantial ideas for consideration by American educators proposing to engage their students in learning about others or in communicating with others in the globalizing world as parts of educational projects (e.g., teleconferencing). Further, they can serve as counterassertions to neoliberal schemes such as "human capital theory," which are becoming important rhetorical influences on education, demanding from it certain responses to meet the demands of a globalizing world (e.g., privatization, efficiency, diminishment of teaching authority in favor of the bureaucratic, etc.).

Seen in this way, the educational scene in its response to migration and new multicultural demographics—part of globalization—becomes a catalyst for new thought on the nature of the American school as laboratory or a model for what American society is becoming.

The American pluralist ideal has come under pressure as its promise of a unifying civic culture, superimposed over a private realm of diverse cultural expression, seems less tenable to some than to its earlier promoters. Thus, contemporary reprises of democratic educational theory by such writers as Gutmann and Feinberg must consider anew how the world beyond the older American self-identity can become more a part of the world within the American school.

This question seems to represent a counterpart to the questions of utopianism discussed by such writers as Boulding and various other peace educators, who would universalize educational motives in ways that transcend national interest and even the academic history that has shaped the schools. So, the question arising with a comparison of these two groups asks: Should the universalization of human values through education be achieved through development of an inclusive form for democracy or through a transcendence of older forms of community, pedagogy, and government?

In addition, one might look at certain government policies on education that have some prominence in the field today, particularly the <u>Nation at Risk</u> policy statement of the United States Department of Education (1988), the recent No Child Left Behind act, and the more recent policy statements of the European Union. These valorize education as preparation for the global economic competition their nations are involved in and individual resourcefulness developed in workers as individual members of their nation-communities capable of earning their own livings in this new economy. In this view, the individual's economic competitiveness serves that of the nation, and vice versa. Education should be a matter of public policy, according to this view, because it serves the function of matching citizens to productive and enriching labor needs. Thus, education should be vocational and community members should have access to it at various crucial moments in their lives when economic change requires them to develop new skills more profitable (to themselves but also to "the economy") than their old ones. The policies of the European Union have been analyzed critically by Spring (1998, 2001), who argues that their deletion of human-rights-based curricular concerns in the 1990's deprives them of their former ideal and impoverishes them by turning them into sheer market strategies for education. The theoretical positions described next stand as alternatives to such possible impoverishment. Although these political policies for education represent ideological or theoretical interests some educators might share, they are not treated here separately as theories because their polemic form gives them a force in the world that theoretical writings cannot have. Thus, we might treat them rather as givens, as markers of what is already in force, rather than of what might be.

Freire might be mentioned in the context of utopian educational thought, although he did not write about American education or offer proposals for it. Nevertheless Freire drew his ideas in part from European and American philosophical and educational thought; he worked for a time at an American university and made frequent visits to speak in the United States. He was also a friend and associate of Horton in their later years, and saw common threads of creative thought and practice in his pedagogy of the oppressed and the work of Horton's Highlander. Further, many American educators have adapted Freire's pedagogical critique to address problems of equity and social change.

Freire called his educational thought "utopian," emphasizing its focus on becoming and his belief that social justice must be the core of any progressive pedagogy. Freire's pedagogy approaches the world in realistic terms. It begins with collaborative groups making "codifications," or images of their world that they can then discuss reflectively rather as an artist might consider a scene. The codification distances the scene slightly from the immediate lives of its creators, but, of course, they remember it is a scene from their lives. Its generality, however crude, allows them to see the scene of their lives more integrally and to relate one thing in it to another and to affective concerns about the conditions these things, as an ensemble, represent. Illiterates learn written language in doing this, as Freire's model teaches syllables for the construction of written words to articulate the codification on paper (which is easier in Portuguese than in English). Cultural meanings tied to the participants' descriptions now become themes in literate discussion, which gives another form to their reflective distancing of themselves from the material conditions that are the scenes of their lives. The participants' distance, achieved by making the codification into a visible figure of their world, allows them to look more closely, as if at a candid photo or stop-action film, in apprehending its reality, but the addition of written words, a new power for them, naturally makes them participate in another realm of meaning as they describe the scenes of their lives. This power belongs more widely to the world than their vernacular language and its acquisition becomes a new political condition in their lives with potential involvements previously not available to them. Freire (1998a), borrowing an idea from European critical theorists, called this pedagogy "education for critical consciousness."

In this way, Freire's students notice things that their everyday immediate involvement in the scene would ignore. They notice contrasting values in their statements about a particular scene, which helps to point out the connectedness of the scene with the world. Their interest extends from the immediate instrumental perception of the environment to critical concern for the justness or beauty of social relations inscribed in it. With this, their interest becomes "epistemological," concerned with the process of knowing as well as with its object (Freire, 1998a). With new knowledge of their own situations, articulated in a new language, Freire's cultural workers might become activists. Their critical knowledge is inherently active. Their knowing becomes an urge to change things to achieve greater harmony and social justice.

Freire wrote with an acute awareness of postcolonial oppression and developed his pedagogy on principles unique to the Portuguese language, but readers in many countries have identified with his images of the cultural worker, the "culture circle," the "codification," and its "epistemological curiosity." Freire's pedagogy has much in common with UNESCO's community education, for example, its reliance on grassroots interest, its *ad hoc* problem solving, its reliance on affordable available resources, its utopian vision of universal practical improvement, and its absence of ideological rhetoric. But, it differs in its theoretical sophistication and its willingness to make education political. Freire has consistently refused to offer suggestions to American educators about the application of his pedagogy to their social environment. To do this would counter his belief in the ability of vernacular people to identify problems and solutions. Implicit in Freire's pedagogy is the belief that education must address the particular problems of a people, which are necessarily different from the problems others experience in the world. Freire respects cultural difference as a given. His utopianism regards the desire for happiness, justice, and freedom in the future as the only universal. This internationalism requires that people seeking to employ Freire's pedagogical principles look critically into their own local societies for the sources of oppression, injustice, and restrictions on freedom and use education as a cultural force for social and political change (Freire, 1998a, 1998b). In shifting the universal to the realm of becoming, which he identifies as the common denominator of human experience, Freire resembles Dewey and American pragmatism.

Another educational form that shares this utopian interest and its egalitarianism is peace education. Peace education (an umbrella term for various pedagogies and theoretical stances) belongs to the utopian category because of its insistence on the possibility of universal harmony of interests. Peace education seeks the abandonment of traditional suppositions about subjectivity and the dominance of cultural forms, including dominant cultural forms of educational research and practice. By abandoning belief in preordained social and ethical structures that foster inequality, oppression, and war in the world, peace educators regard all persons as equally interested in the elimination of such ills, on the grounds that such interests are not ordained in nature. Essentially, peace education follows a postmodernist view of personal subjectivity, which asserts itself as part of being rather than as having its identity only in belonging to an established social order, which would foster its interests through hegemonies and classes.

Peace education has allied itself with action research, an empirical approach to learning that involves participants—students and their teachers—in investigations of questions making the nature of their learning and inquiry part of their interest. Carson describes one such project, undertaken in 1988, in an endeavor called CARPE (Collaborative Action Research in Peace Education). Carson's project grounded itself partly in principles of critical consciousness derived from the same European philosophy that became a formative part of Freire's pedagogy. CARPE's purpose was threefold: to explore the meaning of peace education; to create practices in peace education in the teaching of CARPE's participants; and to begin transforming their educational settings into places that mirrored the "peaceful structures" the researchers had identified as necessary, such as attention to human rights and nonviolent conflict resolution. CARPE drew its framework of "peaceful structures" from a guide published by other peace educators—Toh and Cowagas—that focused on nonviolence, human rights, antimilitarization, intercultural trust, and "attention to questions of personal peace," by which they meant concern about "alienation, substance abuse, family violence, etc." (Pinar & Reynolds, 1992, p. 107). The CARPE group met regularly to discuss their practice, tape-recording their sessions.

Carson's peace education builds on insights from phenomenology, particularly its recognition of a pastoral original condition of being that might be retrieved by thoughtful action attentive to the "hermeneutic" processes by which we make meaning, roughly and inchoately at first, more clearly with practice (*praxis*), in our lives. Hermeneutics takes practice and is a kind of practice and thus a kind of education. Its attention to being in its non-technologized state, phenomenologists believe, draws us away from the potentially divisive reifications of things in their mere instrumental uses as identified by technological development. Peace educators, and phenomenological curriculum theorists, see this as a way of escaping the rigid classifications of things, and of knowledge, according to instrumental schemes that keep people apart from the possibility of recovering the lost original of our being in the world.

Interpretation becomes an essential part of the research for all participants practicing in their classrooms the peace education strategies described by Carson—in contrast to the professionalization of research and its interpretation as functions separate from teaching and from the subjective lives of the researchers (Pinar & Reynolds, 1992, p. 113). Thus, in the project Carson describes, education, reflecting socially on education, recording commentary, and critically exposing limitations that reduce participants to material status, all become part of one activity of learning more about the experience of attempting to educate peacefully. "Peace," then, cannot be described as an object of research, exactly, because it must also be part of the research practice. The nature of peace education cannot be understood as something formed in its theoretical assertions, but rather as something formed in the openness of its researchers to learning more about what happens when they engage in it fully. Carson's project is utopian in various senses, not the least of which is its de-professionalization, an aspect it shares with the work of Freire and Horton.

Such thought is utopian in its generality, optimism, and spurning of corrupt schemes that have tended to diminish human potential and relegate persons to the status of things. Environmental education has been undertaken according to similar principles as a form of peace education, regarding natural resource protection and the health of the earth as an ecosystem including humans as an interest calling on people in their ontological natures. Ecology education of this sort would use action research to empower those who would work for environmental improvement to make such improvement happen in the investigation of environmental ills, rather than differentiating the workers in the environmental movement as mere researchers, field workers, political activists, or conscientious consumers.

Although such action research resembles "community education," it assumes a more radical philosophical foundation, and perhaps a more sophisticated one. Its concern with the ontological status of learning and improving the human condition through subjective investigations makes all its participants searchers after some retrievable condition of being that would eliminate the divisions and violence of the world of human affairs. Its utopianism reaches far beyond the pragmatic concerns of community education in its philosophical sophistication, which might be its limitation.

Another perspective in the field of peace education comes from the work of Boulding. Boulding's utopianism asserts itself through the rhetoric of the United Nations, particularly the educational themes of UNESCO and the possibilities for improving the world through networks of independent nongovernmental agencies (INGOs). Working from the practical premises of the United Nations charter as a given, Boulding builds a theoretical model for world change that would respect and enhance the subjectivities of individuals in self-chosen solidarities with groups joined for common purposes. These purposes would be, because they spring from the grassroots interests that form INGOs in the first place, local, *ad hoc*, and spontaneous and they would have strong practical interest *qua* interests that people really want to get something done about. INGOs can include environmental groups, church groups, hobby groups, heritage groups, nature-interest groups—virtually any interest that joins like-minded people might become the basis for forming an INGO. Boulding (1988) accepts all groups under this umbrella, relying on the dynamics of solidarity and international networking through structures already in place in the United Nations to limit as well as to valorize their potentials.

Boulding looks past national state structures, and past the Security Council functions of the United Nations (without spurning them) to these agencies of solidarity as the purposeful social organizations of the future. She expects that their development might produce in the world something those other structures cannot achieve: purposeful and effective action to meet the interests of people joined in mutual groups formed around the identification of real needs and concerns, which will be expressive and humanizing. Her plan is educational on the grand scale in its recognition that people joined through such activities will learn through their interests. Its insistence that their learning will be applied to betterment in the world and its expectation that such activities might one day outstrip outmoded governmental forms that have proved to be less effective in producing happiness is utopian.

Boulding could be grouped with peace educators for some of the interest and method she shares with them, but also with feminist educators, for her assertion that the new global civic order she foresees would be especially valuable in allowing women access to the project of management and improvement in the world through public structures of education and creative civic work. The localness, responsiveness, and openness of the INGO make this possible.

Another theoretical perspective from feminist thought, the "schoolhome" educational theory of Martin, would merge value interests of the domestic and the public world through a transformation of schooling. Martin's view looks to the domestic scene as the model for cherishing, growth, security, and other essential values that she believes would make society at large more humane. Her critique focuses both on the stresses many American families have felt to be wearing down their coherences, and on the rigidity and unresponsiveness of school structures. Essential values are in danger of being lost from both realms, Martin argues. Her solution is the creation of the schoolhome, which would assume more of the cherishing and nurturing nature of the home, in part to supply the want of such things in our society, and at the same time attach these important ways to the work of learning, in order to re-inspire schooling with more vital purpose (Kohli, 1995, pp. 45–55).

Martin further develops her thought in the concept of "cultural bookkeeping," which regards all cultural legacies as in danger of extinction or degradation in the current scene of domineering and narrowly focused interests in public life. Cultural bookkeeping would become the responsibility of education, making the school and other institutions of learning responsible for assessing the nature of cultural legacies within our society and ways in which these might be protected and used (Martin, 2002).

Martin's critique reprises certain older themes in American educational theory—for instance, the integration of learning and civic life and the reproduction of home interests in school life as a way of compensating for a deficit in the modern experience of children, which Dewey promoted in his Laboratory School in Chicago. But she joins these ideas with contemporary concerns about the crushing effects of a standardizing and domineering public culture that shows little responsiveness to many persons and their cultural inheritances, which it ignores. Much will be lost in this process, Martin (2002) warns Martin.

The interaction between domestic values and social values forms, in Martin's view, the dialogic energy needed to clarify and institute proper values in each. Her philosophy counters the tendencies of abstraction and alienation that many thinkers have blamed for making society inhumane. It resembles Freire's pedagogy in its reliance on actual positive shared beliefs about humanity and its insistence that these be brought into a kind of dialectical relation with the problematic issues that disrupt the public sphere, as resources for humanizing it (Kohli, 1995, pp. 45–55). Martin's theory, like Boulding's, looks to certain social and civic structures already present in the world for renewal through a revalorization rooted in principles of feminine insight.

Nussbaum's new cosmopolitanism presents a challenge to our thinking about world citizenship that springs from an acute diagnosis of contemporary social problems on a world scale without resorting to postmodern pastoral imagining or to the radical political utopianism of thinkers like Boulding or Freire. Nussbaum argues that the modern state has become outmoded because its interests must be served by people too narrowly, preventing them from reaching the full expression of humanity—an educational ideal—that would identify with anyone anywhere who had understood this expression to be a cosmopolitan goal. Nussbaum looks to the ancient Stoics for her cosmopolitan model. Theirs was a critical humane ideal, generated in opposition to the corruption and oppression brought about by political force. Nussbaum argues that cosmopolitan education of this sort should be espoused because it makes us more aware of ourselves in our fully human nature; because it would have us understand the human background of diverse peoples; because it would lead us to recognize, through this perception of otherness, our obligations to people in the world; and because it would call for consistency in our dealings with others.

Arguing for a separation of the humane ideal from political states, Nussbaum asserts that recognizing their limitations and tendencies to distortion of ideals would make us more sympathetic to the people living in the conditions of limitation imposed by such states, this recognition, she argues, would lead us to identify with people in their differences because we would see in them and in ourselves a common condition of limitation; this would then become a sympathetic and dialogic recognition and the basis for a search for something better. The redeeming ideal, Nussbaum et al. (2002) believes, is to be found in a transcendent humanity idealized as something not to be limited by national borders. Nussbaum's cosmopolitanism sounds radically new despite its ancient lineage. It addresses contemporary concerns about the limitations of the modern political state and the protection of cultural identities against oppression by states and offers a new version of the ideal of global citizenship.

Nussbaum's original essay on cosmopolitanism provoked controversy among critics who argued for patriotism as an essential value in contemporary society and education, despite Nussbaum's claim that it had been outmoded (a claim asserted quite differently by postmodernists, e.g., Bamyeh). The democratic educational ideal was treated theoretically by Dewey and others early in the 20th century, but it has come under new challenges recently, particularly from the interests of multiculturalism. Although these are not the only theoretical concerns that question the democratic model as it has been developed in the past as a model of pluralism, they will be treated especially here because they bring up questions closely related to the interests of global citizenship.

Specifically, the problem of multiculturalism and democratic education re-introduces in puzzling ways the questions about the larger polyglot world finding expression within American society as an ideal form that we saw in the earlier history of universalism. Globalization increases the migratory and cosmopolitan phenomena that lead to multicultural community formation, either in regions that were less exposed to such phenomena in recent times or in urban areas where older immigration patterns had led to eventual settled relations among different cultural communities. In addition, postmodern thought, at the same time, has questioned national boundaries as it questions the concept of the state as a transcendent entity, as new demographic configurations as well as economic allegiances tug at the older conceptions of the state as a unified and identifying interest of its peoples (Bamyeh, 2000). Competitive and exploitative interests of states, as well as the tendency of capitalist corporations to exploit state resources, have suggested to some that the modernist concept of the state is outmoded. What will replace it is a matter of conjecture, whose speculations have included some of the world citizenship programs discussed herein. These might not all see themselves as replacement models for the modernist state, certainly; but their interests suggest alternative representations of people in political affiliations that would make the state a less-than-complete boundary on their lives.

Theorists espousing a renewal of the liberal democratic theory of education have worked to reassert the claims of the modern state as necessary to securing stability, dignity, and happiness in people's lives even in a world given to such changes. It is in this context that we will address the question of democratic education. Multiculturalism, presenting itself as a theoretic replacement to pluralism, has challenged the liberal democratic ideal principally in suggesting that the latter fails in its too-exclusive commitment to process rather than substance as a basis for citizenship and citizenship education. The multiculturalist argues that liberal civic societies cannot generate values except in the limited areas demarcated by civil rights. Charles Taylor, for instance, would divide individual rights (e.g., to nondiscrimination on the basis of gender) from rights concerning the integrity and expression of cultural groups (e.g., the right to protect a minority language as representing a culture; (Taylor in Gutmann, 1994, pp. 53–54).

Liberal democratic education might be understood, in its recent theoretical revisions, as an alternative to the utopian strain in educational thought represented by peace education and liberation pedagogy. Recent theorists have suggested that considerable value might be redeemed from the liberal democratic school by effecting certain revisions inspired by the recognition of a problem overlooked in the past when the democratic school was regarded as a laboratory of pluralism. This new critique centers on questions of multiculturalism that challenge the older pluralist ideal.

The pluralist ideal valued the common civic culture of democratic society as the mutual interest and forum for personal expression that would separate private and public lives in a satisfactory way. Building on the ideal of the liberal state, pluralism relegated personal interests and expressions, including cultural ones, to the private realm and expected that persons would transcend these interests in their public lives, where they came together to consider common concerns. This idea is well represented by the writings of Kallen (1956), among others. Recent political and educational theory have challenged this notion with the assertion that not only do people have certain crucial aspects of their identities from the cultural groups to which they belong, but these groups themselves are entitled to political representation as a guarantee of their continued existence. Multiculturalists, such as Taylor, argue that only groups can raise children and create and inculcate values not included among those guaranteed in liberal constitutions (Gutmann, 1994, p. 61, and *passim*). Thus, the right to freedom of speech is a civic value that people achieve through their nature as citizens, but values arising from expression in music or family structures cannot be created taught to children in the public arena, because they belong to people in their natures as cultural groups.

Gutmann develops the theory of democratic education partly in response to such concerns of multiculturalism. Gutmann defends the value of the democratic school as an essential means by which a people can reproduce their way of life, but she seeks to reinvent the formula for such a school to allow for the fair representation of cultural values in schools. Gutmann justifies democratic education as the best way for a society to reproduce itself and still allow its citizens—and cultural groups—expression in the changing identity formation of the society. She describes three political orders: the "family state," the "state of families," and the "state of individuals," each of which continues to exert influence as an ideal among people, although Gutmann's critique exposes them as inadequate. The family state regards the political society as one community with a common identity to which all can belong and in which all can find happiness and justice (the Platonic ideal). The state of families allows separate families to determine the good for themselves and their children, without government norms for morality; and the state of individuals treats all as equal members free to discover the good on their own. The latter represents the form of liberal society as it has been conceived from the philosophy of J. S. Mill and others. The state of families represents the form many feel society should take in order to allow freedom of expression and replication to culture groups within modern society (and one cherished by neoliberal champions of globalization and "human capital" theory).

Gutmann calls on us to imagine a democratic education that would satisfy the concerns for central moral authority, such as the family state promises, the rights of families to determine what values their children will be taught, and the integrity of individuality as a political principle. Her approach would allow the whole society to reproduce itself through mechanisms designed into school structure that provided for expression by cultural groups in certain areas of interest, and by individuals in others. Gutmann believes democratic education could achieve this, provided two safeguarding principles were instituted and protected: the principle of "nonrepression" and the principle "nondiscrimination." The former "forbids using education to restrict *rational* deliberation or consideration of different ways of life" (Gutmann, 1999, p. 45). The latter would require that *"all* educable children be educated adequately to participate as citizens in shaping the future structures of their society" (p. 46). Democratic education could thus reproduce the society it represents by processes that were intrinsically deliberative, without requiring people to quell their culturally formed voices. This form would respect the multicultural reality of contemporary society within a democratic setting. At the same time, the principle of nondiscrimination would assure that all should learn the civic morality democratic society depended on.

Feinberg makes a similar point, addressing the question of the democratic pluralist state's viability in the face of hard-to-dismiss claims that cultural groups within the state should have the right to survival and expression. Feinberg acknowledges the criticism that the liberal pluralist state might promote only process as its essential value, leaving itself open to the charge that it has no substantial values to communicate and foster and that such values, which are produced in its various culture groups, will assert themselves in ways at odds with the civic culture of the society as a whole. Feinberg argues that the liberal state does have a substantial public culture, evidenced in its choices of certain patterns of living, (e.g., monogamy) as acceptable while others are disallowed. Further, he argues that whereas awareness of difference is inevitable and potentially educational in a pluralist society, some means must be in place to manage this awareness so that it becomes reflective and fruitful. Cultures coexisting within the liberal state should learn from one another, Feinberg argues; but that state must have an educational system that insures that they will do this, if the value of cultural interchange as a means to enhanced awareness and effective judgment about matters the public must deliberate is to be maintained. Thus, the process of democratic education is not an empty one; it is substantial and contributory to public deliberation about what sort of people the society would continue to be and become (Feinberg, 1998).

Recognition of the rights and interests of others in a liberal state, Feinberg argues, is not just a matter of process insofar as with such recognition "there is a profound educational change in the way believers relate to that doctrine." Further, "the deliberate attempt to bring about this change is a major concern of citizenship education in a liberal society" (Feinberg, 1998, pp. 219–220). Thus, in the liberal state as Feinberg sees it, persons would learn from cultures, both their own and others of their co-citizens, self-consciously with a "decentering" awareness of the variety of voices expressing the nature of life in their society; and they would assume the deliberative responsibility for making decisions in such an open-minded way as a substantial civic activity rather than a mere process. The activity would be substantial because it entailed the choice of growth and development through decentering mutual awareness of interests and values arising culturally into the public arena.

Gutmann's and Feinberg's approaches might revitalize the democratic ideal for American education and make it amenable to resolving the theoretical problem presented by the multicultural perspective: that values are generated in cultures, as groups, rather than by a civic society itself. Civic society as conceived by the pluralist cannot become a culture in a complete sense of this term, and thus it cannot produce the values people live by in society; it can only produce civic values (Feinberg, 1998, pp. 18–27).

Multiculturalists, Feinberg points out, have argued that in the modern liberal state certain voices become dominant and hegemonic, suppressing or marginalizing all others, a description that should lead us to accept revisions of its form to allow for special protected expression by groups outside this hegemonic stream (Feinberg, 1998, pp. 24–25).

Spring (1998; 2001), advancing a critique of hegemonic tendencies in modern societies in the United States and Europe, argues for democratic education rooted in the assertions of the U.N. Universal Declaration of Human Rights, first promulgated in 1948. Spring conceives world education according to a general model that could be used in various ways respecting and allowing expression to enduring cultural traditions of the major regions of the world (the Confucian, the Islamic, etc.), all of which would be rooted in respect for the Universal Declaration of Human Rights (2001). His critique demonstrates the many ways in which countries, particularly the European Union and the United States, have in recent years tended to make economic competition a more salient goal in education than human rights (Spring, 1998). His argument for human rights-based education is not entirely different from liberal democratic educational theory as interpreted by Feinberg.

In some respects, these theories of democratic education might represent an alternative to the utopian ones. But, they have about them the same sense of an ideal available to humanity, rather than a limited ideal for education in certain modern countries. In this way, they might merge with the utopian ideals we have discussed. Also, several of the utopian ideals can be distinguished according to whether they depend on postmodernist assumptions, hermeneutics, or more pragmatic philosophies.

Teachers writing curricula for international understanding under the rubric of "global citizenship" must consider whether their interests and pedagogical vocabularies (which will evince their interests) entail affirming democratic education as a value, or a new cosmopolitanism, or a postmodern pastoral ideal of solidarity, and so on. Each of these ideals might be voiced in the terms teachers use to create their curricular lessons in global citizenship, but these terms are neither simple nor readily compatible. Some theoretical sophistication is required of teachers undertaking to write such lessons.

REFERENCES

Bamyeh, M. (2000). *The ends of globalization*. Minneapolis: University of Minnesota Press.

Barber, B. (1995). *Jihad vs. MacWorld*. New York: Times Books.

Boulding, E. (1988). *Building a global civic order: education for an interdependent world*. New York: Teachers College Press, Columbia University.

Department of the Interior, Bureau of Education. (1877). *The international conference on education held at Philadelphia, July 17 and 18, in connection with the International Exhibition of 1876*. Washington, DC: U.S. Government Printing Office.

Dewey, J. (1927). *The public and its problems*. Athens: Ohio University Press.

Dewey, J. (1975). *Moral principles in education*. Carbondale and Edwardsville: Southern Illinois University Press. (Original work published 1909)

Feinberg, W. (1998). *Common schools, uncommon identities*. New Haven, CT: Yale University Press.

Freire, P. (1970). *Pedagogy of the Oppressed*. New York: Continuum.

Freire, P. (1998a). *Education for critical consciousness*. New York: Continuum.

Freire, P. (1998b). *Pedagogy of the heart*. New York: Continuum.

Gutek, G. L. (1992). *American education in a global society: Internationalizing teacher education*. New York: Longman.

Gutmann, A. (1999). *Democratic education*. Princeton, NJ: Princeton University Press.

Gutmann, A. (Ed.). (1994). *Multiculturalism*. Princeton, NJ: Princeton University Press.

Henry, N. B. (Ed.). (1945). *American education in the postwar period, part II: structural reorganization. The forty-fourth yearbook of the National Society for the Study of Education*. Chicago: University of Chicago Press.

Henry, N. B. (Ed.). (1959). *Community education: Principles and practices from worldwide experience. The fifty-eighth yearbook of the National Society for the Study of Education*. Chicago: University of Chicago Press.

Horton, M. (1998). The long haul: An autobiography, with Judith Kohl and Herbert Kohl. New York: Teachers College Press, Columbia University.

Kallen, K. (1956). Cultural pluralism and the American idea: An essay in social philosophy. Philadelphia: University of Pennsylvania Press.

Kandel, I. L. & Whipple, G. M. (Eds.). (1937). *International understanding through the public-school curriculum. The thirty-sixth yearbook of the National Society for the Study of Education*, (Part II). Chicago: University of Chicago Press.

Kohli, W. (Ed.). (1995). *Critical conversations in philosophy of education*. New York: Routledge.

Martin, J. R. (2002). *Cultural miseducation: In search of a democratic solution*. New York: Teachers College Press.

National Education Association. (1918). *A national program for education: A statement issued by the National Education Association, Commission on the Emergency in Education and the Program for Readjustment During and After the War*. Commission series number one. Washington, DC.

Nussbaum, M. et al. (2002). *For love of country?* Joshua Cohen (Ed.). Boston: Beacon Press.

Pinar, W. F. & Reynolds, W. M. (Eds.) (1992). *Understanding curriculum and phenomenological and deconstructed text*. New York: Teachers College Press.

Sassen, S. (2001). *The global city: New York, London, Tokyo*. Princeton, NJ: Oxford University Press.

Shane, H. (Ed.). (1969). *The United States and international education. The sixty-eighth yearbook of the National Society for the Study of Education* (part I). Chicago: University of Chicago Press.

Spring, J. (1998). *Education and the rise of the global economy*. Mahwah, NJ: Lawrence Erlbaum Associates.

Spring, J. (2001). *Globalization and educational rights: An intercivilizational analysis*. Mahwah, NJ: Lawrence Erlbaum Associates.

Stromguist, N. & Monkman, K. (2000). *Globalization and education*. Latham, MD: Rowman, Littlefield.

Chapter 7

Global Citizenship: Theoretical and Pedagogical Perspectives

Eric Davis

Rutgers University

The concept of global citizenship is of recent vintage having emerged after World War II, and influenced by the spirit of the United Nations and world federalism. As with the notion of world federalism, global citizenship has always had idealistic objectives. However, in the wake of the terrorist attacks of September 11, 2001, the concept has assumed a new urgency. If Americans ignore the dramatic changes that have taken place in global society, then they do so at their own peril. How should global citizenship be defined in the current international environment of suspicion and hostility between the West and many non-Western countries, especially those of the Middle East? What are the components of global citizenship and what reasons might attract American students to identify with this concept? What types of pedagogy need to be developed to make global citizenship a salient concept to the current generation of American students?

Although there is no moral equivalence when discussing the September 2001 terrorist attacks, we must recognize that they represent a reaction to globalization's impact on the Middle East and non-Western world, as well as a response to the U.S. proclivity to support the political status quo in much of the world, despite its frequent lip service to democracy. The September 2001 attacks reflect the impact of a globalization regime that involves extensive economic integration between the advanced industrialized countries of Europe and North America and less developed countries in the Middle East, Africa, Asia, and South America. The core contradiction caused by globalization is the disjuncture between the high level of global economic integration, on the one hand, and the lack of intercultural understanding and political institutionalization among nation states that are affected by the new global political economy, on the other. This disjuncture is dangerous because ordinary citizens do not comprehend the extent to which international trade, capital and labor flows, consumption patterns, environmental problems, and cultural developments—just to mention some of globalization's impact—affect their daily lives. Even the opportunities provided by the Internet for increased cross-cultural understanding have not overcome this contradiction. If anything, citizens in both the developed and less developed worlds seem to have less understanding of one another because the tensions caused by globalization have fostered stereotypical thinking and undermined trust between the "core" and "periphery."

THE COMPONENTS OF GLOBAL CITIZENSHIP

Global citizenship entails first and foremost the development of a *normative consciousness*. It requires young people to view the world differently than they have in the past. No longer can the world beyond our borders be viewed as either a source of cultural enrichment or an optional focus of interest. Global society is, and will become even more so, a core component of the lives of all Americans, whether in economic, political, environmental, or social terms. For the current secondary school and college generations, careers will increasingly require extensive interaction with global society. Thus, it is not enough for students to simply acquire knowledge about the forces of globalization and their impact on global society. Students also must develop an *empathetic approach* that will enable them to grasp in sophisticated ways what the changes in global society have wrought in other countries, especially non-Western societies where political and economic inequality often produces hostility to the United States.

The challenges involved in inculcating this normative consciousness in the current generation of American youth is daunting. As academic pressures to achieve mount on students seeking to enter the professional and business worlds, and attaining these careers becomes more difficult, the tendency for students to view life in more instrumental and self-centered terms represents a distinct possibility. Without an extensive effort to promote new curricula that will encourage students to think in global terms, current economic and status pressures may lead students to think and act more in terms of a narrowly defined self-interest, further impeding an understanding of international affairs.

Creating the normative consciousness and accompanying empathy that are crucial for developing a sense of global citizenship and being a part of the larger world around us requires a distinct type of pedagogy. First and foremost, it must be *historically oriented*. Ethnocentrism and ahistoricism go hand in hand. American students need to become more sensitized to the concept of *change*. The idea that Americans, especially those from privileged backgrounds, have little to worry about in the future is naive and a result of a consciousness that ignores history and change. The future material well-being of the United States and the integrity of the global environment, just to take two of the more prominent problems influenced by globalization, cannot be taken for granted. An emphasis on change creates a sensitivity to the fact that the existing status quo may not necessarily predict the future.

Understanding that much of what we, as Americans, take for granted, entailed great struggle by multiple generations that came before us, promotes a deeper respect for the societal benefits we enjoy, whether our legal and political rights, or our material abundance. The pragmatism inherent in American culture has frequently produced a future-oriented consciousness that assumes that all problems can be solved with the appropriate application of science and technology. This attitude has resulted in great achievements, but it often causes Americans to ignore the past. The assumption that an understanding of globalization and the complex problems that it has engendered can be solved without a historical memory, substantial intercultural dialogue, and the creation of transnational political and economic institutions is deeply flawed.

Thinking historically encourages global citizenship by drawing student attention to the *multicultural nature* of American society, which of course mirrors global society. Clearly, it is impossible to consider the achievements of American society without taking account of the incredible diversity of the groups that made those achievements possible, whether we think in ethnic, racial, gender, religious, or social class terms. A multicultural perspective challenges the rigid cultural boundaries that often result from a strong sense of nationalism. By understanding that enduring values and institutions are often created through cross-ethnic and cross-national cooperation and effort, a historical method sensitizes students to the fluidity of human interaction and the fallacy of assuming that any one group or nation possesses a monopoly on historical achievement.

A historical methodology helps address the tension between "local" and "global" citizenship. A deep and complex understanding of one's own cultural and political heritage helps inculcate a strong value system. Possessing a complex understanding of our own past helps us interact with others by allowing Americans to bring a strong sense of political and social identity to the intercultural "learning table." A more developed sense and appreciation of one's heritage and the past expands the cultural tableau and "issue matrix" that can be shared with those from other cultures.

Second, a pedagogy designed to enhance global citizenship requires an *interdisciplinary* approach. Interdisciplinary learning not only fosters enrichment and creativity, but encourages students to view issues and problems from multiple perspectives, which is a core element of developing a sense of global citizenship. As the processes of globalization force us to increasingly think of issues beyond our national borders, we will be forced to multiply, by an enormous factor, the number of perspectives that we need to take into account. Interdisciplinary learning helps lay a better foundation for confronting this complexity.

The importance of interdisciplinary learning may become more apparent by reference to particular forms of pedagogy. In teaching a midlevel undergraduate course for second- through fourth-year students, called *Globalization and the Non-Western World*, I seek not only to have class members understand the large macroanalytic framework in which globalization is taking place, but also its impact at the local level, namely on our own society but especially the peoples of non-Western countries. Whereas social studies texts are most effective in transmitting knowledge about the increased interdependence of the global economy, rates of foreign direct investment, and transnational labor migration, works of literature often convey a much more nuanced and sensitive understanding of the impact of these processes on non-Western societies. Using visual imagery in the form of film, photography, and indigenous art also allows students to grasp foreign societies in a way that is often not possible through more abstract and theoretically oriented social science research.

A third form of pedagogy that enhances an understanding of and commitment to global citizenship entails *student-directed learning*. In implementing the *Global Citizen 2000 Project* at Rutgers University (described in detail later), students were able to generate numerous initiatives designed to enhance their comprehension of global society that were impressive in their scope and results. Student-directed learning empowers students at an early age, facilitating their becoming active citizens later in life. Despite much lip service to the ills of what Freire (1970) calls the "banking approach" to education, in which educators "deposit" knowledge in their students, this approach still dominates far too much of the secondary school and college curricula where students make the critical transition from student to citizen.

Student-directed learning, if envisioned as project oriented, also undermines the excessively individualistic experience that most students are exposed to as they go through the education system. As pressures to achieve higher grades and win coveted awards increases, the education system is becoming more competitive and individualistic. Competition is a necessary component of any society, but it does not necessarily promote good local, much less, global citizenship, both of which require a sophisticated understanding of the mechanisms and goals of *cooperative action*.

Student-directed learning, if conceptualized in terms of cooperative projects involving groups of students, can offset the tendency of education to become excessively individual centered and competitive. It not only can enhance the knowledge base of students through project members' sharing of information and views, but it also develops interactive skills that will serve students well in the social and political realms once they complete their education. Teachers frequently report that students are much more enthusiastic about learning when they themselves generate the questions and ideas that inform that learning.

Because global society is so complex, and the processes of globalization are so all encompassing, student-directed learning, understood in terms of group projects, allows an individual student to better understand this complexity through an intellectual division of labor in which each student contributes a portion of the knowledge required to complete a project. Thus, student-directed learning can empower young learners in multiple ways. First, it teaches them to conceptualize and implement their own projects. Second, it helps them better understand how to interact and work collectively. Finally, it makes the process of understanding global society less intimidating because students can divide up intellectual tasks and subsequently combine their collective conceptual and research efforts in producing a final product.

HISTORICAL PERSPECTIVES

To make these points clearer, I would like to discuss the pedagogy involved in two courses that I teach at Rutgers University and the outcome of the three-phase *Global Citizen 2000 Project*. *Critical Perspectives on the Middle East* (see appendix) was developed as a response to the tremendous number of stereotypes and misunderstanding I have encountered while teaching students about the comparative politics of the Middle East at Rutgers University over more than 25 years. In confronting the problem of stereotypical thinking that often prevents my students from gaining a comprehension of Middle Eastern politics and society, I used a pedagogy that embodies a historical and interdisciplinary perspective. The concept behind *Critical Perspectives on the Middle East*—which originates in the Department of Political Science, but also serves as an exit-level seminar for Middle Eastern studies majors and minors—is to examine the manner in which ideas and understandings of the Middle East, especially of its Islamic and Arab components, have entered into American political culture. Through developing a historical and interdisciplinary approach to the ways in which knowledge of the region has developed, especially in stereotypical and distorted forms (but also by examining those authors, artists, and travelers who were able to overcome these stereotypes), students come to understand the manner in which stereotypes are created, the historical causes for their development, as well how they change. Because stereotypes do change over time, students also learn that they are not fixed in nature and can be altered and even eliminated. Likewise, by using an interdisciplinary approach in which students study selected examples of religious texts, art and architecture, photography, travelogues, literary works, and forms of popular culture (e.g., cartoons, film, television, newspaper reporting, and advertising) students learn how stereotypes differ from medium to medium and how different media can combine to reinforce stereotypes (e.g., through a film that is made from a novel).

In *Critical Perspectives in the Middle East*, students learn that the idea of global citizenship has always been an implicit component of American political culture. The course begins by examining the Puritans, one of the most prominent settler groups, who saw themselves as the "new Zionists" who would create the "City on the Hill" that would become a "beacon of light unto all nations" (Sha'ban, 1991). If the North American colonies, later to become the United States of America, represented the new Jerusalem that would show the world the path to prosperity, spiritual health, and political stability, then there was little question that, from its founding, the United States felt destined to play a major role in world affairs. The idea of American exceptionalism, which meant that the United States did not suffer from the problematic historical legacies that plagued so many European and non-Western societies, combined with a purportedly nonideological and pragmatic approach to political and social problems, implied that the United States would assume a special leadership role in global society.

As the course moves to the 19th century, students learn of our first encounters with the Middle East. Shortly after the nation's founding, the United States found itself involved in a series of wars with the so-called Barbary pirates of the northern coast of the Mediterranean Sea. Our role as a global power was evident then and codified not long thereafter in the Monroe Doctrine, which delineated Latin America as a critical sphere of interest for the United States. Nevertheless, American citizens took little heed of the implications of our growing role as an emerging international power as the 19th century progressed. The separation of the United States from the rest of world by two oceans, our strong domestic economy that required little dependence on overseas markets, and the Puritan legacy of the United States as a "beacon unto other nations" developed a self satisfied feeling among the populace at large, especially educated elites, which provided little motivation for interest in other cultures.

The increased interest in foreign affairs following the Civil War reflected less new educational policies in American schools than the impact of U.S. rapid industrial growth between the 1870s and World War I. With increased discretionary income, tourism developed as an industry as more upper-class and upper-middle-class Americans possessed the wherewithal to travel abroad. The motivations for foreign travel were the result of multiple causes. First, the rapid industrialization and increases in immigration that resulted from economic growth during the latter part of the 19th century promoted antimodern impulses. Large sectors of the Protestant middle and upper classes saw the shift from an agrarian to an urban and industrially based economy as threatening the "Republican ideal" of which they had been the primary guardians. Travel to remote and exotic lands in the Middle East and East Asia provided, among other things, the opportunity to either escape into the "exotic" or, in the case of the Holy Lands, reconnect with the religious roots of the United States that many Protestants felt were in decline and threatened. Travel abroad also promoted the construction of fantasy worlds that allowed those who viewed the increasing industrialization and secularization of society with fear and disdain to engage in escapism designed to offset these feelings.[1] Thus, Critical Perspectives attempts to demonstrate the extent to which stereotyping of foreign cultures often results from domestic identity politics, rather than actual interest in the region in question.

As the course moves to the 20th century, it looks at the relationship between the new imperial impulse, promoted by the administration of President Theodore Roosevelt, and the feelings of decline felt by large sectors of the middle and upper middle classes. The move from rural to urban areas and the standardization of life in the new corporate form of economic activity, symbolized by the finite work day and punch clock, created a gender response as WASP males, in particular, greeted the Rooseveltian male ideal of strenuous physical activity and the stoic but forceful male embodied in the motto, "Speak softly and carry a big stick" with enthusiasm. For the middle classes, the new imperial impulse was less about acquiring colonies than about the reassertion of WASP culture, the male desire to recapture the Republican ideal, and the escape into exoticism as a means of confronting many of the tensions caused by the industrialization and standardization of society.[2]

If the fin de siècle entry of the United States into the realm of big power politics and imperial control was not accompanied by increased international understanding among the American populace, then the even greater international role that was epitomized by Wilson's Fourteen Points likewise did little to enhance empathy and understanding for foreign cultures. The so-called Roaring Twenties saw a return to what Warren Harding called "normalcy." Economic prosperity provided little incentive for becoming more globally conscious. Nevertheless, the growth of cities and the urban workforce, which included large numbers of immigrants, combined with more discretionary income among the middle and upper classes, propelled the growth of the film industry, which produced highly popular fantasies with foreign themes (e.g., *The Sheik,* with Rudolph Valentino, and *The Thief of Baghdad,* with Douglas Fairbanks). The debates over immigration by East Asia and during the 1920s and the ultimate

---

[1] For a discussion of these trends, see Lears (1981).

[2] Even the several World's Fairs organized in Philadelphia, but especially in Chicago, Buffalo, St. Louis, and San Francisco, prior to World War I, which were intended to educated the American populace about foreign cultures, found fair goers more interested in the "Midways," which emphasized fantasy and escapism and were more reminiscent of an amusement park than an educational experience. See Davis (2002).

legal restrictions that were imposed on such immigration, which were followed in the film world during the 1930s by the *Charlie Chan* series, Tarzan movies, and the French foreign legionnaire genre set in Middle Eastern deserts, increased the number of demeaning stereotypes about non-Western peoples, all of which did little to foster better international understanding.

As is well known, the period following the end of World War II witnessed a cultural insularity reinforced by the U.S. role as the world's military and economic superpower. Despite the desire of large segments of the populace to return to pre-World War II isolationism, fear of the Soviet Union and the spread of communism forced the United States to remain active in the international arena. McCarthyism was instrumental in not only suppressing communists and alleged communists, but also dampening creativity in many intellectual fields including foreign education. Government funding of area studies in the late 1950s and early 1960s (under the National Defense Education Act) was not conducive to developing innovative pedagogies, but rather a defensive mode of defending American values against the threat posed by the Soviet Union and its Eastern bloc allies. Thus, even the 20th century, with two world wars, the Cold War, and the Korean and Vietnam wars, seems not to have promoted a sense of global awareness, much less citizenship. Indeed, after the end of each of these threats to our national security, Americans sighed a breath of relief and returned to a largely insular view of the world.

If *Critical Perspectives on the Middle East* is designed to foster critical thinking skills through emphasizing a historical and interdisciplinary learning, then *Globalization and the Non-Western World* is intended to foster a greater "hands on" approach to learning and impress on students the reasons why they require a better comprehension of global affairs. The concept of globalization, which is at the core of this course, is indicative of the problems students face in trying to grasp an incredibly complex and misunderstood process. Rather than offering them a fixed definition or set of definitions of globalization, students are required to research at least five definitions of the concept and then offer an evaluation of which they find the most compelling. After gaining a better understanding of the concept, students divide into groups of six to eight students to produce group research papers. In these papers, students are asked to study, in detail, what they consider a positive component of globalization and envision ways in which the impact of this positive component might be enhanced. Alternatively, they may decide to focus on what they consider to be a negative impact of globalization and determine means for ameliorating its negative impact on global society. Through studying the empowering and detrimental impacts of globalization, students learn to become part of the world and hence better global citizens.

As educators, the key question remains as to not only how to conceptualize global citizenship, but also how to inculcate an interest in it among students.

Appealing to their idealistic impulses or an "interest in the exotic" is insuffi-
cient. If young people are to take global citizenship seriously, then educators
need to demonstrate how global forces affect their daily lives. In this sense, the
focus on *interdisciplinary education* is not just one that enhances creativity, but
an approach that allows students to better grasp the complexities and integrated
nature of the processes of globalization and the requirements of global citizenship that flow from these processes. How can we make the process of global
citizenship acquire greater meaning for our students?

First, we need to explain how the processes of globalization have produced
a greater need for global citizenship. The rapid rate of global economic integration acquires more salience for students when they are able to comprehend the
extent to which the United States is economically dependent on foreign societies
as markets for our products, as sources of (cheap) labor, and as sources of raw
materials. When students realize the extent to which their own future life opportunities are contingent on sustaining these relationships, then global citizenship
is no longer an idealistic vision but a necessary goal for all Americans to take
seriously.

Second, we need to emphasize that, whereas globalization has created many
benefits, it has also resulted in problems that cannot be solved by any single
nation-state working on its own. Global warming; air and water pollution; over-
fishing of the world's rivers, seas, and oceans; deforestation; and the AIDS and
other health epidemics that spread quickly from country to country due to
greater contact among nations necessitate a multinational approach if they are to
be solved. Although, as educators, we need not promote a pedagogy of fear, we
do need to help students develop ways of thinking about solving the problems
created by globalization through transnational organizations and institutions.

THE GLOBAL CITIZEN 2000 PROJECT

The *Global Citizen 2000 Project* (GC2000) is an outreach project developed by
the Center for Middle Eastern Studies at Rutgers University that received 3-year
funding from the U.S. Department of Education, Title VI, and supplemental
funding from the Geraldine R. Dodge Foundation. The project emerged from an
awareness that high school and middle school teachers in New Jersey have come
under increasing pressure in recent years to teach a broader curriculum in international education. Many teachers point out that their college training did not
give them the breadth of information required to teach what was being asked of
them in the realm of international studies. GC2000's monthly curriculum development workshops at Rutgers University, held during the 2000–2003 academic
years, developed new lesson plans on a wide variety of topics. These workshops
sought to offer teachers the types of resources that would help them overcome

their lack of training. Lesson plans were grouped in a set of curriculum modules from which teachers could choose not only lesson plans, but also a wide variety of resources with which to organize the teaching of issues relating to international affairs. These curriculum modules became part of the Global Citizen 2000 Web site (http://www.gc2000.rutgers.edu) and easily accessible to anyone with a computer.

One of the core principles guiding the lesson plans were that they be interdisciplinary. An effort was also made to incorporate a historical perspective. An interdisciplinary approach was emphasized through relating each lesson plan to comparable plans in other modules. By interrelating social studies and world literature modules, for example, GC2000 seeks to encourage students to view issues and problems in international education from multiple perspectives, thereby increasing knowledge and creative ideas about how to confront these issues and problems. By incorporating curriculum modules such as the U.S. Immigrant Experience, not only did we seek to encourage teachers and students to question the boundaries between "domestic" and "international," which often separate social studies teachers, but we also sought to encourage students to think historically and processually. If American students can see issues as always in a state of change or "becoming," then they will internalize a more open-ended approach to studying international affairs, thereby contributing to our goal of enhancing an understanding of global citizenship.

During the second year of the GC2000 Project, the United States was subject to the terrorist attacks of September 11, 2001. One of the funders of the GC2000 Project, the Geraldine R. Dodge Foundation, generated a new grant program to commemorate the victims of September 11. From this call for proposals, GC2000 developed *Citizens Across Borders: The Student Initiative in Global Citizenship in the Wake of September 11, 2001* (CAB). In developing this project, the goal was to empower students as they commemorated September 11. Thus, we asked participating teachers in the *Global Citizen 2000 Project* to identify students who would generate appropriate projects on their own. All of the projects submitted for consideration by the CAB Project were designed and implemented by students.

If the CAB Project's first phase was *commemoration*, then the second phase involved *civic engagement*. It was our view that one of the goals of the terrorist attacks was not only "cultural policing," namely, to impede intercultural contact and understanding, but also to strike fear in the hearts of Americans, thereby undermining their political and social solidarity. The project organizers felt that it was not enough just to ask students to commemorate the victims of the terrorist attacks. We also felt that students should share their projects with the community, thereby drawing in larger numbers of citizens and engaging them in a dialogue about the meaning of the attacks and appropriate responses to them. This second phase would underscore one of the core components of American society, and one that successive generations have struggled to maintain, namely, the right of free speech and assembly, and the ability to encourage a sense of community through the free exchange of ideas.

The third phase of the project involved *global representation*. After an exhibition of the CAB projects at Rutgers University on May 11, 2002, which represented the efforts of almost 200 students from many central New Jersey school districts, prizes were awarded and the winning projects were placed on a new section of the Global Citizen 2000 Web site. Award-winning projects were placed on the CAB segment of the Global Citizen 2000 Web site, and translated into the five official languages of the United Nations: Arabic, Chinese, French, Russian, and Spanish.[3] The purpose of this third phase of CAB was to demonstrate to the world that many American students are globally literate and highly conscious of their role as citizens in a larger global society.

The sum total of the *Citizens Across Borders Project* was to encourage students to define their role in global society and relate this role to groups in their own communities. The problem with much curriculum at all levels of the educational system is that it does not encourage students to generate their own knowledge. CAB thus was concerned with encouraging creativity on the part of students. One of the best projects, which was the first prize winner, was a videotape project completed by the Odyssey of the Mind Club at Perth Amboy High School entitled, "How Have the Terrorist Attacks of September 11 Affected Your Views of Patriotism?" Students traveled to "Ground Zero" in New York City, where they conducted interviews of New Yorkers, which were then contrasted with interviews with citizens and students in Perth Amboy, which were then shaped into a highly thoughtful video essay on the meaning of being an American in the post-September 11 era.

If *Citizens Across Borders* sought to empower students by encouraging them to think creatively and in civic terms, and represent their projects globally, then the final phase of the *Global Citizen 2000 Project* was designed to create actual contact between New Jersey students and students in foreign countries via teleconferencing projects. During early 2002, the Center for Middle Eastern Studies received a 2-year grant from the Verizon Foundation, *Across the Cultural Divide: Bridging the Knowledge Gap in Middle Eastern and Global Studies* (ACD). One component of the ACD project was to develop teleconferencing links with schools and Non-Governmental Organizations (NGOs) in foreign countries as part of the process of increasing the understanding of global society on the part of New Jersey students.

---

[3] For a description of the award-winning projects from high school and middle school students, including visual imagery and student essays, see the CAB portion of the Global Citizen 2000 Project Web site (http://www.gc2000.rutgers.edu).

Using foreign contacts developed by international studies faculty and graduate students at Rutgers University, projects were established in the People's Republic of China, Taiwan, Lebanon, Jordan, Israel, Poland, South Africa, and the Amazon ecosystem in Brazil. Through a process that first involves e-mail contact centered around a document entitled, "A Day in Your Life," which contains a list of questions designed to help students in the United States and abroad gain a better familiarity of their daily lives, and through adding photo essays of the schools and communities involved in the teleconferencing projects, students develop knowledge of each other's cultures. Once this familiarity is established, students move to develop a mutually agreed on project. After a project is established, students engage in two to three teleconferencing sessions through which they develop, along with their continuing e-mail correspondence, their projects. Once the projects are completed, they are uploaded to the *Across the Cultural Divide* component of the GC2000 Web site.

ACD projects included a wide range of topics but are oriented toward solving problems affecting both participating groups, American and foreign. In the Amazon ecosystem teleconferencing project, New Jersey students and Brazilian students in Sao Paulo exchanged information about how their respective governments are attempting to cope with issues of economic development, while protecting the environment and educating local populaces on environmental issues. Arab and Jewish students in Israel shared their efforts to bridge ethnic differences through peace education with American students who are studying bias and hate crime legislation as a means to cope with ethnic conflict. American students teleconferencing with South Africa compared the experience of slavery in the United States and efforts to achieve racial equality with South Africa's Apartheid system and efforts of the Truth and Reconciliation Commission to transcend it now that it has been dissolved. In teleconferencing with Poland, understanding how Poles and the Romani (gypsy) people are attempting to overcome their ethnic differences and also how Poles are coming to terms with the Holocaust that Jewish Poles suffered during World War II, was contrasted with American efforts to appreciate difference in school districts with rapidly changing ethnic populations.[4]

---

[4] There are numerous ways to generate contacts with educators abroad, for example, through the Web sites of *Global Leap* (http://www.global-leap.com) and *ePALS Classroom Exchange* (http://www.epals.com) Teleconferencing software, such as New Meeting and Yahoo Messenger, can be downloaded at no cost. All that is needed for teleconferencing is a computer and a web camera that is set near the computer and contains a microphone. These web cameras can be purchased at the time of this writing for approximately $50 per camera. For school districts with MAC systems, Apple Computers has its own teleconferencing software that can be downloaded at no cost.

Once the projects are completed at the end of the 2004 academic year, video clips of the teleconferencing sessions, the final projects, and teacher and student assessments of the year's activities will be posted to the *Across the Cultural Divide* portion of the Global Citizen 2000 website and translated into the 5 languages of the United Nations as well as appropriate local languages.

CONCLUSIONS

Global citizenship is an educational imperative that all schools must incorporate into their curricula. In light of the complexities and all encompassing impact of globalization, students should be encouraged to develop self-initiated projects that are completed in groups. Instructors and administrators at all levels of the education system should avail themselves of the technology that is currently available at little or no cost to take advantage of the many teleconferencing opportunities that can easily become an integral part of the school curriculum. Whereas the challenges of creating global citizens are many, the potential benefits for the United States and the societies with which we develop better and hopefully enduring ties far out way the effort involved.

APPENDIX: CRITICAL PERSPECTIVES ON THE MIDDLE EAST

Course Description

No other non-Western region of the world has evoked such strong emotions as the Middle East. Historically, how have Americans developed their attitudes and images of the region? Have these attitudes and images distorted their understandings of it? To what extent are such attitudes indicative of American attitudes toward the non-Western world as a whole? Which historical processes have shaped the way in which American society has approached the problem of social difference/otherness? How have these historical processes affected the way in which Americans view the non-Western world? What role has the Middle East played in the formation of American political culture?

In the contemporary era, how has the power imbalance between the United States and the Middle East, as reflected in American regional strategic and economic interests, shaped prevailing conceptualizations of Middle Eastern peoples and societies? In what ways can scholars and educated laypersons escape some of the constraints imposed by faulty conceptualizations of the region?

Course requirements include periodic presentations of readings by seminar members as a means of opening our session discussions and a 25-page research paper that is due at the end of the course.

Required Readings

Bernstein, Matthew, and Gaylyn Studlar, eds., *Visions of the East: Orientalism in Film* (Rutgers).
Michalak, Laurence, *Cruel and Unusual: Negative Images of Arabs in American Popular Culture* (ADC).
Sabbagh, Suha J., *Sex, Lies and Stereotypes: The Image of Arabs in American Fiction* (ADC).
Said, Edward, *Orientalism* (Pantheon).

Course Outline

I. INTRODUCTION

II. CONCEPTUALIZING THE MIDDLE EAST

Said, *Orientalism*, 1–110
>   al-'Azm, Sadek Jalal, "Orientalism and Orientalism in Re-
>   verse," *Khamsin*, no. 8 (1981), 5–26
>   Paulo Freire, *Pedagogy of the Oppressed*, 57–74
>   Thompson, James, "Mapping the Mind: The Quest for Eastern
>   Metaphors," in *The East, Imagined, Experienced, Remem-
>   bered*, 18-35
>   Videos: *Jihad in America/ Islam in America*
>   Recommended:
>   Bernal, Martin, *Black Athenea: The Afroasiastic Roots of
>   Classical Civilization*, esp. v. I, 1–73
>   MacKenzie, John, *Orientalism and the Arts*
>   Young, Robert, *White Mythologies: Writing History and the
>   West*

*Initial paper proposal and annotated bibliography due

III. AMERICA'S ORIENT: EARLY ENCOUNTERS

A. Religion and Literature
>   Fuad Shaban, *Islam and Arabs in Early American Thought*, 1–
>   63, 141–176
B. Missionary Activity
>   Sha'ban, 83–114

IV. THE MIDDLE EAST IN WESTERN SOCIOPOLITICAL CONSCIOUSNESS: NINETEENTH- AND TWENTIETH-CENTURY PERSPECTIVES

A. Orientalist Art
>   Stevens, MaryAnne, ed., *The Orientalists: Delacroix to Ma-
>   tisse* survey paintings designated by instructor in
>   class
>   Ackerman, Gerald, *The American Orientalists* survey paint-
>   ings designated in class
>   Graham-Brown, Sarah, "Orientalism in Color: Review Essay
>   of The Orientalists: Delacroix to Matisse," *MERIP
>   Reports*, nos. 124–125 (July–Sept., 1984), 56–59
>   Nochlin, Linda, "The Imaginary Orient," in *The Politics of Vi-
>   sion*, 33–59
>   Davis, John, *The Landscape of Belief*, 3–51
>   Recommended:

Sweetman, John, "The American Story," *The Oriental Obses-sion*, 211–250

Berger, John, *Ways of Seeing*

Rosenthal, Donald, *The Near East in French Painting, 800–1880*

Jullian, Philippe, *The Orientalists*

Thornton, Lynne, *Les Orientalistes*

B. Travelogues and Domestic Tourism

Sha'ban, 115–140

Mark Twain, *The Innocents Abroad*, v. II, Chap. XVI, 480–529; Chap. XXIV, 586-630, Chap. XXXI, 684–702

Celik, Zeftep. *Displaying the Orient*, 1–15, 17–49, 80–88, 153–198

Dos Passos, John, *Orient Express*, 73–75, 96–102

Hansen, Eric, *Motoring With Mohammed: Journeys to Yemen*

Recommended:

Lears, Jackson, *No Place of Grace: Anti-Modernism and the Transformation of American Culture, 1880–1920*, 4–58, 98–139

*Updated project proposal due

C. Photography

Perez, Nissan N., *Focus East: Early Photography in the Near East, 1839–1885*, 15–119 skim text and survey des-ignated photographs

Graham-Brown, *Palestinians and Their Society, 1880–1946: A Photographic Essay*, skim text and survey desig-nated photographs

Graham-Brown, Sarah, *Images of Women: The Portrayal of Women in the Photography of the Middle East, 1860–1950*, skim text and survey designated photographs

Recommended:

Alloula, Malek, *The Colonial Harem*

D. Film and Popular Culture

Slide, Anthony, "The Sheik," in *Selected Film Criticism*, 261–262

Kupferberg, Audrey, "The Sheik," in Frank Magill, ed., *Magill's Survey of Cinema*, 964–968

Bodeen, DeWitt, "Beau Geste," *Magill's Survey of Cinema*, 135–137

Hansen, Miriam, *Babel & Babylon: Spectatorship in American Silent Film*, 245–294

Michalak, *Cruel and Unusual: Negative Images of Arabs in American Popular Culture*, entire

Bernstein and Studlar, *Orientalism in Film*, 19–98

*Third update on research paper due

V. CONCEPTUALIZING THE MIDDLE EAST IN THE POST-COLONIAL ERA

A. The Middle East Through the Prism of Religion

R. Singerman, "The Jew As Racial Alien: The Genetic Component of American Anti-Semitism," in D. Gerber, ed., *Anti-Semitism in American History*, 103-128

Said, Edward, *Covering Islam*, 75–125

Naipaul, V.S., *Among the Believers*, 3–82

B. The Middle East Through the Prism of Terrorism

Lewis, Bernard, "Islamic Terrorism?," in Benjamin Netanyahu, ed., *Terrorism: How the West Can Win*, 65–69

Chomsky, Noam, "Middle East Terrorism and the American Ideological System," in E. Said and C. Hitchens, eds., *Blaming the Victims*, 97–147

Rifas, Leonard, "The Image of Arabs in U.S. Comic Books," *Itchy Planet*, no. 2 (Summer 1988), 11–14

C. The Middle East Through the Prism of the Mass Media

Kellner, Douglas, *The Persian Gulf TV War*, 56–108

Nimmo, Dan and Jack Coombs, *Nightly Horrors: Crisis Coverage by Television Network News*, 140–178

Shaheen, Jack, *The TV Arab*, 21–39, 55–70, 113–134

Selected political cartoons comparing anti-Semitism and Arab stereotypes, to be distributed by instructor

*Final research paper update due

D. The Middle East Through the Prism of Modern Literature

Sabbagh, *Sex, Lies and Stereotypes*, entire

Uris, Leon, *The Hajj*, 5–140

Livingston, Harold, *To Die in Babylon*, 3–106

VII. PRESENTATION OF RESEARCH PROJECTS

VII. COURSE EVALUATION

VIII. SUBMISSION OF RESEARCH PAPER

REFERENCES

Davis, E. (2002). The representation of the middle east in American world's fairs, 1987–1904. In A. Amanat & M. Bernhardsson (Eds.), *The United States and the middle east: Cultural encounters* (pp. 342–381). New Haven, CT: Yale University Press.

Freire, P. (1970). *Pedagogy of the oppressed*. New York: Continuum Books.

Lears, T. J. (1981). No place of grace: Anti-modernism and the transformation of American culture. New York: Pantheon.

Sha'ban, F. (1991). *Islam and Arabs in early American thought: Roots of Orientalism in America*. Durham, NC: Acorn Press.

PART III

NEW APPROACHES TO CIVIC RESEARCH AND PRACTICE

Chapter 8

Teaching Democracy Appreciation

John R. Hibbing
University of Nebraska

Alan Rosenthal
Rutgers University

Civic education in the United States is failing. Yet progress is still possible if we, as a nation, take the challenge seriously, develop leadership, allocate resources, and persist. The social studies community is well aware of the problem of a decline in voting, especially among youth. Many teachers have signed on to efforts to persuade youngsters to vote and, more generally, to stimulate their civic engagement. Voting and civic engagement are important, but a major threat to representative democracy in the nation and states is being ignored—that is, the public's misconception of and cynicism toward politics, politicians, and political institutions.

What are the consequences of this misunderstanding and scorn? Able people are being discouraged from seeking political office because potential candidates are often unwilling to endure the hardships and nastiness faced by elected public officials today. Our legislative institutions are weakened by public distrust, thus making the job of governing more problematic than it would otherwise be. Finally, the entire system of representative democracy is being undermined and, without conscious thought or decision, alternative systems are gaining strength. One alternative system is executive dominance, whereby presidents and governors work their will and legislatures act as rubber stamps. Another alternative is direct democracy, whereby the study, deliberation, and negotiation of representative assemblies is supplanted by public initiatives or referenda that vote major issues up or down.

This chapter explores the problem of declining support for the practices—if not the overall principles—of representative democracy.[1] The first task is to specify what Americans think about the system. Then, we argue that Americans are wrong in what they think. Next, we discuss reasons for the disconnect between what people think and how the political system actually works. Most importantly, we maintain that part of the disconnect is attributable to the way civic education is taught in the schools. Finally, and admittedly from the perspective not of pedagogues but of political scientists who are long time students of Congress and state legislatures, we offer ideas about what should be taught and how it should be taught.

WHAT DO AMERICANS THINK ABOUT POLITICS?

Americans are cynical and distrustful when they think about politics. They do not want to take part personally in politics and they are suspicious of those who do. People do not believe that government works in their interest, except perhaps for national defense and the military. According to public opinion polls, they feel that public officials do not care much what "people like them" think. If public officials are not listening to ordinary people, then to whom do ordinary people think they are listening? When asked, "Would you say the government is pretty much run by a few interests looking out for themselves or that it is run for the benefit of all the people," only one third answer the latter.

One of the problems, in the mind of the public, is that those who are elected to office, if not already corrupt, are soon corrupted by the system. Only 12% rate members of Congress and only 17% rate state officeholders as "very high" or "high" on honesty and ethical standards. At the state level, for example, New Jerseyans were asked in a *Star-Ledger*/Eagleton-Rutgers Poll (dated June 26, 2002) why they thought people went into politics. According to 64% of the respondents, most do so for personal gain; only 25% thought it was to serve the public. Similarly, 69% thought that, once in office, politicians look out more for their own interests, whereas only 20% felt they looked out more for the interests of the public. These attitudes have changed little over the past two decades. In the same poll, New Jerseyans were asked how many politicians they thought were corrupt. Half the respondents thought that anywhere from 50% to 100% of politicians were corrupt. In an earlier survey, New Jerseyans were asked what percentage of state legislators in Trenton they believed took bribes. One third of the respondents answered that between 50% and 100% took bribes.

---

[1] This chapter, except for the section on how civics is taught in the high schools, is based largely on the recent work of the authors and their colleagues. Their findings are published in Hibbing and Theiss-Morse (2002) and Rosenthal, Loomis, Hibbing, and Kurtz (2002).

The younger generation is more tuned out and turned off than their older counterparts. In a 2002 survey, 1,166 individuals, ranging from age 15 to 25, were asked to check off "the words that come to mind when you hear that word POLITICS." Only 18% checked "interesting," whereas 47% checked "boring." On the positive side, "public service" came to the minds of 26% and "responsive" to the minds of 7%. On the negative side, "lying" came to the minds of 54%, "corrupt" to 48%, and "for the rich" to 40%.[2]

ARE AMERICANS RIGHT IN WHAT THEY THINK?

The system of representative democracy and the people involved in making it work are far from perfect. Anyone can point to problems. Most people would place campaign finance at the top of the list. Extreme partisanship would also be mentioned. Problems vary from one legislature to another and from one session to the next. The problems in the California legislature are not the same as those in the Indiana legislature, which are different from those in legislatures in Louisiana and Vermont, and Congress is something else entirely.

Among the 535 members of Congress and 7,424 members of the 50 state legislatures, some are bound to be corrupt, some ethically challenged, and some simply stupid. But these legislators have been sent to Washington, DC, and to state capitals by voters in their districts. The overwhelming majority is not corrupt, unethical, stupid. But, that is the way they appear, because citizens base their assessment of the whole on the extremely small parts that they see, hear about, and recall, abetted by the news media's proclivity to focus on the bad ones.

People generalize from the worst, not the best, cases. So they assume that what they see is only the tip of the iceberg; below the water line, elected public officials are just as bad or even worse. If Americans generalized from their own representative to Congress as a whole or from their own legislator to the state legislature as a whole, then the result would be very different. Approval ratings by constituents for their own individual representative are 80%–90% percent positive, whereas the ratings of Congress and state legislatures as a whole are less than half that figure.

Despite what people think, the systems of representative democracy in the nation and states are working—not perfectly perhaps, but remarkably well. They function generally as the framers had intended over 200 years ago when they

---

[2] The Youth Civic Engagement Survey was funded by a grant from the Pew Charitable Trusts to Cliff Zukin, Scott Keeter, and Molly Andolina. The survey was administered January 29, 2002 through February 25, 2002, to Knowledge Networks panel members.

drafted the U.S. Constitution. The framers created a government more powerful than the one that existed under the Articles of Confederation, but they also divided power among three branches, each of which checked and balanced the other. They further constrained the legislative branch, by providing for bicameralism. They required consensus to be built for laws to be enacted. To get anything done, factional interests would have to be overcome and a succession of majorities would have to be crafted. The framers' creation was ingenious, practical, and with adaptation, has stood the test of time.

An assessment of representative democracy in terms of a number of agreed-on standards shows that the system not only is performing well, but has actually improved during the past 30 to 40 years:

1. Representativeness. Since the U.S. Supreme Court decisions on reapportionment in the 1960s, legislatures have become more politically representative than before. Descriptively as well, legislatures are more representative. Although the demographic characteristics of lawmakers in Congress and state legislatures do not mirror the public they represent, the proportions of members who are women and racial and ethnic minorities have increased. And the proportion of lawyers has diminished. Members are closely tied to the districts they represent and work assiduously to promote the interests of their constituents.

2. Capacity. Legislatures today have the wherewithal to do the job, which most did not have in the 1960s. Members spend more time on the job. They have better facilities at their disposal and, most important, able professional staffs, both partisan and nonpartisan, to back them up. Consequently, they have better information to use in debating policy and crafting laws.

3. Integrity. Legislators and legislatures are more ethical than they used to be. At both the congressional and state legislative levels, the ethics of members are highly regulated. Nearly everywhere, legislators are required to file financial disclosure statements. Depending on the particular state, legislators must disclose gifts they receive or are limited as to the dollar value of gifts they can accept. Some states (e.g., Wisconsin, South Carolina, and Minnesota) have a "no cup of coffee" law, which bars legislators from accepting anything at all. Conflict-of-interest laws, which apply to "citizen legislators" who earn income at jobs outside the legislature, are much tougher than they used to be.

4. Transparency. Citizens today have access to large amounts of information about both their legislators and their legislatures—that is, if they want it. Votes in committee and on the floor are recorded. Citizens can find agendas, calendars, bill status, and analyses on legislative web pages. They can view C-SPAN coverage of Congress and of about one third of the legislatures.

5. Competitiveness. If competitive politics—in which each side has a reasonable chance to win—are of value, then legislative systems have made substantial progress. The political parties are highly competitive today—for the presidency and statewide office, for the U.S. Senate and U.S. House, and for about two-thirds of the 99 legislative bodies in the states. The parties, just about everywhere, represent different constituent groups, have contrasting agendas, and behave differently when in power. The people have a choice.

6. Democracy. Internally, legislative bodies are more democratic than they used to be. Indeed, they have always been relatively democratic, because every member has an equal vote in the chamber and the same number of constituents outside.[3] As compared to the past, however, power is even more dispersed, with leaders (who are elected by members) having somewhat less and rank and file having somewhat more. Newer generations of members are more independent than older ones used to be. Nowadays, leaders as well as members have staff and informational resources to bolster their positions. The tenure of leaders is shorter than formerly, which weakens them. In the 17 term-limited states, their tenure will last no longer than 2, 3, or 4 years.

7. Responsiveness. Legislative bodies today are taking on issues that were rarely addressed before, and many of these (e.g., abortion and gun control) are highly contentious. Legislatures cannot satisfy everyone, and perhaps not anyone completely, but they are responsive to needs and demands. The needs and demands of constituents and of interest groups, along with the agendas of the political parties and the values and beliefs of individual members, are what drive the process. When legislators are criticized for playing politics, what they are really being criticized for is being attentive to the wishes of the people.

The framers saw the need in a representative democracy for a balance between independence and responsiveness. That balance has shifted today toward the responsiveness side. Congress and state legislatures have less insulation, less autonomy—" less wiggle room," if you will—than formerly. The distance between legislatures and their publics has narrowed. In fact, legislatures now may be too responsive.

WHY DO AMERICANS BELIEVE WHAT THEY DO?

---

[3] This is not exactly true, because some state legislative bodies have multimember districts along with single-member ones—New Hampshire and Vermont being examples.

Americans are mainly wrong in what they think about politics, politicians, and political institutions. Their beliefs do not derive from the way representative democracy actually works, because it works pretty well. Where, then, do people's beliefs come from? Three sets of explanations largely account for people's negative and cynical views. The first set relates to the environment in which politics have been conducted since Watergate and the Vietnam war. The second set relates to the nature of the process itself and how it looks to the uninitiated (and to many of the initiated as well). The third relates to the teaching of civic education in America's schools.

Environment

Throughout the history of the republic, Americans have been critical of their government. Skepticism has been a constant. Yet, the American discontent since the traumatic events of the Watergate scandal and the Vietnam war is of a distinctive nature, with the skepticism of the past becoming the cynicism of the present. In large part, this is due to the change in the way the media covers government and politics. In the period before these watershed events, the media conceived of its role as not only reporting the news, but also choosing what not to report because the consequences might be harmful. Journalists and legislators shared a community of interests. This is no longer true; now the relationship between journalists and legislators is adversarial. Public officials are fair game — indeed, big game for the media.

How Americans orient themselves toward their political institutions depends on the impressions they get from the media. No single story in print or on television shapes people's orientations, but the accumulation of coverage has effects. For the media, the very definition of news is a negative one. When legislatures are working well, they are not newsworthy. Controversy, conflict, or deadlock is newsworthy. The media goes further in an effort to give people what they want, thereby attracting readers, viewers, and thus advertisers. It seeks the sensational, the scandalous. And it finds it, or infers it, often enough to give Americans the impression that the political system is completely out of whack.

Political campaigns add to the negative image. They often stress the negative because the negative has more appeal to voters than the positive. One candidate wins the election, but neither the candidates nor the political system come out unscathed. Moreover, the widespread use of the legislature itself as a target in political campaigns further undermines the public trust. Even incumbent members of Congress and state legislatures run against the institutions in which they serve. "It's the system that's at fault," incumbents and challengers alike charge. "Elect me and I will change it."

Reform efforts also have effects on what people think. Take the discussion of campaign finance, for example. The proponents of reform and the media both engage in hyperbole and innuendo. In order to make their argument, but without pointing fingers at individuals, they accuse the system of being corrupt. Yet, few cases of corruption have been charged and fewer public officials have been convicted of selling their votes for campaign contributions. But Americans think that it is common practice for lawmakers to sell themselves to the highest bidders. After all, that is what they are told during attempts to improve the system.

Issue campaigns, conducted by interest groups trying to mobilize members and persuade large publics, also have a negative cast. Grassroots and media strategies depend on strident appeals, which result in disappointment when a group does not get everything it wants. The explanation from the group's leadership is not that opposition groups were also making legitimate demands, but rather that the system was not fair and did not work as it should. Otherwise, the argument goes, the group's position naturally would have prevailed.

Process

The American political system was not designed for people to understand easily, so it is not surprising that Americans today have little idea of how representative democracy works. Even if they are among the relatively few who observe the legislative process firsthand, by visiting a capitol or by watching C-SPAN, they will probably find it mystifying. A close-up view can also be disillusioning, because people naturally prefer order, efficiency, and regularity—even in a legislature. Indeed, about half the respondents in a national survey indicated that they would like to see legislatures run more like a business or administrative agency in the executive branch. Instead, they see a process that looks dilatory, messy, even chaotic.

Add to this lack of understanding the distaste people have for critical features of the process itself. Americans are devoted to democracy in principle, but they have little appreciation for what democracy entails in practice. They assume that there is consensus on important issues. People agree, so why don't politicians? They attribute the lack of political agreement to selfish groups and interests: political parties that are most interested in winning elections and not representing people and interest groups that insist on their narrow agendas, which are irrelevant to ordinary people. The legislative process in Congress and state legislatures, most Americans believe, is too contentious. Americans like conflict in sports, but they do not like it in governance. Moreover, in order to resolve conflicts, lawmakers compromise too readily instead of standing up for principle. In short, people think, politicians sell out.

People simply do not want to see competing parties and competing interests, uncertainty and messiness, bargaining, compromise, and conflict, or any of the other features central to a legislative body in a representative democracy. As our research has shown, they simply do not like the normal practices of democratic politics and political institutions.

Civic Education

Given the environment in which most Americans have grown up and people's natural distaste for democratic practices, the public's perspective toward politics is to be expected. Maybe the public perspective could be more informed and less negative if civic education had been doing its job. Although society often expects more from civic education than it can possibly provide, there is little doubt in our minds that students are not presently being exposed to the realities of representative democracy.

HOW IS CIVICS TAUGHT IN THE HIGH SCHOOLS?

It is not a simple matter to figure out how civic education is being taught in the schools. The focus here is on high schools, where some data are available despite the decentralized nature of education in the United States. Perhaps the best summary data come from student surveys conducted by the National Assessment of Educational Progress (NAEP), with the most useful for our purposes being a major 1988 national survey of 4,275 high school seniors in 302 different schools. This survey contained background items on the civics courses each student reported taking during high school, as well as more traditional survey items on political attitudes and, especially, political knowledge. Extensive use of this survey is made by Niemi and Junn (1998).

Scope

At first blush, it would seem easiest to determine how much civics education students typically receive, but even this more objective matter is open to different interpretations. In the NAEP survey, more than 87% of the high school seniors report having taken a civics or government course that lasted at least one semester. Inspection of the actual transcripts of large numbers of graduating seniors suggests a slightly different answer. It reveals that, in 1987, only 72% of high school graduates had at least a semester of civics. Interestingly, by 1994, well after the survey, the figure had grown to 78% (Legum, 1997; Niemi & Junn, 1998, p.64). In any event, the transcript data lead to the conclusion that although students tend to over-report their civics training, they do not do so by much, and it seems safe to conclude that somewhere around four out of five graduating high school seniors have had at least one semester.

But one semester of study devoted to something as central as citizenship and the governing process is minimal. Is this all most students receive? In a word, no. The NAEP survey also asked the students to report the total amount of coursework they received in government/civics. Forty percent reported having more than 1 year; 23% had exactly 1 year; 25% had less than 1 year but at least one semester; and as mentioned earlier, about 13% reported having no coursework at all. And subjects other than those formally labeled as civics/government (e.g., history), regularly contain substantial portions of civics subject matter. So, exposure to the topic is probably even greater than suggested by the figures listed.

An important related issue involves when in their high school careers students are most likely to take coursework on civics/government. The NAEP survey provides a clear answer: the senior year. More specifically, 41% of the students said they had taken a civics-type course in 9th grade year; 31% in 10th grade; 52% in 11th grade; and 61% in 12th grade. A fairly common, although certainly not universal, curriculum entails a semester-long civics course in the 9th grade and then some type of citizenship issues course during one of the students' last four semesters in high school. The issue of when civics courses are taken may seem minor, however it turns out to have an effect—at least in the eyes of many analysts. Studies have revealed that government courses taken in the senior year are more effective in getting students to retain information than are courses taken earlier, perhaps because "some material about government and politics may be impossible for younger students to comprehend fully" (Niemi & Junn, 1998, p.156).

This finding has led many reformers to urge concentrated government instruction in the 12th grade. Although there may be merit to this idea, two cautions are in order. First, classes taken in the 12th grade have been found to have the greatest effect in virtually all subject matter areas, not just civics/government. If all classes were taught when they did the most good (i.e., during the 12th grade), then students would have nothing to do during their early high school years and would not have enough time in their schedules during their senior year. Moreover, it is legitimate to ask if information retention from 12th grade classes is really better if it only appears to be better because when the survey soundings are taken those classes are either recently concluded or still in progress, whereas 9th and 10th grade classes are distant memories. In sum, 80% of high school students have at least one semester of formal civics/government instruction; around two thirds have more than one semester; and 61% take a civics/government class during their senior year, the time during which it does the most good.

In some respects, even more important than the number and timing of civics classes are the topics covered and the pedagogy employed by teachers in these classes. As to what is covered, the NAEP survey made an effort to identify the topics students reported studying "a lot," "some," and "none." The findings seem to confirm Katz's suspicion that civics teaching often stresses "dry institutional descriptions" (1986, p.91). The U.S. Constitution, Congress, rights and responsibilities of citizens, elections and voting, and the presidency top the list of topics students report studying "a lot" in their classes.[4] At the bottom of the list of 10 topics are "principles of democratic government" and "other forms of government." Apparently, civics classes do not do much in the way of comparing American democracy to government in other countries or, even more important, to acquainting students with the elements of governing in a democratic fashion. And, it is interesting to note that the drafters of the survey did not even feel it was worth their time to ask about topics such as public opinion, interest groups, governmental policies, and debate.

Finally, students in the NAEP survey were asked about the frequency of their exposure in civics classes to 10 possible methods of instruction. Students said the most common activities in their classes were "reading material from the textbook," "discussing material they had read," "discussing current events," and "taking a test or quiz." The least utilized activities were "reading material not in the textbook," "working on a group project," and "writing a report of at least three pages." Again, the list is notable for what is not included: activities such as mock courts, mock legislatures, simulations, and debates. Even if these were considered "group projects," such activities are, according to the students, quite rare. Only 18% of the students said group activities occurred weekly. All told, civics classes appear to be heavily textbook oriented and equally heavily tilted toward institutional, structural approaches. To the extent that ordinary people surface in civics/government classes, it is usually only in connection to the rights and responsibilities they have, and not to describe the widely varying opinions they hold and behaviors in which they engage.

Textbooks

Because the students claim that "reading material from the textbook" is their most common activity while taking civics/government classes, examining textbooks is a valuable way of determining the content of these classes. Examining textbook content will also make it possible for us to begin to look more specifically at the content of classes as opposed to NAEP's broad summary data on the number and timing of civics classes within the high school career. Such a task is made easier by virtue of the fact that there is a clearly dominant textbook in the field. *Magruder's American Government* (McClenaghan, 1999) is used by the majority of 11th and 12th grade government classes. So we analyzed the organization, content, and pedagogical emphases of this most widely used text.

The book consists of seven units: foundations of American government, political behavior, the legislative branch, the executive branch, the judicial branch, comparative political and economic systems, and state and local gov-

---

[4] Similar conclusions are found in Niemi (2001, pp. 37–64).

ernment. Given this organization, it is obvious that the emphasis is on history and especially institutions, with each branch of government receiving three to five separate chapters. And within these chapters, the structural, constitutional, and functional emphasis carries right on through. Each chapter contains a listing of the main objectives, and to illustrate typical emphases consider the learning objectives of the three chapters on Congress:

10.1 the place, the role, and the structure of Congress,
10.2 the structure of the House of Representatives,
10.3 the structure of the Senate,
10.4 the general characteristics of members of Congress,
11.1 the scope of the powers of Congress,
11.2 the many and important expressed powers of Congress,
11.3 the nature and extent of the implied powers of Congress,
11.4 the several non-legislative powers of Congress,
12.1 the organizational structure of the houses of Congress,
12.2 the committee system in both houses,
12.3 the legislative process in the House of Representatives,
12.4 the legislative process in the Senate.

Perhaps the most startling omission in this list involves representation or any sense of Congress as an institution that must sort out the conflicting views of an incredibly diverse citizenry. Everything seems to be about constitutional powers and institutional organization. There is a brief distinction made between the trustee and delegate role, but no message about the difficulties facing a legislator who needs to cast a "yea" or a "nay" roll call vote even though the range of opinion in the legislator's district or state often is large and ambiguous. On most issues, most citizens do not communicate their wishes to their legislator—and the few people who do communicate often are at odds with others. So what is a member of a legislature to do? The textbook contains no discussion of this vital matter, moving from the definitions of the delegate and trustee roles into a brief discussion of constituency service and then to a listing of the compensation, perquisites, and privileges of members. The impression given is that the only thing members of Congress do to earn all the benefits they receive is occasionally serving as errand boys and girls for selected constituents. The laborious, but essential, task of working through conflicting opinions to arrive at a compromise solution is not mentioned at all.

Maybe the exciting, albeit bewildering, diversity of political opinions held by Americans comes through in the chapter on public opinion. As logical as such an expectation might be, it does not happen. The chapter or public opinion in *Magruder's American Government* is actually entitled "Mass Media and Public Opinion," and it deals almost exclusively with the factors that shape public opinion (primarily the media, according to the text) and the manner in which public opinion is measured (primarily polls). There is not a single reference to the actual beliefs that real Americans hold on issues or even on just one issue.[5] The chapter does not specify what the public thinks about major political issues, so it is unable to make it apparent to students that different people have different thoughts; that some favor gun control and some do not; that some are willing to sacrifice selected civil liberties for increased safety from terrorists and criminals and some are not; and that some support affirmative action and some do not.

The chapters on political parties, interest groups, and elections/voting behavior are of no help in familiarizing students with the nature and inevitability of political conflict. To the author's credit, these chapters are not overtly critical of interest groups, political parties, and candidates for office. Rather, in these chapters, the author is so eager not to pass judgment that the text is almost exclusively confined to historical, factual, and conceptual matters: the requirements to be a voter, the historical struggle to expand suffrage to disadvantaged groups, the problem of nonvoting, the organization of the major parties, the different party systems the country has had over the centuries, the purposes of political parties, the primary system, campaign finance, the stages of the campaign, the mechanics of the act of voting, the types of interest groups, and the strategies of interest groups.

In sum, one key message contained in the book is that the American people not only do not disagree with each other, they do not seem to have any positions at all on major policy issues of the day. A second key message is that elected representatives do not so much represent the wishes of their people as they merely become part of an elaborate and impersonal governmental machine. The following are among the most telling phrases in the book: "The United States is a pluralistic society—one consisting of several distinct cultures and groups . . . still, there is a broad consensus—a general agreement among various groups— on fundamental matters"; and later, "The nation has not been regularly plagued by sharp cleavages in politics"[6] (1994, p. 104).

This "one big happy family" approach to American politics is not peculiar to *Magruder's American Government*. The leading civics text for younger high school students is *American Civics* (various editions) by Hartley and Vincent (1983). Perhaps reflecting the younger (primarily ninth grade) intended clientele, this text gives even shorter shrift to the diversity of actual political views

---

[5] Actually, some data are given on public attitudes toward housing programs, but they come from 1981 and are employed only to show that responses change when question wording changes (1994, p. 195).

[6] Hepburn and Bullock accurately note that "typically teachers of social science are very cautious about dealing with social-political conflict and controversy" (1999, p. 114; see also Hepburn, 1983).

and the implications of this diversity for representative democracy. There is no chapter on public opinion, but the topic is briefly discussed in a chapter entitled "Taking Part in Our Political System." To be fair, the authors make a quick concession that "the opinions of individual people often differ," but they go on to say that "the term 'public opinion' is generally used to refer to the opinion held about any issue by a majority of the people" (p. 221). This is a startling assertion in that it implies that if a majority of the people do not agree, then public opinion does not exist. Apparently, on controversial issues of the day that typically see less than 50% agreeing and less than 50% disagreeing with the remainder undecided, there is no public opinion. No public consensus, no public opinion. Once beyond this statement, the lion's share of the "public opinion" section deals with propaganda, a topic that in the authors' eyes, leads directly into interest groups. The rambling chapter then concludes with the ritual call for everyone to take an active part in government.

As with *Magruder's American Government*, the chapter on Congress in *American Civics* is devoid of any reference to the representation of divided public opinion and to the difficulty of trying to come to a solution in the face of diversity. In the chapter, the authors are content to discuss the organization of Congress, leadership structure, committee assignments, powers of Congress, how a bill becomes a law, and constitutional restrictions on eligibility for membership. Discussions of representation—let alone representation of maddeningly diverse interests—are absent. Overall, as Hepburn and Bullock put it, "Texts and teachers provide a multitude of facts but too often fail to convey an understanding of the politics" (1999, p. 126).[7]

Service Learning and Other Techniques

One of the most important educational trends in the last couple of decades has been the movement toward service learning and especially service-learning requirements.[8] Service learning is generally defined as using community-based service experiences as tools for teaching students about politics. Students are coerced (either as a class or a graduation requirement) to spend a certain number of hours "volunteering" in a community organization or group. Procedures vary widely and for some students punching the time clock is the end of it, but most are required to prepare reports, to engage in group discussions of their experiences, or to keep journals. One of the main purposes of these requirements is to get students to "do politics" (Battistoni, 2000, p. 615).

Careful evaluation of the consequences of service learning has revealed few

---

[7] Elsewhere they note that "only a very small portion of the textbook material focuses on the multiple actors, issues, and actions" (1999, p. 112).

[8] For a good discussion, see Battistoni (2000).

concrete benefits. On completion of their analysis, Hunter and Brisbin (2000) conclude that "service learning did not affect students' thinking about democracy or about their role as a citizen" and more generally, "service does not appear to bring about consistent and comprehensive changes in students' general cognitive skills, attitudes, and political values" (pp. 624, 626). These findings are corroborated at the aggregate level by the widely cited UCLA surveys of college freshmen. As service-learning requirements have proliferated during the last 10 to 15 years, the number of first-year college students who report having participated in a local project or community betterment effort shot up. The problem is, this increase in group work was not accompanied by an increase in any measure of favorable attitudes toward the political system, understanding of the political system, or participation in the political system. Well intentioned as the service-learning movement might be, the truth of the matter is that working with a small, local group of like-minded citizens to achieve noncontroversial goals should not have been expected to make young people more understanding of the rough and tumble, zero-sum world of real politics.

Speaking more broadly, enlightened government instructors around the country are engaged in efforts to provide their students with "hands on" activities, as opposed to the more traditional textbook, lecture, and quiz approach. We have met many teachers who are trying all kinds of creative ways of getting students to be informed of and involved in politics. For example, some students build voting booths, some participate in simulations, some work in campaigns, and some hold mock trials or mock legislatures; however, the results of the NAEP survey suggest that the number of students with these kinds of experiences is dwarfed by the number enduring traditional lecture and textbook classroom setting. Moreover, some of these hands-on activities are unlikely to achieve the objectives that we feel are most desirable.

Civic Engagement

Both traditional textbook-centered instruction, as well as service-learning/hands-on teaching techniques, tend to stress civic engagement. Perhaps because of the fairly abysmal rates of youth involvement, everyone's primary goal these days seems to be to get young people to participate more in politics. Textbooks badger students to get more politically involved and hands-on techniques are designed to expose students to various aspects of the political process with the hope that this exposure will lead to more involvement. To the extent we can tell, civics/government classes seem to be filled with exhortations to be politically active.

Although securing greater participation levels among American youth is an unquestionably desirable objective, we believe current approaches to civics/government instruction may focus too exclusively on participation. If people think ill of the political process, rubbing their noses in that process is unlikely to make them feel any better about it. In 1998, a series of focus groups was conducted across the country. A participant in one of those sessions gave the following testimonial: "Politics was never an interest and then the last election was the first time I just said, 'hey, you know, I'm always bitching about this and this and that.' So I registered and voted. You know and I think that out of . . . all the changes that I wanted, I think only one of them happened . . . I couldn't care less right now because it's just like everything you wanted to see changed still hasn't happened" (Hibbing & Theiss-Morse, 2002, p.120).

It is clear that, for this individual, the simple act of participation was not enough to trigger an improved attitude toward politics and additional subsequent participation. The reason is that his participation was not based on a realistic understanding of democratic governance. If he realized how many people wanted "changes" different from those he wanted and if he appreciated that, because desired changes vary from person to person, not everyone is going to get their way, he might have been satisfied with getting one of his changes and he might not have been turned off by the political process. As this individual illustrates, unless it is accompanied by a deeper appreciation for the dissatisfying nature of democracy in a diverse society, participation in and of itself will not create satisfied, long-term political participants.

One of the authors has held several focus groups with college students who were interning in the Minnesota and Ohio legislatures. The internships were for academic credit, but the participating universities and colleges did not provide a class to accompany the placements. Consequently, most of the students had little perspective on the legislature and the legislative process. Still, their hands-on participation had an effect on their attitudes. They generally came away from their experience convinced that the legislators they recently observed at close quarters were well-motivated, tried to do right by their constituents, and worked very hard at a tough job. But, they had little idea of the legislative process itself. Working in a member's office, attending a committee meeting, or observing a floor session was not enough to give them any real understanding. And several of the interns admitted they found the process unappealing, saying it confirmed their cynicism. They needed perspective on the process, which they apparently did not get through their internship experience.

Thus, whether students are implored by their textbook and instructor to get more involved in politics or whether they are subjected to hands-on exercises, experiences, and internships designed to achieve the same objective, a fixation on getting students to engage civically will do little to improve their appreciation of democracy, their interest in government, or their level of involvement with government. After all, for decades civics/government teachers and textbooks have been cajoling students to get more involved and the participation rate in political activities has done nothing but drop. Because the "participation at all costs" approach to civics has failed, we urge a more balanced set of objectives in which gaining a perspective on and an appreciation of democracy become the central objectives—objectives that we think may lead to more participation and we are certain will lead to more enlightened and meaningful participation. But just how do we teach democracy appreciation?

WHAT NEEDS TO BE TAUGHT AND HOW?

What is now being taught in high schools by way of civic education does not make the grade, not if a goal of civic education is to give students an appreciation of the functioning of representative democracy. Providing this appreciation is not achieved by concentrating mainly on the U.S. Constitution, the organization and structure of government, or the procedures by which a bill becomes a law. Neither is it achieved by service learning or a focus on civic engagement and voting. Youngsters, and adults as well, need a perspective that enables them to figure out what they can and cannot expect from the political system.

The Lessons

A reasonable perspective on representative democracy would include as major lessons the following:

> 1. Fundamental is the diversity of our nation and states. People have different values, interests, and priorities. They may see eye-to-eye at a general level—favoring better health, education, and welfare—but at more specific levels disagreements are common. Opinion is divided on whether government or private enterprise should play a greater role in health, on whether school vouchers should be tried, and on what work requirements should be connected to welfare reform. There is disagreement on abortion, gun control, capital punishment, the environment, and development, among other issues.
> 2. The different values, interests, and preferences of people are all represented in three principal ways. First, they are represented directly by those elected to serve in Congress and the state legislatures. These individuals take into account their district's needs and constituents' views as they decide on policy, revenues, and appropriations. Second, they are represented by one of the political parties, even if their own elected representative does not belong to that party. Most identify with either the Democratic party or the Republican party, and they vote generally for candidates of the party with which they identify. The Democratic and Republican parties have different constituent bases and take different positions on many of the major issues of the day, such as taxes and spending and the role of government. Third, they are represented by one or a number of political interest groups.

Seven out of 10 Americans belong to at least one group, whereas 4 out of 10 belong to more than one. And even those who are not members have their values and interests represented by one group or another. These groups, singly, or more often in coalition, try to advance their agendas and serve their members.

3. The legislative process in Washington, DC, and the state capitals involves the clash of values, interests, and priorities over policies and budgets. Participants include individual constituents, elected representatives, the political parties, and political interest groups. Some issues that legislatures have to decide are not controversial, but many are fraught with division and conflict. Disagreements may be fought out, with one side prevailing; they may also be negotiated, with both sides compromising in order to resolve conflict. In any case, the legislative process is a continuing one, with settlements in effect as long as they command majority support and are not challenged.

4. The system of representative democracy is an accountable one. It is relatively transparent. Information on the associations, behavior, and policy positions of elected public officials is available. Elections are held regularly: every 2 years in the case of members of the U.S. House and house members in most states; every 4 years in the case of senate members in most of the states; and every 6 years in the case of members of the U.S. Senate. The political parties, as well as individual members, can be and are held accountable by the voters. Currently, either party is well-positioned to win control of either house of Congress and of most legislatures.

The Teachers

Such are the lessons that need to be taught if students are to develop a proper appreciation for representative democracy. Whether or not social studies teachers will be able to teach these lessons depends on a number of factors. First, and most important, do teachers themselves appreciate democratic practices? Or are they, like most everyone else, cynical about politicians and political institutions. On the basis of our limited experience with social studies teachers, we believe that their perspectives are not very different than those held by most people.

One of the authors delivered the keynote address at the 2001 annual meeting of the New Jersey Social Studies Teachers Association. In the course of addressing about 400 teachers in a plenary session, he brought up the issue of cynicism and mentioned a survey conducted in New Jersey. People had been asked in the survey, he told the teachers, what percentages of legislators in Trenton they thought took bribes. He then addressed that same question to the assembled teachers, asking them to raise their hands where appropriate. How many would say that 75% to 100% of the legislators in Trenton took bribes? How many would say 50% to 75%? What about 25% to 50%? And 0% to 25%?

Hands went up after each percentage range was mentioned, with an equal distribution of hands in each of the four categories. That means that half the teachers in the audience thought that anywhere from 50% to 100% of the legislators in New Jersey took bribes. As a matter of fact, the responses of teachers were somewhat more cynical than the responses of the public that was surveyed earlier. Even allowing for a misinterpretation of the word "bribe," the expression of cynicism by social studies teachers is remarkable. No New Jersey state legislators in recent memory have been convicted, none indicted, and none even accused of taking bribes. But, somehow, politicians routinely are perceived to take bribes.

We are about to undertake a study of civic education on representative democracy, focusing on five states. In a first phase, we will be interviewing high school social studies teachers in Nebraska and New Jersey, inquiring into their orientations toward the politicians, institutions, and practices of representative democracy. We will be measuring their orientations on two scales, one on democracy appreciation and the other on cynicism. On the basis of the initial interviews, we plan to organize a number of focus groups in each state, where we will try out the lessons outlined earlier on teachers with a variety of orientations. The aim is to see which teachers are willing to adopt the overall perspective that we believe has to be communicated to youngsters. Is it possible to sway any teachers who score high on cynicism and low on democracy appreciation? What about those who score low on cynicism and high on appreciation? Our intention is to determine which social studies teachers would be most open to teaching an alternative perspective on representative democracy.[9] Those teachers who buy into the lessons on representative democracy will be invited to help develop curricular materials for classrooms.

The Methods

As was suggested in our review of civic education, the ways in which the subject is taught will affect how well lessons are learned. The required lessons of representative democracy cannot be conveyed by lectures. Students have to be engaged, but, at the same time, they cannot just be engaged in noncontroversial tasks such as building voting booths or picking up litter along the highway. Rather, the lessons probably require analogy or simulation exercises, whereby the legislative process is demystified and brought closer to the lives of students.

For example, on point one, which relates to disagreement, it would be pos-

---

[9] Even so-called eligible teachers might not choose to change what they do. Discussions that we have had with very committed teachers suggest that they are confident that what they do is what they should be doing, and are not particularly open to different approaches.

sible to have the students imagine that a group of them has to decide on a movie to see from among a dozen or so playing in the vicinity. Do they agree or disagree on which movie? How do they resolve disagreements that are likely to exist? The challenge facing legislative bodies is not that different. The teacher might use national poll results, which can be found on the Web to show issues on which the country is split 55% to 45% or 60% to 40% indicating that people disagree on policy. It is not surprising, the teacher can point out, that legislators who represent diverse constituencies will also disagree on policies. On point two, which relates to representation, the teacher may invite a legislator to the class so that the students can ask questions about the legislator's connection to his/her constituency. The teacher can ask each student to indicate one or two of their own beliefs and figure out whether and by which interest group their beliefs are expressed in Congress and/or the state legislature.

These illustrations suggest that the needed lessons can be taught in an interactive fashion, but specific curricular materials still have to be prepared. In the project we are undertaking, our plan is to recruit teachers to help develop materials for the classroom. These teachers will then use the materials to teach a 3- or 4-hour module on representative democracy and will report back on how the materials work. We shall try to assess the effects of the lessons we have formulated and how they are delivered by the teachers involved.

WHO SHOULD TAKE RESPONSIBILITY?

Responsibility for something as important as civic education on representative democracy has to be shared. Certainly, the schools in the 50 states have to take the job more seriously than in the past. Social studies teachers—through the National Council on the Social Studies and state associations—are key to such an endeavor. There is also a role for the Center for Civic Education and its networks of teachers in the states. Public information is not new to state legislatures, but recently legislatures have also begun to take on the civic education function. Leadership in this area is being provided by the National Conference of State Legislatures (NCSL), which through its Trust for Representative Democracy is sponsoring a number of projects and activities to get the message out. Explaining to the American people how representative democracy works and should work is part of the representational responsibility of legislatures. This enterprise will, of course, require effort and persistence to counterbalance the natural distaste people have for democratic practices. Working toward balance, however, is absolutely necessary and is a job that cannot be done without the schools and their teachers.

REFERENCES

Battistoni, R. M. (2000). Service learning in political science: An introduction. *PS, 33,* 615–616.

Hartley, W. H., & Vincent, W. S. (1983). *American civics.* New York: Harcourt Brace Jovanovich.

Hepburn, M. A. (1983). Can schools, teachers, and administrators make a difference? The Research Evidence." In M. A. Hepburn, (Ed.), *Democratic education in schools and classrooms* (pp. 5–29). Washington, DC: National Council for Social Studies.

Hepburn, M. A., & Bullock, C. S. (1999). Congress, public, and education. In J. Cooper (Ed.), *Congress and the decline of public trust,* (pp. 101–130). Boulder, Co: Westview.

Hibbing, J. R., & Theiss-Morse. E. (2002). *Stealth democracy: Americans' beliefs about how government should work.* New York: Cambridge University Press.

Hunter, S., & Brisbin, R. A. Jr. (2000). The impact of service learning on democratic and civic values. *PS, 33,* 623–626.

Katz, E. (1986). Federalism in secondary school American history and government textbooks. In S. L. Schechter (Ed.), *Teaching about American federal democracy.* Philadelphia: Center for the Study of Federalism.

Legum, S. (1997). *The 1994 high school transcript study tabulations.* Washington, DC: U.S. Department of Education.

McClenaghan, W. A. (1999). *Magruder's American government.* Needham, MA: Prentice-Hall.

Niemi, R. G. (2001). Trends in political science as they relate to pre-college curriculum and teaching. In C. S. White (Ed.), *Sea changes in social science education* (pp. 37–64). Boulder, Co.: Social Science Education Consortium.

Niemi, R. G., & Junn, J. (1998). *Civic education: What makes students learn.* New Haven, CO: Yale University Press.

Rosenthal, A., Loomis, B., Hibbing, J., & Kurtz, K. (2002). *Republic on trial: The case for representative democracy.* Washington, DC: CQ Press.

Chapter 9

The Limits of Efficacy:
Educating Citizens for a Democratic Society

Joseph Kahne
Mills College

Joel Westheimer
University of Ottawa

Justin, a teenager from a West Coast City, delivered the following harsh indictment when we asked him about the semester he spent working to improve his community: "You can try and change things, but basically it will just make you feel bad for trying. They didn't even want to hear what I was saying. They don't care."

Unfortunately, more youth today are coming to the same conclusion. Indeed, a national survey of youth from age 15 to 24 revealed that 57% agree with the strong statement that "you can't trust politicians because most are dishonest." Two thirds of all young people agreed that "our generation has an important voice, but no one seems to hear it." Moreover, those youth who were least trusting were also the least likely to vote, to believe that government can affect their lives, or to pay attention to politics (see National Association of Secretaries of State, 1999).

What makes this statement and similar findings even more alarming is that they reflect data indicating a long-term decline in young people's political engagement. For example, whereas 50% of 18- to 24-year-olds exercised their right to vote in 1972, only 32% did so in 2000. Similarly, a recent survey of college freshmen (Sax, Astin, Korn, & Mahoney, 1999) found that interest in social activism is declining. Only 35.8% felt it "very important" or "essential" to "influence social values" (its lowest point since 1986), and students' desire to participate in community action programs fell to 21.3% (its lowest point in over a decade).

In response to these trends, a growing number of educators and policymak-ers are looking for ways to promote young people's participation in political and civic affairs. A common strategy for doing so is to provide youth with opportu-nities to make a difference in their communities. Indeed, much research demon-strates a strong connection between an individual's sense that they can make a difference—their sense of efficacy—and their level of civic participation[1]. As Almond and Verba (1963) write in *The Civic Culture*: "The belief in one's com-petence is a key political attitude. The self-confident citizen appears to be the democratic citizen. Not only does he [sic] think he can participate, he thinks others ought to participate as well. Furthermore, he does not merely think he can take part in politics; he is likely to be more active" (p. 257). Similarly, Conway found that those with high levels of political efficacy are 20% to 30% more likely to vote than those with low levels of efficacy, and similar relationships have been found to other forms of civic participation (in Berman, 1997, p. 44; also, see Niemi & Associates, 1974, and National Association of Secretaries of State, 1999).

The connection between efficacy and civic engagement, however, is com-plex. Scholars, for example, draw a significant distinction between internal and external political efficacy (Balch, 1974). *Internal political efficacy* refers to the individuals' sense of their own ability to participate effectively in the political process. People with high degrees of internal political efficacy believe they are capable when it comes to civic affairs. Measures of *external political efficacy,* on the other hand, reflect perceptions of governmental and institutional respon-siveness to citizens' needs and demands.

Although findings are not uniform, internal political efficacy has generally been found to have a positive relationship to political activity and the closer the alignment of a specified measure of efficacy to the form of activity, the stronger the relationship (Wollman & Stouder, 1991). Measures of external efficacy, on the other hand, have not exhibited a consistent relationship to activity. Indeed, Shingles (1981) and others have found high internal political efficacy and low external political efficacy prompted political activity among African Americans (see also, Ennis & Schrener, 1987; Harris, 1999). Feeling both personal compe-tence *and* that government is not responsive to the needs of African American citizens prompted many African Americans to participate in political affairs (often through activities like litigation and protest) to bring about more just laws and increased government awareness and action.

---

[1] We adopt a relatively traditional conception of efficacy in political and civic endeavors: the belief that what you or those in the community do can bring posi-tive change (see Bandura, 1977).

THE CHALLENGE FOR EDUCATORS

What might these relationships imply for educators and those creating curriculum? Given what we know about the relationship between internal and external political efficacy and civic participation, does a curricular emphasis on opportunities for students to develop a sense of efficacy make sense? Should program leaders structure their programs so that students always have successful civic experiences?

Over 2 years, we studied 10 nationally recognized programs that engaged students in community-based experiences and aimed to develop students' civic and political commitments. By drawing on observations, interviews, and pre–post surveys focusing on changes in attitudes related to civic participation, we were able to consider both the benefits and the potentially problematic consequences of a curricular emphasis on efficacy in relation to civic and political engagement. To illustrate our findings, we focus on two of the programs, both of which worked with high school seniors in their social studies classes. Data collected in one of the programs indicated that students experienced a great deal of both internal and external efficacy and their commitment to participation expanded as well. In the second program, the reverse occurred. Students became frustrated by their inability to bring about change and, like Justin, the West Coast teenager mentioned earlier, their interest in future involvement declined. They also became critical of the broader society.

Based on this data, one might expect that we concur with educators who advocate providing students with opportunities for efficacy. The strong relationship that social scientists have identified between young people's sense that they are competent civic actors and their desire to participate seems to provide a clear rationale for such experiences. Intuitively, this relationship also makes sense. If students are rewarded through their civic participation, then they will be more inclined toward political participation in the future. The logic of this thinking seems reasonable and, in many respects, the data from our study support these conclusions.

In discussing the implications of our findings, however, we argue that interpretations of such findings are not as straightforward as they may seem. Indeed, we argue that although efficacious experiences (particularly those that seek to promote internal political efficacy) can support the development of stronger commitments and may often be desirable, opportunities for students to learn about and experience the barriers and constraints they and other civic actors frequently face can also be important. Not only may exposure to these constraints prepare students for some of the frustrations they will likely face in future civic participation, but it can also help students learn about the ways power structures, interest group influences, and technical challenges can hamper the effectiveness of both individuals and groups. In fact, if "structuring projects for success" obscures these barriers and constraints, we worry that such curriculum may be miseducative—reinforcing the conservative political assumption that if individual citizens would just help out where help is needed, then these acts of kindness and charity (multiplied across a citizenry) will transform society and offer redress for complex social problems. This approach may also promote a false sense of efficacy by obscuring real-world complexities, power structures, and other barriers to change—meaningful and controversial social realities that many educators agree should be a central focus of study for schooling in a democracy (Noddings, 1999; Oakes et al., 2000; Wood, 1992).

Thus, educators face the potential conundrum: How can they create curriculum that helps students make informed judgments regarding barriers that must be faced for meaningful change to occur without undermining students' sense of internal political efficacy? Drawing on examples from our study, we conclude by discussing several curricular strategies.

METHODS

Sample

This chapter focuses on data from 2 of the 10 programs studied as part of the Surdna Foundation's Democratic Values Initiative. "Madison County Youth in Public Service" was located in a suburban/rural East Coast community outside a city of roughly 23,000 people. Two teachers were involved in this project, one from each of the county's high schools. Each year, the teachers worked with one of their government classes. Over 2 years, four classes participated. Students needed to request to participate in this version of the 12th-grade government class, and teachers characterized participants in both schools as slightly better than average in terms of academic background. Students who enrolled in the advanced placement government course could not participate. More girls (59%) than boys (41%) participated. Although we were not able to collect reports on students' ethnicity, teachers characterized the student population as almost entirely European American (with a few recent immigrants). An estimated 3% of the schools' students are persons of color.

Bayside Students for Justice was a curriculum developed as part of a 12th-grade social studies course for students in a comprehensive urban high school in a large West Coast city. During the first year, 67 students took part in the program. The group tested roughly at national norms and was relatively low income, with 40% living in public housing (data provided by the instructor).

Procedures

We collected four forms of data: observations, interviews, surveys, and documents prepared by program staff. Each year, our observations took place over a

2- to 3-day period in classrooms and at service sites. In some instances, we were also able to observe formal public presentations by the participating students. These observations took place during the spring semester. Over the 2 years of the study, we interviewed 59 students from Madison County (in groups of 3 or 4) and 27 students from Bayside (either individually or in groups of 2 to 3). We also interviewed at least 3 staff members for each program toward the end (April or May) of each year. Several staff members were also interviewed at the beginning of the first year. Interviews lasted between 20 and 45 minutes, and all interviews were both taped and transcribed. Finally, we conducted pre and post surveys of all participating students in September and June. In the case of Madison County Youth in Public Service, we studied the same program for 2 years. During the second year, we also were able to administer pre and post surveys to two control classrooms. These classrooms were also 12th-grade government classrooms, served students of similar academic ability, and were taught by the same two teachers. Bayside's program changed significantly after the first year of operation, and we discuss the second year briefly later in this chapter.[2] An appropriate control classroom was not available in the case of Bayside, and we therefore rely on changes in the pre- and post-survey data and on our observations and interviews of students and staff. To receive feedback and as a check on our interpretations, we shared analysis on both quantitative and qualitative findings with those who ran the programs.

Measures and Analysis

Survey items were selected in an effort to assess varied outcomes commonly associated with civic priorities. We employed measures of students' commitment to community involvement, personal responsibility to help others, desire to volunteer, desire to work for justice, interest in politics, and commitment to following the news.[3] We also employed several scales to assess varied outcomes related to students' sense of efficacy. These included measures of civic efficacy, leadership efficacy, and their sense of their knowledge or social capital for

---

[2] For a detailed discussion of the second year experience and findings see Westheimer and Kahne (2002).

[3] Measures of commitment to community involvement, personal responsibility, volunteering, and vision, are adapted from the National Learning Through Service Survey developed by the Search Institute. Some of these measures, in turn were adapted from instruments developed by Conrad and Hedin (1981). Items related to social capital and leadership efficacy draw on a leadership measure developed for the Community Service Leadership Workshop. Contact Jim Seiber, Issaquah School District 411, Issaquah, WA 98027. For a complete list of items, please contact the authors.

community development. These measures emphasized internal efficacy. The measure of civic efficacy, for example, asked whether students felt that, "I personally can make a difference in my community." Similarly, the measure of leadership efficacy assessed students' sense of their leadership effectiveness with questions such as, "Once I know what needs to be done, I am good at planning how to do it." The measure of social capital for community development assessed their sense of their own knowledge and ability to promote community development. It asked, for example, if students feel they "know how to contact and work effectively with organizations in my community such as schools, businesses, and social service organizations." We did not employ survey measures of external civic efficacy. External efficacy, however, received extensive attention in our focus group interviews. We conducted confirmatory factor analyses to verify that the items in each scale loaded on a single factor. We also computed a Cronbach's alpha for each scale to assess the internal consistency reliability. As detailed in Tables 8.2 and 8.3, alphas for all but two of the scales were greater than .6.

Our interviews and observations complement the surveys. Specifically, student and faculty interviews focused on students' beliefs regarding citizenship and on ways features of the curriculum may have affected those perspectives. We asked: What does it mean to you to be a good citizen? Did the program affect that vision? What people or experiences have influenced your behaviors and beliefs?

We also asked participants to identify and discuss particular social issues that are important to them and to community members. We encouraged them to describe their perspective on the nature of these problems, their causes, and possible ways of responding. Next we asked participants to describe any ways their participation in the given program might have altered their attitudes, knowledge, or skills in relation to either particular civic issues or their perspectives on responsible and effective citizenship. These questions drew out student beliefs regarding their internal and external efficacy. They spoke, for example, about their sense of competence in civic affairs and about their confidence that they could or could not have an impact. We also asked them directly if they thought that government and other important social institutions were or were not responsive to the social issues about which they cared and about the experiences that shaped these beliefs.

Our observations took place in classrooms and at service sites. These observations (of at least 4 classroom sessions of each program each year) helped us understand and illustrate program practices. In some instances we were also able to observe formal public presentations by the participating students. Though we are hesitant to generalize from a small number of observations, they were a helpful check on interpretations of interviews and surveys and we sometimes drew on these observations during interviews.

We analyzed this data in conjunction with our statistical analysis of survey results. We found that the interviews enriched, explained, and allowed us to corroborate our interpretation of survey results. The interviews and observations also deepened our understanding of and ability to articulate the meaning of responses to survey items and provided us with insight regarding particular findings. In the case of observations and interviews, the process of data collection and data analysis was recursive, cycling "between thinking about the existing data and generating strategies for collecting new—often better quality—data" (Miles & Huberman, 1994, p.50).

The analysis occurred throughout data collection as well as after data collection was complete, and followed the process described by Strauss (1990) as the constant comparative method. This iterative process occurred through reflective and analytical memos between the researchers, as well as the ongoing coding of field notes. In particular, we analyzed the interviews for recurring themes and patterns regarding student and teacher perceptions of how participation had affected students' beliefs regarding citizenship and democratic values. We also asked teachers to reflect on our observations not only to test the accuracy of statements but also to reexamine perceptions and conclusions, drawing on their insider knowledge.

The following descriptions were captured from field notes and audiotapes. The quotations are verbatim. Names of schools, students, teachers, and geographical references are pseudonyms.

FINDINGS PART I: OPPORTUNITIES FOR EFFICACY ARE OFTEN DESIRABLE

This section explores two common assumptions: First, when students' sense of efficacy grows, their commitment to future civic involvement grows as well; second, and conversely, when students become frustrated or come to believe that problems are intractable, their commitment often declines. We found both of these suppositions to carry significant weight. As is explored in the following section, however, the conclusions to draw from such findings are not as straightforward as they may seem. But first, we describe data from two programs we studied that support both of these propositions.

Madison County Youth in Public Service

The story of Madison County Youth in Public Service demonstrates the ways an emerging sense of internal and external efficacy can contribute to students' civic commitments. As part of a high school government course, the Youth in Public

Service curriculum first engaged students in intensive study of the traditional government curriculum content over the course of a semester. During the second semester, students worked in small groups with various government agencies and programs on community-based projects. These internships required that small groups of students work on public service projects in their county's administrative offices. One group studied the feasibility of curbside recycling. They conducted phone interviews of 150 residents, undertook a cost analysis, and examined maps of the city's population density to determine which parts of the city should be served in this way. These students examined charts of projected housing growth to estimate growth in trash and its cost and environmental implications. Another group identified jobs that prisoners incarcerated for less than 90 days could perform and analyzed the cost and efficacy of similar programs in other localities. Other students helped to develop a 5-year plan for the fire and rescue department. Another group examined ways cellular telephone service providers might share communications towers.

In all of these projects, students were responsible for interacting with government agencies, writing reports, and presenting findings. Each project required students to conduct research in order to fully understand the issues. There was latitude within each project for students to define their specific civic concern. The students' considerable successes, however, were aided by a great deal of administrative footwork beforehand. For each of the projects, the school district's instructional supervisor coordinated contacts at the appropriate government agencies, worked with those agencies to structure appropriate and engaging projects, and found liaisons that were excited about working with students. In short, Madison County Youth in Public Service was designed so that students would succeed in what they set out to do.

And succeed they did. The group of students organizing the recycling drive wrote an editorial based on their analysis that was published in their local newspaper. The group studying a plan to reduce the number of cellular telephone towers wrote a detailed analysis of the legal requirements of such towers and presented their findings to the Board of Supervisors highlighting issues of which many were unaware and, ultimately, influencing policy. Making the case for improved funding for the fire and rescue department, one group of students calculated the number of minutes it would take for fire trucks to reach the widely disparate elementary schools in their rural district. Their calculations were publicized and the community responded with interest.

Table 8.1. Madison County Youth in Public Service

Factors (Chronbach's Alpha pre, post)	Sample	Change	Pre-test	Post-test	p Level	N of Students
Personal Responsibility to Help Others (.62, .74)	Intervention	.21*	4.00	4.21	.01	61
	Control	- .06	3.99	3.92	.63	37
Commitment to Community Involvement (.54, .71)	Intervention	.19^	4.27	4.46	.06	61
	Control	-.10	3.89	3.99	.54	37
Desire to Work For Justice (.65, .73)	Intervention	.07	3.07	3.14	.31	61
	Control	.03	2.84	2.88	.81	37
I Will Volunteer (.80, .86)	Intervention	.10	3.59	3.70	.14	61
	Control	-.09	3.28	3.18	.43	37
Follow The News (.43, .41)	Intervention	.24**	3.35	3.59	.00	60
	Control	-.12	3.22	3.10	.27	37
Interest In Politics (.81, .81)	Intervention	.03	3.41	3.44	.55	61
	Control	-.05	2.76	2.71	.63	37
Civic Efficacy (.66, .71)	Intervention	.34**	3.78	4.12	.00	61
	Control	.10	3.38	3.48	.34	37
Vision (.65, .71)	Intervention	.30*	2.65	2.95	.01	61
	Control	.12	2.63	2.75	.35	37
Knowledge/Social Capital For Community Development (.67, .72)	Intervention	.94**	3.95	4.89	.00	60
	Control	-.23	3.13	2.90	.25	37
Leadership Efficacy (.78, .81)	Intervention	.31**	3.60	3.91	.00	61
	Control	.03	3.57	3.60	.72	37

^$p < .10$; *$p < .05$; **$p < .01$.

Consistently, when discussing their experiences in this program, students expressed significant satisfaction with all they had accomplished and with the recognition they received for these accomplishments. As one student explained, "I thought it was just going to be another project. You know, we do some research, it gets written down and we leave and it gets put on the shelf somewhere. But . . . this [curbside recycling] is going to be a real thing . . . It's really going to happen." A different student told us, "I didn't realize this was going to be as big as what it is. I mean, we've been in the newspaper…four times." And another student reported:

> I didn't expect it to have such an impact. I thought it would be one of those classes where we all talk about it and . . . they'd nod and smile [but] we really had an effect on what is happening. And we're learning a lot more than I thought we would, because if you just take the standard government classes, you're just going to learn about government. Now you're learning about government and how to deal with people and how to collect information.

Indeed, the program provided numerous opportunities for students to learn skills and to be exposed to information that, in addition to their accomplishments, enhanced their sense of both internal and external efficacy. For example, when high school students needed to make their presentation to their county's Board of Supervisors, each group worked with their teacher and with their field site supervisor to plan their presentation. They got tips on how to make their brief presentations interesting, on how to generate visual aids with computer software, and on how to insure that their primary message was communicated.

Perhaps most importantly from the standpoint of civic involvement, students linked their sense of efficacy (stemming from their emerging sense of capacity and from the impact of their work) to their desire for continued civic participation. For example, Eddie noted, "I didn't realize we had as much influence as we did. One person can really make a change in the community." When we asked him whether this changed the way he thought about being a citizen, he replied that, after the experience with local government agencies, he thought that "All citizens have a responsibility to voice their opinion by either writing letters or talk[ing] to people who control the county government, or state and federal government. Just let them know what you think about something that they're trying out. Maybe give new opinions or new ideas that you think would help." Other students expressed similar satisfaction from what they accomplished as well as commitments to remain engaged in civic affairs in the future.

Our quantitative data was consistent with what we heard during interviews and saw during site visits. Specifically, as detailed in Table 8.1, there were statistically significant ($p < .05$) changes in pre–post Likert scale scores on several of our measures. In fact, we found a significant increase in all three measures related to efficacy: civic efficacy, leadership efficacy, and students' sense that they had the knowledge and social capital needed to effectively promote community development. These gains were matched by increases in reports of personal responsibility to help others, following the news, and vision of how to help others, and a marginally significant ($p < .06$) commitment to community involvement.

The robust nature of these results became even clearer during the second year of our study because a control group was also surveyed. This group had similar academic skills and was taught by the same two teachers. This control group did not show statistically significant changes on any of the items we measured.

To summarize, the developers of the Madison County Youth in Public Service program structured their program to provide efficacious experiences working with government agencies. They wanted students to succeed in their community activities and thereby to develop confidence that they could be effective civic actors. They structured the curriculum and the students' experiences in the community accordingly. Both qualitative and quantitative data indicate that their efforts paid off. The students gained a sense that they "made a difference"—that they were capable leaders and change agents in their communities. Moreover, students reported that they were more inclined to engage in civic affairs in the future.

Bayside Students for Justice

Bayside Students for Justice provides an interesting contrast to the Youth in Public Service program. The Bayside Students for Justice program, part of a district-wide collaborative effort, was created by the teachers at Woodrow Wilson High School.[4] One class enrolled "Academy" students who are "at risk" of dropping out and another worked with students preparing for advanced placement (AP) exams. The Academy classes are populated primarily but not exclusively by minority students, whereas the AP classes enroll mostly but not exclusively white and Asian students. Students chose their own projects based on discussions in class, readings, and research about problems facing their communities. One group of students investigated the lack of access to adequate health care for women and sought to get the city Board of Supervisors to allocate funds to erect a new women's health center in an underserved area. Another group sought to challenge a state Senate bill that could put students and their parents in jail for truancy and try juveniles as adults for certain crimes. Other groups investigated child labor practices and bias in standardized testing. In addition to work

---

[4] All the classes used the Active Citizenship Today materials developed by the Constitutional Rights Foundation and the Close-Up Foundation.

in the community, students also participated in three "summits" where they publicly presented both their projects and what they accomplished.

Students' experiences working on these community-based activities were uneven. Some students were engaged in powerful in-depth projects; others were engaged in projects that were badly thwarted. Their problems stemmed from two related dynamics. First, the government, school, and community agencies were not prepared beforehand to expect contact from the students. Consequently, when students sought to investigate issues, they frequently were turned away, ignored, or, in the students' words, "not taken seriously." In addition, and more importantly for our purposes here, the projects students pursued challenged the status quo. Whereas students in Madison County worked with city officials on projects, those at Bayside criticized and sought to change various governmental and educational policies and programs. Not surprisingly, they encountered resistance.

Both qualitative and quantitative data regarding the students' frustrating experiences indicate that these experiences decreased their commitment to future civic involvement. In interviews, students reported high levels of frustration and a growing sense of hopelessness. They expressed low levels of both internal and external efficacy related to community improvement and questioned whether it is their responsibility to try. One student recalled her frustration this way: "We were trying to get anyone to listen to us but never got all the way through because we kept running into all this red tape that said 'no you can't do that' [or] 'Oh, you want to do that, well you'll have to go to that office over there.' [We] kind of got the impression that nobody really wanted to do anything about it."

This sense of frustration was widespread. In response to other interview and in-class reflection questions, such as "What did you learn from these activities?", other students answered "If you go out into the community and try to do good, someone will pull you down," "Basically, they were wasting our time and theirs too," and "It's hard to get anyone to listen to you."

In most cases, the survey results, as shown in Table 8.2, were consistent with the interview data, reflecting the frustration students experienced in connection with their community-based activities. With a few important exceptions (discussed in the next section), virtually all measures of students' orientation towards civic participation and community engagement declined. Their sense of personal responsibility to help others declined and they were marginally ($p = .1$) less likely to express a commitment to community involvement or a desire to work for social justice. Two measures related to efficacy (measures of civic efficacy and of students' sense of their knowledge related to community development) showed no change and the measure of leadership efficacy declined significantly. Most notably, students reported a sizable (-.50) and statistically significant ($p < .01$) decline when asked to indicate their level of agreement with the statement, "I want to become an effective leader in my community." These

declines occurred despite thorough and carefully developed classroom curriculum in which teachers hoped students would emerge ready to work to improve
society as active leaders and citizens.

Table 8.2: Bayside Students for Justice

Factors (Chron-bach's Pre, Post)	Change	Pretest	Posttest	Significance Level	Number of Students
Personal Responsibility to Help Others (.62, .74)	-.41**	4.17	3.76	.00	54
Commitment To Community Involvement (.54, .71)	-.23^	3.98	3.75	.10	54
Desire To Work For Justice (.65, .73)	-.14^	3.05	2.91	.10	55
I Will Volunteer (.80, .86)	-.10	3.27	3.17	.26	54
Follow The News (.43, .41)	.01	3.13	3.14	.95	51
Interest In Politics (.81, .81)	.08	2.97	3.04	.31	61
Civic Efficacy (.66, .71)	.12	3.24	3.35	.29	55
Vision (.65, .71)	-.09	2.81	2.72	.39	55
Knowledge/Social Capital For Community Development (.67, .72)	.03	2.87	2.89	.81	52
Leadership Efficacy (.78, .81)	-.21*	3.31	3.10	.03	55

$^\wedge p < .10$, $* p < .05$, $** p < .01$

Thus, whereas efficacious experiences promoted civic commitment among Madison County Students, the reverse occurred at Bayside. The commonly assumed connections between the successful or unsuccessful nature of student experiences working in the community, their self confidence as agents of change, and the impact on students' commitment to future civic involvement were supported by our study.

FINDINGS PART II: THE LIMITS OF EFFICACY AS A CURRICULAR GOAL

So far, these findings seem unremarkable. Given that Madison County's approach promoted civic commitments and Bayside's program did not, educators might be tempted to promote the Madison County approach over that employed at Bayside. Similarly, policymakers might be tempted to support civic education that provides students with the sense that they can make a difference as a means of promoting young people's political engagement. We would argue, however, that the choice between these two programs or approaches is not straightforward. Giving students a chance to "make a difference" clearly may have benefits, but this approach may also have costs. Our perspective on the issues can be clarified by considering the difference between internal and external efficacy and by revisiting attention to the two programs already discussed.

Specifically, it is important to consider the difference between internal and external political efficacy as educational aims. In many cases, it seems reasonable, for example, to structure curriculum to promote students' sense of internal efficacy—their sense of personal competence. As discussed earlier, the literature indicates that higher internal efficacy is related to active engagement. This goal might be pursued by developing that competence and by engaging students in efforts where a sense of success is possible.

Structuring curriculum so as to promote students' sense of external efficacy, however, may be problematic. Political scientists use self-reported measures of feelings of external political efficacy to capture differences across various population groups. African Americans and Latinos, for example, tend to have a lower sense of political efficacy than do their White counterparts (see Abramson, 1983; Niemi & Junn, 1998). Such results likely reflect the fact that government and community institutions are less responsive to African Americans than to Whites. These lower measures of external efficacy thus reflect a reality. The appropriate response, therefore, is to increase government responsiveness—not to try and convince a disempowered group that mainstream institutions want to respond to their concerns. To do otherwise is to alter *indicators* of a healthy democracy without challenging the underlying ills.[5]

What makes attention to broad notions of efficacy as a goal particularly complex, therefore, is that curricular strategies that deal sensibly with external efficacy may not promote internal efficacy. Conversely, attending primarily to internal efficacy may not help students consider issues related to external efficacy.

Our two cases illustrate these dynamics. The Bayside program, for example, engaged high stakes problems that students found difficult to solve. Although many school-based programs might have students clean up a nearby park or collect clothing or food for a local charity, the Bayside students were engaged in ambitious projects that sought to expose structural injustices, sometimes forgoing more typical and bounded projects that do less to challenge existing power structures. Whether to support a publicly funded health care center for women or how to investigate bias in standardized tests, for example, are controversial and unresolved social policy questions.

Naturally, these projects were more likely to meet with opposition than less ambitious projects. As a result, students reported doubts about their ability to effect change in social institutions such as better attention to women's health care. As already detailed, this appears to have lessened their desire to participate in political and civic endeavors. However, at the same time that these experiences may have diminished students' sense of internal efficacy and thus undermined their commitment to civic action, they also appear to have sparked valuable insights related to questions of external efficacy. Kira reported, for example "I think it's really hard to get things done that count for anything. I mean we can pick up litter all day long and get something done [that is temporary], but to try and get them to build a women's health center in our community, that's a tough task and no one wants to do it." In interviews and in class, students expressed an often-realistic assessment of how difficult it is to accomplish meaningful and, at times, controversial tasks. And, interviews and observations reveal that students were deeply engaged in these activities and that most took them very seriously. For example, another student, Tony, observed that "We really had no clue that so many people would be *against* a [publicly funded] health center, but when we started to see where people stood on this, it seemed like, well those who wouldn't get 'nothing from it; they were the ones who didn't

---

[5] Highlighting a similar set of issues, Thomas (1970) identified a conservative bias in measures of personal efficacy. He found that those holding a conservative political ideology were more likely to express personal efficacy than those holding liberal beliefs. Because these judgments may reflect reasonable interpretations of lived experience, he argued that it therefore makes no more sense to try and convince liberals that they should have more efficacy than it does to convince conservatives that they should have less.

want it." When asked what it would take to get a women's health center built, Kira responded, "You'd have to change a lot of people's minds about stuff and organize. . . . You'd have to fight for it."

Further analysis of the survey data reveals important distinctions as well. For example, the scale measuring interest in politics showed no change. However, if we consider three of its items (see Table 8.3), we find movement in opposing directions. Two items related to political action ("interest in voting" and "interest in working on a campaign") showed statistically significant declines of .38 and .31, respectively. At the same time, students reported a dramatic (+1.00) and statistically significant (p < .01) increase in "talking about politics and political issues." In fact, this was the largest pre–post change of any item across all the programs we studied. Thus, the curriculum appears to have diminished students' sense of internal efficacy and, as a result, to have diminished their interest in related political activity, but not their overall interest in politics. Specifically, their interest in politically charged concerns and debates increased.

Table 8.3: Notable Individual Item Scores in "Interest in Politics" Scale for Bayside

Factors/Items	Change	Prettest	Posttest	Significance Level
Interest In Politics	.08	2.97	3.04	.31
I enjoy talking about politics and political issues	+1.00**	3.16	4.16	.00
I expect that I will vote in every election	-.38*	3.79	3.40	.03
In the next 3 years I expect to work on at least one political campaign	-.31*	2.77	2.46	.04

The Madison County Youth in Public Service curriculum offers lessons in this regard as well. Both qualitative and quantitative data indicate that these students showed impressive gains in their sense of internal efficacy, but neither their interest in political discussion nor their intention to engage in explicitly political activity changed (see Table 8.1). More generally, we did not find evidence in student interviews, our observations, or our analysis of survey data that student projects examined ideological and political issues related to interest groups and the political process, the causes of poverty, different groups' access to health care, or the fairness of different systems of taxation (even though two projects focused on issues related to health care and taxation). Students focused on particular programs and policies and aimed for technocratic/value neutral analysis. Accordingly, neither survey data nor interview data indicated changes in our measures of these students' knowledge of or interest in structural dynamics, collective or root causes of social problems, or political participation (see Westheimer & Kahne, 2002, for details).

In short, the Madison County curriculum appears to have fostered internal efficacy as well as civic commitments, but the manner in which this was achieved appears to have avoided attention to structural issues and political dynamics—foci that might have diminished students' sense of internal efficacy, but that are essential to informed and effective efforts to promote democratic citizenship and democratic social change.

A WIDESPREAD TREND?

What is particularly troubling about this dynamic is that educators often are making this choice—emphasizing curricular strategies that develop internal efficacy but that obscure the importance of politics, social critique, and collective pursuit of systemic change (Barber, 1992; Robinson, 2000; Westheimer & Kahne, 2000). Data that the Department of Housing and Urban Development (HUD) collected on 599 college service-learning programs, for example, revealed that 50% were direct service (e.g., tutoring, serving food, clothes collections, blood drives), 42% provided technical assistance (e.g., leadership classes and computer training), 7% emphasized physical revitalization (e.g., tree planting and housing renovation), and only 1% were for political advocacy (e.g., drafting legislation or building tenant councils) (Robinson, 2000, p. 145). In addition, surveys of young people indicate movement in exactly this direction. As noted earlier, a recent survey of college freshmen (Sax et al., 1999) found that students' interest in social activism is declining, whereas their volunteer activities are reaching new highs. Similarly, a study commissioned by the National Association of Secretaries of State (1999) found that less than 32% of eligible voters between ages 18 and 24 voted in the 1996 presidential election (in 1972, the comparable number was 50%), but a whopping 94% of those from age 15 to 24 believed that "the most important thing I can do as a citizen is to help others." In a very real sense, youth seem to be "learning" that citizenship does not require government, politics, or social action.

Tobi Walker, drawing on her teaching experiences with service learning at Rutgers University's Eagleton Institute of Politics, labels this phenomenon a "service/politics split" (2000). She describes the disposition of the students she has worked with this way: "Most of them were filled with disgust, disillusionment, and even dread toward politics. They wanted to "make a difference" and they believed that the best way to do that was by helping another person one-on-one . . . [C]hallenging decision-making structures . . . rarely entered their thinking" (p. 647). Walker goes on to note that students involved in noncontroversial activities that allow young people to "'get things done' and immediately see results" tend to think of civic engagement as "results driven activity" that does not challenge institutions in power. They are eager to feed the hungry but not to think about the causes of poverty or injustice; they tutor inner-city children, but they do not ask why the schools have little in the way of resources. She concludes that her students learned a great deal about how to serve but little about effecting political change (Walker, 2000).

Thus, whereas Madison County Youth in Public Service, and other similar programs, may foster internal political efficacy and may well be an effective way to lever enthusiasm for engagement, it also appears to diminish or obscure both the importance of politics and the need to think about the impact and design of social institutions and structures.[6] The pursuit of a more just and equitable society requires more than individual efforts to "make a difference"—because politics and attention to the design and impact of social structures are also essential— but those designing curriculum must find ways to maintain and promote students' sense of internal efficacy while also attending to the importance of politics and analysis of social institutions.

---

[6] We also suspect that an emphasis on experiencing efficacy can sometimes lead to a focus on doing rather than thinking. Specifically, because careful analysis takes time away from action and because such analysis often highlights potential shortcomings of efforts that, on the surface, appear desirable, a commitment to efficacy may lead some educators to downplay analysis. This outcome is not inevitable, however. The programs we studied all emphasized academic and analytical work related to students' experiences.

CURRICULAR POSSIBILITIES

Faced with this tension, what can educators do? In particular, how can good programs promote commitments to both politics and participation? Given the importance of experiences that promote internal forms of efficacy, how can these be promoted without obscuring structural issues and attention to social justice?

Our study of these and other programs have helped us identify curricular strategies that may help educators respond to this challenge allowing programs to foster both students' sense of internal efficacy and their commitment to engagement while simultaneously recognizing and analyzing broader structural dynamics that may constrain many efforts at societal improvement.

Small Successes—Bigger Agendas

Several programs we studied sought to carefully plan activities so that small successes were possible, with the understanding that they are part of something larger, perhaps less immediately attainable. Like Madison County Youth in Public Service, these programs offered students successful experiences and minimized difficult implementation snafus by careful attention to small, achievable, intermediary tasks. Unlike their Madison County peers, however, teachers in these programs connected small projects substantively with broader explorations into root causes of social problems and accompanying political struggles. Like Bayside Students for Justice, these programs sought to equip students with the analytical and critical thinking skills needed to address structural obstacles to change.

In one program, for example, students from a private high school who were enrolled in an advanced Spanish language class were brought together with adults in a nearby Hispanic community who were studying for their U.S. citizenship exam. The students had opportunities for intensive Spanish speaking as they examined their own and others' ideas about citizenship and the value of democratic participation. They also gained direct experience with the Hispanic immigrant community and a sense of accomplishment from their work in that community. As one student noted, "What I like best about the class is really working hands-on with someone else and also being able to use Spanish in a real life situation."

From the standpoint of implementation, this Spanish language program was successful. But the lessons did more than provide efficacious opportunities through tutoring and related opportunities to reflect in class on the people they met. Although such experiences, like those of their Madison County peers, might have spurred greater commitment to future voluntary acts, had the curriculum ended with tutoring, tutoring would have been framed as an "answer" to the challenges these recent immigrants face.

To highlight the kind of deeper analysis of social, political, and economic issues that the leaders of Bayside aimed for, the teachers of this course arranged for students to tour the community and to study the social, political, and economic conditions of the local town, and of other Hispanic communities in the United States and in Latin America. Through this work, students gained an increased awareness of underlying political concerns. Students spoke (in Spanish), for example, about the high incidence of lead paint in houses in this community, about cycles of poverty, and about inadequate public services. After reading articles on poverty and housing conditions in this town, several students questioned how the state legislature could be considering lowering taxes when such poverty exist. When asked about the curriculum, students often demonstrated a new awareness of these underlying, broader challenges. Statements like the one that follows were typical:

> Learning first-hand about some of the experiences of the immigrants here in [our town] reflects on other places like Washington Heights in New York where there is a huge Dominican population; And not just Hispanics, because all immigrants share some similar experiences. . . .
> They face the same kinds of problems finding jobs and facing racism.

This student went on to highlight the importance of addressing these deeper social ills. In short, this program, while giving students a strong sense of success in preparing adults for the citizenship exam, also required that they examine broader social, political, and economic dynamics in relation to the lives of the immigrants they met. In doing so, they linked individual relationships and actions to policy issues and analysis of social structures.

Whereas students may have felt no more optimistic about their potential to change policies affecting immigrants than the students who participated in the Bayside program, the sense of despair that characterized many Bayside interviews was notably absent in the statements made by those who were part of this citizenship project. In the parlance of the 1980s Nuclear Freeze Movement, their projects were "small enough to appear doable but big enough to be inspiring."[7]

Interestingly, during the second year, the Bayside program adopted a related approach. The class decided to focus on violence and to study this issue from a structural perspective. Rather than doing a service project, the students took part in a retreat and focused on personal transformation and the role that violence plays in their lives and in the lives of fellow community members. These discus-

---

[7] This phrase appeared on a popular Nuclear Freeze Movement bumper sticker.

sions were coupled with discussions of broader social dynamics that might promote violence in the society. Whereas it was clearly difficult for students to talk honestly and openly about their behavior and about the ways in which violence had affected their lives, the experience left students energized rather than depleted. Survey results indicated growth in some conventional measures of civic capacities and commitments as well as in student interest in political engagement and ability to discuss root causes of social problems (see Westheimer & Kahne, 2002).

Similarly, it is important to note that the successful strategy employed in Madison County—placing students in efficacious organizations and having them join others in meaningful work—can be structured to emphasize themes of social justice while minimizing the potential sense of frustration and alienation that can occur when students work on their own on often intractable social problems. A clear and powerful example of this approach is provided in James Youniss, McClellan, and Yates's (1997) study of mostly African American students enrolled in a Washington, DC Catholic school. These students worked in soup kitchens and their accompanying classroom analyses of poverty and homelessness provided them not necessarily with a sense of complete success—but rather a vision of an ideal for which they and others could collectively strive. Frustration did not take hold of these students despite the fact that homelessness was not eliminated. Students became engaged in thinking about these issues and began to be able to see themselves as effective political participants.

There are other strategies programs might use to carry students' sense of hope and possibility through difficult and broader political projects. The Highlander Folk School in Tennessee, for example, seeks to engage students in a supportive community that can motivate and affirm the importance of challenging political structures and working for systemic change even when—or especially because—participants encounter strong resistance from governmental and other social institutions. Indeed, other studies have suggested that social bonds, a sense of affiliation, and support from a community of students and others who share commitments can nurture and sustain civic involvement despite intimidating challenges and frustrating experiences (McAdam, 1988; Youniss et al., 1997). Similarly, we studied a program at Berea College in Kentucky called the Overground Railroad. Participants visited historic landmarks in the civil rights movement and met individuals who helped make the civil rights movement happen. These individuals who were active in the movement and who in some cases are still active in social change efforts today—individuals who stayed true to their convictions despite the challenges of their work—seemed to inspire students and buttress their sense of hope and civic commitments. They offered a compelling vision of a meaningful life and of the potential efficacy of collective social action.[8]

CONCLUSIONS: RETHINKING THE GOAL OF EFFICACY

Young people today have too few opportunities to recognize their potential contributions to civic and political life. The Madison County Youth in Public Service program highlights the substantial impact that experiences of success can provide. By integrating government curriculum with meaningful work in the public sector, students' civic commitments and capacities expanded significantly. Many similar programs seek to engage students in successful community work so that they might develop a sense of efficacy in relation to their participation in community efforts. Certainly providing positive experiences that develop young people's sense that they can make a difference in their community is a worthwhile educational project. But this is not the complete story.

The impact of the frustration Bayside Students for Justice experienced is also worthy of careful attention. The experiences of students at Bayside demonstrates that exposure to some authentic community dynamics can diminish students' sense of internal efficacy and in the process limit their commitment to future civic or political involvement, but other indicators demonstrate the value of engaging students in analysis of significant and difficult-to-solve social problems. Part of the frustration Bayside students experienced resulted from real-world barriers to change. Students appeared to report low external efficacy because, in fact, external factors were barriers to change. We are reluctant to reject the value of these authentic experiences even though they appeared to diminish students' internal efficacy as well as their motivation for active involvement in civic action. Our study indicates that structuring curriculum to avoid real world barriers may obscure important social forces and thus be mis-educative.

At the same time, authenticity alone—to the extent that it conveys a sense of hopelessness—is not desirable. The Bayside curriculum aimed to promote commitments to active civic engagement. The democratic promise of such curriculum is not fulfilled if students "learn" that civic engagement is pointless.

Numerous societal norms and incentives will lead teachers and students to focus on civic activities that avoid major social problems and analysis of root causes of injustice and inequality. Such service activities are less controversial,

---

[8] A detailed discussion of these and other strategies programs employ to effectively promote active democratic citizenship can be found in Kahne, J., & Westheimer, J. (2003). Teaching Democracy: What school need to do. *Ph. Delta Kappan, 85*(1), September, 34-40, 57–66.

easier to fund, and enjoy widespread public support. They also provide opportunities for promoting internal efficacy. Although increasingly common, we are concerned that such activities will not provide sufficient preparation for the often contentious and difficult challenge of working to understand and change the social, economic, and political dynamics that surround complex issues such as poverty, caring for the environment, or racism. If teachers and students decide that such problems are hopeless or, alternatively, that it is easier to pursue a vision of citizenship that avoids conflict, the full promise of democracy will not be realized.

Democracy achieves its potential when citizens are both capable of and committed to working to improve society, and schools have an important role to play in preparing students accordingly. Avoiding projects that focus on difficult-to-solve structural issues in an effort to foster efficacy can result in missed educational opportunities. Capacities for structural analysis and for persevering despite frustration are essential for those who hope to be effective actors in a democratic society. Emphasizing only efficacious acts of charity can advance a politically conservative understanding of civic responsibilities—one that sees direct service and individual acts of kindness and charity rather than efforts to examine and address root causes of problems as the primary engine for social improvement.

Educating citizens for a democratic society requires that students gain both a sense that they can "make a difference" and also the ability to analyze and challenge social and institutional practices as they work to create a more just society.

ACKNOWLEDGMENTS

This research was generously supported by a grant from the Surdna Foundation. We also wish to thank Melinda Fine, Barbara Leckie, Tobi Walker, and James Youniss for helpful feedback on earlier drafts. The authors are solely responsible for any and all conclusions. A shorter essay on this topic appeared in *Political Science and Politics*, April 2006, 39(2), 289-296.

REFERENCES

Abramson, P. (1983). *Political attitudes in America: Formation and change.* San Francisco: Freeman.

Almond, G. A., & Verba, S. (1963). *The civic culture: Political attitudes and democracy in five nations.* Princeton, NJ: Princeton University Press.

Bandura, A. (1997). *Self–efficacy: The exercise of control.* New York: Freeman.

Barber, B. (1992). *An aristocracy of everyone: The politics of education and the future of America.* New York: Ballantine.

Berman, S. (1997). *Children's social consciousness and the development of social responsibility.* New York: State University of New York Press.

Balch, G. (1974). Multiple indicators in survey research: The concept "Sense of Political Efficacy." *Political Methodology,* 1, 1–43.

Conrad, D. & Hedin, D. (1981). *Instruments and scoring guide of the Experimental Education Evaluation project.* St. Paul, MN: Center for Youth Development and Research, University of Minnesota.

Ennis, J. G., & Schrener, R. (1987). Mobilizing weak support for social movements: The role of grievance, efficacy, and cost. *Social Forces,* 66, 390–409.

Harris, F.C. (1999). Will the circle be unbroken? The erosion and transformation of African-American civic life. In R. Fullinwider, (Ed.) *Civil society, democracy, and civic renewal* (pp. 317–338). New York: Rowman & Littlefield.

Kahne, J., & Westheimer, J. (2003). Teaching democracy: What schools and colleges need to do. *Phi Delta Kappan,* 85(1) September, 34-40, 57-66.

McAdam, D. (1988). *Freedom summer.* New York: Oxford University Press.

Miles, M., & Huberman, A. (1994). *Qualitative data analysis* (2nd ed.) CA: Thousand Oaks, CA: Sage Publications.

National Association of Secretaries of State. (1999). *New millennium project— phase I: A nationwide study of 15–24 year old youth.* Alexandria, VA: The Tarrance Group.

Niemi, R. G., & Junn, J. (1998). *Civic education: What makes students learn.* New Haven: Yale University Press.

Niemi, R. G., & Associates. (1974). *The politics of future citizens.* San Francisco: Jossey-Bass.

Noddings, N. (1999). Renewing democracy in schools. *Phi Delta Kappan,* 80(8), 579–583.

Oakes, J., et al. (2000). *Becoming good American schools: The struggle for civic virtue in education reform.* New York: Jossey-Bass.

Robinson, T. (2000). Dare the school build a new social order? *Michigan Journal of Community Service Learning,* 7, 142–157.

Sax, L. J., Astin, A., Korn, W. S., & Mahoney, K. (1999). *The American freshman: National norms for fall 1999*. Los Angeles: Higher Education Research Institute, UCLA.

Shingles, R. D. (1981). Black consciousness and political participation: The missing link. *American Political Science Review*, 75, 76–91.

Strauss, A. (1990). *Basics of qualitative research: Grounded theory, procedures and techniques*. Newbury Park, CA: Sage.

Thomas, L. E. (1970). The internal-external scale, ideological bias and political participation. *Journal of Personality*, 38: 273–286.

Walker, T. (2000). The service/politics split: Rethinking service to teach political engagement. *PS: Political Science and Politics*, 33(3), 647–649.

Westheimer, J., & Kahne, J. (2000, January 26). Service learning required—but what exactly do students learn? *Education Week*, p.42.

Westheimer, J., & Kahne, J. (2004). What kind of citizen? The politics of educating for democracy. *American Educational Research Journal*. Summer, 41(2), 237-269.

Wollman, N., & Stouder, R. (1991). Believed efficacy and political activity: A cast of the specificity hypothesis. *Journal of Social Psychology*, 131(4), 557–567.

Wood, G. (1992). *Schools that work: America's most innovative public education programs*. New York: Dutton.

Youniss, J., McClellan, J. A., & Yates, M. (1997). What we know about engendering civic identity. *American Behavioral Scientist*, 40(5), 620–631.

Chapter 10

Civics and Citizenship in Students' Daily Lives: Towards a Sociocultural Understanding of Civic Knowledge and Engagement

Beth C. Rubin
Rutgers University

> *I grew up in Arkansas in the forties and fifties in a society
> marked by racial segregation that was supported by both laws
> and customs. We learned about liberty and justice in school,
> and said—repeating the Pledge of Allegiance in our segre-
> gated school each morning— that our nation had "liberty and
> justice for all." As a child who took school and my teachers
> seriously, I internalized that notion. However, much in society
> told me that liberty and justice was for some but not for all.*
> *—Banks (1996, p. xii)*

Preeminent multicultural education scholar James Banks, reflecting on his youth
in the segregated South, writes movingly of the disjuncture between formal expressions of citizenship in his school classroom and his daily experiences with
inequality beyond the classroom setting. This passage suggests that both formal
and informal civic experiences molded his sense of himself as a citizen and a
civic being. Yet, traditional measures of civic knowledge tend to focus on the
assessment of facts learned through direct instruction in schools, and measures
of civic engagement frequently center on recording students' intentions to vote
and familiarity with current events. Students' out-of-school civic experiences are
rarely included in such measures. The research base resulting from these extensive and long-term investigations is impressive, and raises a number of questions
for further investigation. This chapter explores the possibility of enriching the
current civic education literature—and perhaps shedding light on troubling issues raised therein—through a broader conceptualization of civic learning and

engagement, and suggests an interpretive research methodology as one possible means of doing so.

Civic knowledge is conceptualized in the existing literature as a set of understandings—knowledge of facts about U.S. history and the workings of our government—that young people should master and that can be readily measured with close-ended surveys and tests. Civic engagement, in this literature, is defined as formal participation in civic institutions through voting and other political activity, and more informal participation, most commonly defined as following current events through newspaper reading, television watching, and holding discussions with family and friends about politics. Thus, measurements of civic knowledge commonly seek to understand the extent to which students have mastered the material that has been presented to them, and measures of civic engagement attempt to quantify the degree to which students intend to participate in civic life, as conceptualized earlier.

Yet, as Bank's reflections indicate, students have meaningful civic experiences outside of the classroom, both within schools and beyond, which shape their understandings of what it means to be an American citizen and a participant in the civic life of a democracy. These experiences may differ sharply depending on how students' are situated socially, historically, and culturally amidst the institutional and economic structures of the United States. Two examples illustrate this idea. Compare, for instance, feelings about a primary institution of civic life—the police—held by students with differing life experiences. Would an African American male student who is frequently stopped by the police as a result of racial profiling bring the same sense of civic identity to his civics and government courses as would a European American student who has only had positive interactions with the police? Or, compare the sense of civic efficacy held by students situated differently within U.S. educational institutions, another primary point of contact between young Americans and their government. Would a student in a suburban school whose well-educated parents were able, with a few well placed calls, to have her placed in the best classes with the most coveted teachers at her school, have the same sense of civic efficacy as a student in an under resourced inner-city school who has had to wait for weeks, along with the rest of her classmates, before receiving her final course schedule?

What might such differences in out-of-classroom civic experience mean for formal, classroom-based civic education, which generally proceeds as though all students draw on an identical well of experiences to meaning from the curriculum? How might the practice of civic education be informed by a deeper and more nuanced understanding of diverse students' daily (and differing) experiences with civic life? This chapter is an attempt to link together several schools of thought as a means for exploring a familiar issue from a different and perhaps productive angle. A sociocultural frame and an interpretive research methodology may be possible tools for unearthing and explicating the meaning of students' daily experiences as citizens and civic beings, as distinct from their knowledge abut the workings of the democratic system and their more formal participation (or intent to participate) in traditional markers of civic life.

This chapter is organized in the following manner. This next section reviews current literature assessing students' civic knowledge and engagement, attempting to uncover the conceptions of civic learning and engagement that underlie this body of work. The following section explores how a sociocultural frame and an interpretive research methodology might be employed to broaden our notions of civic learning and engagement and to develop a fuller understanding of how diverse students become citizens and civic beings. A final section explores the implications for the research and practice of civic education that emerge from these approaches, describing a new direction for civic education research that centers on better understanding how civic identity is constructed by diverse students.

CIVIC LEARNING, KNOWLEDGE, AND ENGAGEMENT: PREVIOUS ASSESSMENTS

Students' civic knowledge and engagement are frequently the subjects of analysis by researchers from educational psychology, political science, social education, and other fields. Measures of civic learning have been administered to large cohorts of students, some repeatedly over the course of several decades (i.e., NAEP). The result is a wealth of data and analysis, an impressive body of research documenting students' civic achievement over time. This section provides a brief review of this literature and its major findings. It highlights the methods and conceptions of civic knowledge and engagement underlying this established literature, noting unresolved questions that consistently emerge.

Major Findings in the Literature

Students Lack Civic Knowledge. The National Assessment of Educational Progress (NAEP) is an ongoing assessment project established in 1969 by congressional mandate to gather inclusive information about the educational achievement of U.S. students in a variety of content areas. The NAEP Civics Assessment focused on students' knowledge in three areas. Knowledge of "context" was based on questions about national, state, and local government. "Cognition" was ascertained through "the ability to recall specific facts and concepts" and to apply these concepts (NAEP, 1990, p. 10). "Content" knowledge involved information in four categories: democratic principals and the purpose of government; political institutions; political processes; and rights, responsibilities, and the law.

Working with this definition, the NAEP has repeatedly documented a lack of civic knowledge among students in the United States. The most recent NAEP, conducted in 1998, revealed that less than 25% of students scored at a proficient level in the civics and government area of the exam (Lutkus, et al., 1999). Other studies and polls support this assessment, documenting young peoples' inability to answer questions about "key historical facts" and their lack of understanding of how government works (Bennett, 2000Gallup, 2000; Mann, 1999; Morin, 2000; Vanishing Voter, 2000).

U. S. Students Compare Well Internationally in Their Civic Knowledge. The recent International Association for the Evaluation of Educational Achievement (IEA) Civic Education Study (CivEd) conducted in 1999, on the other hand, sounded a reassuring note about the "civic achievement" of U.S. students as compared with their peers in other countries (Baldi, Perie, Skidmore, Greenberg, & Hahn, 2001; Hahn, 2001; Torney-Purta, Lehmann, Oswald, & Schulz, 2001). The IEA study measured the "civic achievement" of ninth-grade students in 28 democratic countries. This was measured with a "total civic knowledge" scale consisting of two subscales. One subscale measured students' mastery of "civic content," including knowledge of key civic principals and features ("key features of democracies" is the example given), using a multiple-choice format (*Highlights*, 2001, p. 2). The second subscale measured students' "civic skills," that is, their skills in using civic knowledge ("understanding a brief political article or a political cartoon" is the example), also determined through students' answers to multiple-choice questions (*Highlights*, 2001 p. 2). Additional survey items measured students' conceptions of democracy, citizenship, and government, attitudes toward civic issues, and expected political participation.

Using these measures, U.S. students scored above the international mean in overall civic knowledge, scoring substantially higher than their peers in other countries on the "civic skills" subscale, and within the international average on the "civic content" subscale. "Overall," the report states, "the results indicate that ninth-grade U.S. students performed well when compared with students in the other 27 participating countries" (*Highlights*, 2001, p. 4).

Disturbing Patterns in Students' Civic Achievement. Multiple studies concur that there are differences in the civic achievement of U.S. students that appear to be linked to the racial and socioeconomic background of the students being tested (Lutkus et al., 1999; Bald et al., 2001). The IEA CivEd study showed that students in "high poverty" schools, as determined by percentage of student body eligible for the free and reduced lunch program (25% for "high poverty" schools), scored lower on the civic achievement measure than their peers in "low poverty" (less than 25% eligible for free and reduced lunch) schools. The IEA study also reported White and multiracial students scoring higher than their African American and Latino peers (Baldi et al., 2001). On the 1988 NAEP, White students scored on average 13 percentage points higher than their African American peers, and 11 percentage points above their Hispanic[1] classmates (Niemi & Junn, 1998, p. 110). Niemi and Junn note that African American students scored relatively better on the few questions that had to do with racial matters, and Hispanic students scored equal with Whites on the one question having to do with the "contemporary Hispanic experience" (p. 112). Interestingly, the IEA reported no differences in students' expected level of political participation by race or country of origin.

Students' Civic Knowledge is Linked to Their Years in School, Educational Goals, and Their Parents' Educational Attainment. There appears to be a link between years in school (both students' own and that of their parents) and students' civic achievement, although this link may not be directly related to coursework in civics, government and social studies. Niemi and Junn (1998) note that "formal education is the strongest, most consistent correlate (and is widely considered the central causal determinant) of political knowledge" (p. 13). The longer students stay in school the more likely they are to show a high degree of political knowledge (Delli Carpini & Keeter, 1996; Hyman, Wright, & Reed, 1975; Nie et al., 1996), although researchers are not sure why this is the case. Niemi and Junn report "difficulties associated with trying to assess exactly how education leads to greater political knowledge" (p. 13).

Students holding high expectations for their own education (who expected to complete college) did better on the IEA than those who intended to drop out of high school or stop school after graduating high school (Baldi et al., 2001). Furthermore, parents' educational attainment is noticeably correlated with student performance on measures of civic achievement (Baldi et al., 2001; Hahn, 2001; Niemi & Junn, 1998).

Effects of Civics and Social Studies Instruction on Civic Knowledge Participation Are Difficult to Discern. There was disagreement in the literature over the extent to which civic and social studies instruction affects students' civic achievement and participation, and how such an effect might be measured. Niemi and Junn (1998) concluded from their examination of the 1988 NAEP data that "the school civics curriculum does indeed enhance what and how much they [high school seniors] know." (p.147). Hahn (2001), writing about the IEA study, concluded that higher quality and greater quantity of social studies instruction increased meaningful learning among students.

---

[1] "Hispanic" is the term used by the NAEP.

Other researchers argued, however, that civics classes had little or no effect on most students (e.g. Corbett, 1991; Erikson & Tedin, 1995; Gutmann, 1987). These researchers questioned the effect of schools and classroom instruction to motivate students to participate civically, and claimed that it was difficult to determine the effects of classroom civics instruction independent from other variables, such as learning from parental attitudes, school "climate" (Leming, 1985), and the "hidden curriculum" of classroom and school interactions, discourse and procedures (Patrick & Hoge, 1991).

There Is a Decline in Civic Engagement among Today's Youth. Most researchers concurred that civic knowledge and engagement were in decline. Multiple studies reported poor voting rates among young peoples (New Millennium Youth Voters Project, 1999; Vanishing Voter, 2000) and their lack of engagement with civic issues at both school and national levels (Jennings & Stoker 2001; National Election Studies 2000;). Bennett (2000), summarizing the results of recent studies of youth civic engagement, lamented that young people did not have enough basic knowledge to act intelligently as voters, and were "profoundly disconnected from public affairs" (p. 9).

Rothstein (2001) notes that although civic knowledge has remained steady over the past 10 years, levels of voting have declined. Researchers report declines in other measures of engagement as well. The National Election Studies (2000) report states that 14% of people born between 1970 and 1982 never discuss politics with friends or family. Despairing, Bennett (2000) concluded his review of youth civic engagement with the plaint, "some means must be found to overcome youthful indifference to politics; otherwise the future of America's democratic experiment looks bleak" (p. 9). The picture is similar to Putnam's compelling portrayal (1995) of the disappearance of civil society, with a focus on teens and people in their early twenties. It appears surprising, then, that on the IEA, most ninth-grade students (85%) said they intended to vote in national elections when they became adults. In contrast with the low voting rates of young Americans, this statistic is strikingly optimistic and points to a possible gap between students' civic ideals and the realization of those ideas. As Hahn (2001) notes, "The challenge for social studies educators is to build upon the idealism of students, so that as graduating seniors they become citizens who vote and express their views on public issues" (p. 459).

Active Participation in Civic Activities in Youth May Increase Civic Participation in Adulthood. A number of studies note a connection between youth participation in organized groups and their later civic participation as adults (e.g., Beane, Turner, Jones, & Lipkqa, 1981; Ladewig & Thomas, 1987; Verba, Scholzman & Brady, 1995). Youniss, McLellan, and Yates (1997) argue that youth organizations that "provide direct exposure to explicit ideological orientations or worldviews" (i.e., 4-H, public service with homeless people) help young people to "construct" positive civic identities (p. 624). This is a conception of civic knowledge and engagement that differs considerably from that typically found in the literature, and is discussed further later. In a related finding, the IEA reported that students who participated in extracurricular activities scored higher on the civic knowledge section than those who were not involved (Baldi et al., 2001).

Understandings of Civic Knowledge and Engagement Embedded in the Existing Research

In general, this body of literature is based on a conception of civic knowledge as content and skills that teachers can attempt to transmit to students within civics and government courses. Students' mastery of this content, then, can best be assessed through close-ended questions assessing their command of set body of knowledge. In this way, researchers will be able to determine what large numbers of students do and do not know about civic life in the United States.

Political knowledge, in this conception of civic learning, refers to what people know about politics in a formal sense. Thus, political awareness and/or engagement can be determined through an assessment of students' participation in formal markers of civic engagement (e.g., voting), along with some less formal indicators (e.g., keeping up with the news or discussing political affairs). Civic participation, in this literature, mainly refers to one's participation in these formal processes.

Research questions underlying this literature might be summarized most broadly as: "How much civic knowledge do students hold?", "Where did they gain this civic knowledge?", "What might lead them to hold more knowledge?", "How much do they participate (or intend to participate) in civic life?", and "What might lead them to participate more, and more broadly?" The best research methodology for answering such questions is a large-scale, close-ended survey holding to a singular definition of civic knowledge and engagement in order to ascertain the extent to which students have mastered it.

Limitations of the Existing Civic Research

Much has been and continues to be learned from these approaches to understanding civic achievement. This impressive and continually expanding body of research tracks changes over time and allows for numerous analytical possibilities. The studies reviewed also raise important questions about civic learning and engagement, questions that previous approaches may not be able to fully address. Although it is clear from established measures of civic attainment that race, socioeconomic class, and educational attainment are somehow related to students' civic learning it is unclear how or why. The actual impact of classroom instruction and out-of-school involvement is also unclear.

The limitation of this established literature is that, due to conceptual frame and research methods, it can only shed light on whether or not kids have accomplished what researchers define as civic learning and engagement. The meaning civic life has for the students themselves cannot be discerned from such measures, as civic life is a predefined assessment tool itself. Understandings of the relevance of race, class, and educational attainment in this literature are limited by the static and decontexualized quality such factors take on within objective measures of civic achievement. A connection between race and civic knowledge cannot be made, for example, unless we have some understanding of what each of those concepts means to individual students. Without this sort of data, we can only guess at how sociocultural context shapes civic knowledge and engagement, and how these concepts take on meaning in students' daily lives.

A NEW APPROACH TO RESEARCH ON CIVIC LEARNING, KNOWLEDGE, AND ENGAGEMENT

A Sociocultural Framework

There is, perhaps, an additional way to conceptualize civic learning, knowledge, and engagement that is not encompassed by traditional approaches to the question. Let us reconsider James Bank's words, quoted at the beginning of this chapter. Banks' civic identity was shaped by experiences in segregated schools amidst a segregated society in which inequalities were manifest in his daily life. His example raises the question of whether there are other sources of civic knowledge beyond those assumed to be most relevant in the prevailing research. Might students know or have learned something relevant to their civic knowledge and engagement beyond what can be elicited through surveys, polls, and other standardized measures?

Such questions entail a shift from the attempt to determine what kids do not know, to trying to understand what they do know about civic life from their experiences as citizens. Although what they do know may in no way resemble the answers to the questions on standard assessments of civic knowledge, understanding the meaning of civic life from the perspective of its participants may shed light on the curious gap between knowledge and action, as well as the patterns we see and are troubled by. This idea is based on an altered conception of civic knowledge and engagement positing that kids (and their families) are continually civically engaged, that is, they are constantly engaged in interactions with the civic institutions of our society. Students go to school, sign up for classes, interact with adults in positions of authority, ask a police officer for directions, go to the department of motor vehicles to get a driver's license, sit in the waiting rooms of public health clinics, are interviewed by social workers for the state child protective service, accompany their parents to pick up welfare checks and apply for food stamps, and so on. A sociocultural approach would allow researchers to consider how such experiences are part of how students construct their evolving understandings of what being a citizen entails, their relative value and importance within U.S. civic institutions, and their ability to affect the system.

Such an approach might well be a way to address some of the troubling questions that arise from the civic education literature—why do scores vary by race, class, and educational attainment? What actually does spur civic activity? A shift to a sociocultural frame might allow us to view the issue of civic learning and engagement more broadly. It may assist in the exploration of unanswered questions in the literature—why these race and class patterns? Why such a strong correlation between civic attainment and educational attainment? A sociocultural approach to civic knowledge and learning would reframe the question as one of construction of "civic identity" rather than attainment of civic knowledge. In this view, civic identity is fluid, situated, and contingent on social, cultural, and historical location.

Youniss et al. (1997) argue that "formative civic experiences" have the potential to shape the construction of civic identity in powerful ways. Their review describes a study conducted by Fendrich (1993), which concluded that African Americans who attended and graduated college during the civil rights era, both those who had and had not been actively involved in politics, were more civically active than the general population 10 and 25 years after college. Fendrich hypothesized that "Black college graduates in this era were participants to some degree in a generational experience that shaped the trajectory of their life course. This generation was offered novel opportunities to further its education, enter careers previously closed to Blacks, and achieve financial rewards well beyond what was available to their parents' generation" (Youniss et al., 1997, p. 628). Formative civic experiences that offered an opportunity to participate in civic life and gain a sense of efficacy speak to issues of difference, power. Youniss and Yates call their analysis a "developmental analysis," which frames students as constructing civic identities rather than receiving them in a top-down fashion. Perhaps it is more accurate to see it as a sociocultural analysis, which situates construction of civic identity within the social structure of the United States, cultural frameworks, and historical events.

With this in mind, consider the following excerpt, below, in which Haitian American student Neptune (1998) shares her thoughts about applying for U.S. citizenship after Abner Louima's beating and torture at the hands of the New York Police Department:

When I head that Louima had been beaten by the police and harassed because he was Haitian, I remembered all these things, and questions filled my mind. Why should I be part of a country that doesn't want to open its arms to people who seek refuge here? Why should I be part of this country if I have to fear the people who are supposed to protect me just like my parents feared the police in Haiti?   If it hadn't been for the Louima case, I probably would have filled out the forms anyway and become a citizen. Now, though, I've decided to wait. I guess I feel a little hopeless, and I just don't believe that I can change this country. I don't see anyone I would want to vote for or anyone who thinks like me.

I want to become an American citizen for the right reasons—I don't just want to do it so I can get government aid for college or for some other financial benefits. I want to feel passionate about my country and I want to feel like I can bring about change. (p. 29)

Neptune, far from being disengaged civically, is deeply concerned about her ability to effect change in the United States. The brutalization of Abner Louima at the hands of the police affected her powerfully, causing her to question her place in this country as a child of Haitian immigrants.

In this way, a sociocultural approach would allow us to look outside the classroom and other settings traditionally assumed to be the main sites of civic learning to investigate students' daily civic experiences. Such an approach would consider any experience with a civic institution (or its representatives) that held meaning for an individual to be part of his or her "construction" of civic identity. The next section considers the utility of interpretive research methods as a means of gathering such data and presents a few relevant examples from existing interpretive studies.

An Interpretive Research Approach

A sociocultural approach can provide a theoretical frame for a nuanced and contexualized understanding of the construction of civic identity. An interpretive research methodology, in which the researcher "seeks to understand the ways which teachers and students, in their actions together, constitute environments for one another" (Erickson, 1986, p. 128), is one means by which such understandings can be empirically defined and substantiated. Such an approach is grounded in the belief that "patterns of behavior are *constructed* in social scenes; they are assembled by people in their interaction together" (Mehan, 1992, p. 64). Although societal structures form a frame within which individuals interact, the meaning of social actions is negotiated on a moment-by-moment basis by those participating in that action. Meaning is seen as co-constructed, negotiated, and renegotiated among the participants in any given situation, who all simultaneously constrain and create one another's possibilities. "Local meanings" are best discovered through an interpretive research method that focuses on the meaning perspectives of the participants in any event.

Interpretive methods are predicated on a consideration of the "situated" nature of experience. That is, where a subject is socially and historically located in terms of race, class, gender, among other aspects of experience, has implications for understanding how individuals experience their worlds, although not in any easily predictable way. For example, that he was an African American child living in the historical time period of segregation was critical to Bank's sense of himself as a civic being, as described in the epigraph. However, we cannot extrapolate the texture of his civic self from those bare facts. An interpretive approach allows the researcher to be attentive both to how each individual is situated amidst larger social and historical structures, as well as the daily interactions through which humans construct meaning.

Interpretive fieldwork involves careful, reflective and extended observation of everyday events in an attempt to identify the significance of those events from the various points of views of the participants themselves. According to Erickson (1986) interpretive research entails intensive long-term participation in a field setting; careful recording of what happens in the setting; ongoing analysis of the documentary record created; and use of detailed descriptions, such as narrative vignettes and direct quotes, along with analytic charts, summary tables, and descriptive statistics, to report conclusions.

Interpretive methods are most useful when a researcher wishes to learn more about the following (Erickson, 1986, p. 121):

1. The specific structure of occurrences rather than their general character and overall distribution;
2. The meaning-perspectives of the particular actors in the particular events.
3. The location of naturally occurring points of contrast that can be observed as natural experiments;
4. The identification of specific causal linkages that were not identified by experimental methods, and the development of new theories about causes and other influences on the patterns that are identified in survey data or experiments.

In the case of civic education, an interpretive approach has the potential both to reveal dimensions of an individual's experience that traditional approaches cannot and to shed light on achievement patterns identified in survey data.

Examples of Interpretive Research Illuminating Civic Identity

Valenzuela's interpretive study of Latino (immigrant and U.S. born) students in a Texas high school provides an example of how an interpretive research method can be used to enrich understandings of how civic identity is constructed. Valenzuela (1999) presents the words of a woman she interviewed who was a student at Seguin High School during a student walk-out in the 1980s:

> I remember I was in a classroom without a teacher for the whole first six weeks. I showed up every day and hanged out or did my homework but half the class dropped out. I ended up getting a grade for just showing p. This was the first time I really saw how the school didn't care for me or any of us. If I learned or if I didn't learn, so what? I remember feeling very depressed about that. Then I got angry. (p. 51)

Institutional inaction sparked sadness and anger in this student and others, laying the groundwork for the events that followed. Valenzuela continues the "story," weaving together an analytical narrative drawn from interview and observational data:

> Other problems aggravated an already bad situation. The bathrooms were in need of repair, with toilets that did not flush and stalls without doors. Some classrooms had no seats or books; others were overcrowded; and still others had scarcely any students in them . . .
>
> The demands the students made when they walked out point to additional problem areas at the school. They called for bilingual counselors, computerized schedules, and more books and resources, including computers. . . . The students also asked for dropout prevention and retention programs, an expansion of their honors, magnet, and special education programs, and equal funding across all district schools.
>
> Some of the honors students traced their willingness to orchestrate a walkout to the galvanizing effects of a history class discussion on the First Amendment right of free speech and peaceful assembly that had been a part of a more general discussion of the Civil Rights Movement and Martin Luther King's strategy of peaceful non-violent protest. An episode from the television show "21 Jump Street" a week earlier provided added impetus, That episode focused on a walkout students had organized to protest what they deemed to be the unreasonable demands of their principal. Thus, the idea that protesting the conditions of one's schooling was acceptable as long as it was peaceful, took root. (Valenzuela, 1999, p.53)

Although Valenzuela's primary purpose in her book is to expose the institutional processes by which schools "subtract" resources from U.S.-Mexican youth, this excerpt describes an instance of civic action taken by high school students that was sparked by a combination of despair over poor educational conditions, the inspirational effects of a history lesson, and an example of student action seen on a popular television show. Complex and illuminating, such an account could only be generated through interpretive fieldwork and analysis. The sources and manifestations of this emerging activist civic identity among these high school students could not be uncovered through surveys or tests of civic knowledge.

Interpretive research can unearth intricate connections between intertwining aspects of identity. Olsen, in her research with diverse immigrant students in a California high school, found that race, class, and gender were all powerfully implicated in the process of immigrant students coming to think of themselves as American citizens. In *Made in America* (Olsen, 1997), she describes how, for students from various non-Western countries, becoming American was also a process of "racialization" in which immigrant students, in pursuit of a social place in the high school setting, felt they had to align themselves with a particular racial identity and, in so doing, place themselves within an inequitable social structure of the United States.

Olsen's research also explores the complex ways that gender was in the process of becoming American for immigrant girls from religious or "traditional" families. For the young women she interviewed and observed, navigating the competing notions of gender roles and expectations held by family and home culture on the one hand, and by peer, youth, and popular culture on the other hand, were part of the process of Americanization. This process was fraught with intergenerational and personal conflict. For these students, being American had particular meanings and implications, often in conflict with deeply held family and cultural values. For these girls, identification with "American" attitudes about women's dress, behavior, relationships with males, and future goals, could entail a rejection of family and community. Repudiation of these Americanized values meant social ostracism at school and sacrifice of the personal aspirations that were encouraged by teachers, Americanized peers, and popular culture. These difficult choices were central issues of citizenship for immigrant young women at the high school Olsen studied, aspects of emerging civic identity that certainly could not be captured by a standardized assessment of civic knowledge and engagement.

Devine drew a different set of understandings from his research in poor New York City schools. In Maximum Security (Devine, 1996) he notes that immigrant students, mainly from Caribbean countries, were frequently shocked to experience the lack of control adults exercise over young people in the school setting:

> The primary and shocking first impression the immigrant student re-
> ceives is the unwillingness of the school staff to enforce behavioral
> standards that would have been routinely enforced in the home country.
> The fifteen-year-old just arrived from St. Lucia does not immediately
> discern differences in academic standards; but nuances of dress codes,
> execution of norms of politeness, and enforcement of rules of conduct
> transmit latent values . . . from day one . . . The most disruptive stu-
> dents are rarely or ineffectually chastised. As growing adolescents, in-
> clined to test rules and expecting to find a system that upholds stan-
> dards, such as they might have encountered in the more traditional
> schools of the Caribbean, they find instead that the system yields to
> their youthful pressure at every turn. . . .The space of the school be-
> comes a locus of terror for the immigrant student, who suddenly real-
> izes that the school is a presocietal state where anything goes and
> where the strong may prey upon the weak more or less at will. (p.108)

Devine's research depicts the process of immigrant students learning about
U.S. civic institutions from their experiences in violent urban schools. Students
in such schools developed particular understandings of their own worth as citizens within institutional settings marked by chaos and lack of caring on the part
of the adults who were ostensibly in charge.

As these examples illustrate, an interpretive approach is useful for understanding how students make sense of their own daily experiences and the larger
ramifications of this meaning making. Such a method could be fruitfully employed to shed light on some of the questions that emerge from previous work
assessing students' civic knowledge and engagement, supplementing this established literature with a complementary data and analysis that explores the civic
identities of diverse students from a different theoretical perspective.

IMPLICATIONS FOR RESEARCH AND FOR
CLASSROOM-BASED CIVIC INSTRUCTION

This reconceptualization of theoretical frame and research methodologies for
understanding students' civic learning has ramifications both for research and
for classroom-based instruction in civics and government. If we begin to take
seriously students' out-of-school and informal experiences with government
institutions and their agents, our sense of what students bring with them to their
classroom encounters with civics and government curricula are altered. The distinct civic experiences individual students have had, their varying senses of civic
efficacy and worth, and the various ways that race, class, and gender are implicated in students' emerging civic identities all matter for classroom instruction.

There is great potential to design curricula and teaching practices that can tap into deep-seated personal beliefs and significant experiences, developing civics and government instruction that may be more relevant and meaningful for high school students.

Before this can happen, however, we must know more about the dimensions of civic identity, as apprehended from a sociocultural, interpretive perspective. This chapter points to the need for research that uncovers locally constructed meanings of civic engagement, that investigates students' actual civic experiences and the meaning they make from these experiences, and that attempts to understand how students' situated civic experiences come into play in civics and government classrooms. Such research will result in a deeper understanding of how civic learning, knowledge, and engagement take shape in students' daily lives and will point to new directions for the practice of civic education.

REFERENCES

Baldi, S., Perie, M., Skidmore, D., Greenberg, E., & Hahn, C. (2001). *What democracy means to ninth graders: U.S. results from the international IEA Civic Education Study.* Washington, DC: National Center for Education Statistics, U.S. Department of Education.

Banks, J. (1996) Foreword. In W. Parker (Ed.), *Educating the democratic mind* (pp. xi – xiii). New York: State University of New York.

Beane, J., Turner, J., Jones, D. & Lipka, R. (1981). Long-term effects of community service programs. *Curriculum Inquiry, 11,* 143–155.

Bennett, S. (2000). Political apathy and avoidance of news media among generations X and Y: America's continuing problem. In S. Mann & J. Patrick (Eds.), *Education for civic engagement in democracy.* Bloomington, Indiana: ERIC Clearinghouse for Social Studies.

Corbett, M. (1991). *American public opinion: Trends, processes, and patterns.* White Plains, NY: Longman.

Delli Carpini, M. & Keeter, S. (1996). *What Americans know about politics and why it matters.* New Haven, CT: Yale University Press.

Devine, J. (1997). *Maximum security: The culture of violence in inner-city schools.* Chicago: University of Chicago Press.

Erickson, F. (1986). Qualitative methods in research on teaching. In Merlin C. Wittrock (Ed.), *Handbook of research on teaching* (3rd edition, pp. 119–161). New York: Holt, Rinehart & Winston.

Erikson, R. S., & Tedin, K. L. (1995). *American public opinion: Its origins, content, and impact* (5th ed.) Needham Heights, MA: Allyn & Bacon.

Fendrich, J. (1993). *Ideal citizens.* Albany: State University of New York Press.

Gallup (2000). Retrieved 10/2/06 from http://www.gallup.com/Election2000/

Gutmann, A. (1987). *Democratic education.* Princeton, NJ: Princeton University Press.

Hahn, C. (2001). Student views of democracy: The good and bad news. *Social Education, 65*(7), 456–460.

Highlights of U.S. results from the International IEA Civic Education Study (CivEd). (2001). Washington, DC: National Center for Education Statistics, U.S. Department of Education. Retrieved 10/2/06 from http://www.nces.ed.gov/pubs2001/cived/

Hyman, H., Wright, C., & Reed, J. (1975). *The enduring effects of education.* Chicago: University of Chicago Press.

Jennings, M., & Stoker, L. (2001, August 30–September 2). *Generations and civic engagement: A longitudinal multiple-generation analysis.* Paper presented at the 2001 annual meeting of the American Political Science Association, San Francisco.

Ladewig, H., & Thomas, J. K. (1987). Assessing the impact of 4-H on former members. College Station: Texas A&M University, Cooperative Extension Service.

Leming, J. S. (1985). Research on social studies curriculum and instruction: Interventions and outcomes in the socio-moral domain. In W. B. Stanley (Ed.), *Review of Research in Social Studies Education: 1976–1983.* Washington, DC: National Council for the Social Studies.

Lutkus, A., Weiss, A. R., Campbell, J. R., Mazzeo, J., & Lazer, S. (1999). *The NAEP 1998 civics report card for the nation.* Washington, DC: National Center for Education Statistics. Washington, DC: U.S. Government Printing Office. U.S. Department of Education.

Mann, S. (1999). What the survey of American college freshmen tells us about their interest in politics and political science. *PS: Political Science and Politics, 32*, 749–754.

Mehan, H. (1992). Understanding inequality in schools: The contribution of interpretive studies. *Sociology of Education*, 65, 1–20.

Morin, R. (2000, April 17). What Americans think: Don't know much about history. *The Washington Post, national weekly edition*, p. 34.

National Assessment of Educational Progress. (1990). The civics report card. Princeton, NJ: Educational Testing Service (ERIC Document Reproduction Service No. ED315376.)

National Election Studies. (2000). Retrieved 10/2/2006 from http://www.umich.edu/~nes/index.htm

National Center for Education Statistics. (1998). National Assessment of Educational Progress for Civics. Retrieved 10/2/2006 from http://www.nces.ed.gov/nationsreportcard/civics/newresults.asp

New Millennium Young Voters Project (1999). Retrieved 10/2/2006 from http://www.stateofthevote.org/. National Association of Secretaries of State.

Nie, N., Junn, S., & Stehlik-Barry, K. (1996). *Education and democratic citizenship in America.* Chicago: University of Chicago Press.

Niemi, R., & Junn, J. (1998). *Civic education: What makes students learn.* New Haven, CT: Yale University Press.

Neptune, N. (1998). What happened to my American dream? In P. Kay, A. Estepa, & A. Desetta (Eds.), *Things get hectic: Teens write about the violence that surrounds them* (pp. 26–29). New York: Touchstone Press.

Olsen, L. (1997). *Made in America: Immigrant students in our public schools.* New York: The New Press.

Patrick, J. & Hoge, J. (1991). Teaching government, civics, and the law. In J. Shaver (Ed.), *Handbook of research on social studies teaching and learning.* New York: Macmillan.

Putnam, R. (1995). Bowling alone: America' declining social capital. *Journal of Democracy*, *6*, 65–78.

Rothstein, R. (2001). What produces a voter? Seemingly not civics class. *New York Times*, July 11.

Torney-Purta, J., Lehmann, R., Oswald, H., & Schulz, W. (2001) *Citizenship and education in twenty-eight countries: Civic knowledge and engagement at age fourteen.* Amsterdam: International Association for the Evaluation of Educational Achievement.

Torney-Purta, J., Schwille, J., & Amadeo, J. (Eds.). (1999). *Civic education across countries: Twenty-four case studies from the IEA civic education project.* Amsterdam, The Netherlands: International Association for the Evaluation of Educational Achievement (in cooperation with Eburon Publishers, Delft).

Valenzuela, A. (1999). *Subtractive schooling: U.S.-Mexican youth and the politics of caring.* Albany: State University of New York Press.

Vanishing Voter (2000). *Election apathy pervasive among young adults.* Cambridge, MA: The Joan Shorenstein Center, John F. Kennedy School of Government, Harvard University. Retrieved May 12, 2000, from http://www.vanishingvoter.org

Verba, S., Schlozman, K., & Brady, H. (1995). *Voice and equality: Civic volunteerism in American politics.* Cambridge, MA: Harvard University Press.

Youniss, J., McLellan, J.A., & Yates, M. (1997). What we know about engendering civic identity. *American Behavioral Scientist*, *40*, 620–631.

PART IV

CIVIC EDUCATION IN A CHANGING WORLD

Public Time versus Emergency Time after September 11th: Democracy, Schooling, and the Culture of Fear

Henry A. Giroux
Macalester University

On January 29, 2002, 5 months after the horrific terrorist attacks on the Pentagon and the World Trade Center, President George W. Bush announced in his State of the Union Address that the "war against terror is only just beginning" and if other governments exhibit timidity in the face of terror, then America will act without them. Claiming that the security of the nation was his first priority, Bush proclaimed a war without end, and suggested that the United States would act unilaterally throughout the world to enforce what he called "our responsibility to fight freedom's fight." Appealing to what he described as a resurgent sense of unity and community in the country, Bush announced that American citizens were no longer willing to simply live their lives devoted to material pursuits and a "feel good" attitude. According to Bush, in the aftermath of the events of September 11th, America had been reborn with a renewed sense of patriotism, community, and public spiritedness. Painting the United States as a beacon of civilization, Bush urged Americans to perform voluntary acts of public service; be alert for signs of potential terrorism at home; support massive increases in the military budget; endorse an energy policy that involves more drilling for oil; accept a huge tax cut for the rich and major corporations; and tolerate the suspensions of some basic civil liberties and freedoms, especially those granting more power to the police, FBI, CIA, and other security forces.

Although Bush and his associates are quick to remind the American people that much has changed in the United States since September 11th, almost nothing has been said about what has not changed. I am referring to the aggressive attempts on the part of many liberal and conservative politicians to undermine those public spaces that encourage informed debate, promote a remorseless drive to privatization, and invoke patriotism as a cloak for carrying out a reactionary economic and political agenda on the domestic front while simultaneously cultivating an arrogant self-righteousness in foreign affairs in which the United States positions itself uncritically on the side of purity, goodness, and freedom while its opposition is equated with the forces of absolute evil.

As a "wartime" president, Bush enjoys incredibly high popular ratings, but beneath the inflated ratings and the President's call for unity, there is a disturbing appeal to modes of community and patriotism buttressed by moral absolutes in which the discourse of evil, terrorism, and security work to stifle dissent, empty democracy of any substance, and exile politics "to the space occupied by those discontented with the West, and dispossessed by it" (Hesse & Sayyid, 2001, p. 3). Shamelessly pandering to the fever of emergency time and the economy of fear, President Bush and his administrative cohorts are rewriting the rhetoric of community so as to remove it from the realm of politics and democracy. In doing so, Bush and his followers are not only concentrating their political power, they are also pushing through harsh policies and regressive measures that cut basic services and public assistance for the poor, offer school children more standardized testing but do not guarantee them decent health care and adequate food, sacrifice American democracy and individual autonomy for the promise of domestic security, and allocate resources and tax breaks to the rich through the airline bail out and retroactive tax cuts. Under the auspices of a belligerent nationalism and militarism, community is constructed "through shared fears rather than shared responsibilities" and the strongest appeals to civic discourse are focused primarily on military defense, civil order, and domestic security (Anton, 2000, p. 29). Within the rhetoric and culture of shared fears, patriotism becomes synonymous with an uncritical acceptance of governmental authority and a discourse "that encourages ignorance as it overrides real politics, real history, and moral issues" (Said, 2002, p. 5).

The longing for community seems so desperate in the United States, steeped as it is in the ethic of neoliberalism with its utter disregard for public life, democratic public spheres, and moral responsibility, that in such ruthless times any invocation of community seems nourishing, even when the term is invoked to demand an "unconditional loyalty and treats everything short of such loyalty as an act of unforgivable treason" (Bauman, 2001, p. 4). How can any notion of democratic community or critical citizenship be embraced through the rhetoric of a debased patriotism that is outraged by dissent in the streets? What notion of community allows Peter Beinart, editor of *The New Republic*, to wrap himself in the flag of patriotism and moral absolutism while excoriating those who are critical of Bush policies? He writes, "This nation is now at war. And, in such an environment, domestic political dissent is immoral without a prior statement of national solidarity, a choosing of sides" (cited in Lapham, 2002b, p. 7).

Charges of unpatriotic dissent are not restricted to either protesters in the streets or to those academics who incurred the wrath of Lynne Cheney's American Council of Trustees and Alumni for not responding with due Americanist fervor to the terrorist attacks of September 11th. It was also applied to former Senate majority leader, Tom Daschle, when he offered a mild critique of President Bush's plan to launch what appears to be a never-ending war against terrorism. Trent Lott, the Republican leader, responded with a crude rebuke, suggesting that Daschle had no right to criticize President Bush "while we are fighting our war on terrorism" (Rich, 2002, p. A27). It appears that the leadership of the Republican Party along with its strong supporters has no qualms about dismissing critics by impugning their patriotism. Tom Davis of Virginia, the head of the GOP.'s House campaign committee, branded those who criticize Bush's policies as "giving aid and comfort to our enemies" (cited in Rich, 2002, p. A27). The Family Research council went even further by running ads in South Dakota "likening Tom Daschle to Saddam Hussein because the Senate majority leader opposed oil drilling in the Arctic National Wildlife Refuge" (cited in Rich, 2002, p. A27). Community in this instance demands not courage, dialogue, and responsibility, but silence and complicity.

According to Hobsbawm (1994) "never was the word 'community' used more indiscriminately and emptily than in the decades when communities in the sociological sense became hard to find in real life" (p. 428). Maybe it is the absence of viable communities organized around democratic values and basic freedoms that accounts for the way in which the language of community has currently "degraded into the currency of propaganda" (Lapham, 2002a, p. 8). How else can one explain the outrage exhibited by the dominant media against anyone who seems to question, among other things, U.S. support of friendly dictatorships, including Afghanistan and Saudi Arabia, the USA Patriot Act with its suppression of civil liberties, or even suggest the need for a serious discussion about how U.S. foreign policy contributes to the widespread poverty, despair, and hopelessness throughout the world, offering in return terrorist nihilism the opportunity "to thrive in the rich soil of exclusion and victimhood" (George, 2002, p. 12). Actual democratic communities are completely at odds with a smug self-righteousness that refuses to make a distinction between explaining events and justifying them. As Butler (2002) points out:

> To ask how certain political and social actions come into being, such as the recent terrorist attack on the U. S., and even to identify a set of causes, is not the same as locating the source of the responsibility for those actions, or indeed, paralyzing our capacity to make ethical judgments on what is right or wrong . . . But it does ask the U.S. to assume a different kind of responsibility for producing more egalitarian global conditions for equality, sovereignty, and the egalitarian redistribution of resources." (pp. 8, 16)

Such questions do not suggest that the United States is responsible for the acts of terrorism that took place on September 11th. On the contrary, they perform the obligatory work of politics by attempting to situate individual acts of responsibility within those broader sets of conditions that give rise to individual acts of terrorism while simultaneously asking how the United States can intervene more productively in global politics to produce conditions that undercut rather than reinforce the breeding grounds for such terrorism. At the same time, such questions suggest that the exercise of massive power cannot be removed from the practice of politics and ethics and such a recognition demands a measure of accountability to be responsible for the consequences of our actions as one of the most powerful countries in the world. As Lapham (2002b) observes, "It is precisely at the moments of our greatest peril that we stand in need of as many questions as anybody can think to ask" (p. 7).

The rhetoric of terrorism is important not only because it operates on many registers to both inflict human misery and call into question the delicate balance of freedom and security crucial to any democratic society, but also because it carries with it an enormous sense of urgency that often redefines community against its most democratic possibilities and realized forms. Rising from the ashes of impoverishment and religious fundamentalism, terrorism, at its worse, evokes a culture of fear, unquestioning loyalty, and a narrow definition of security from those who treat it as a pathology rather than as a politics. In part, this is evident in Bush's "war against terrorism," which, fueled by calls for public sacrifice, appears to exhaust itself in a discourse of moral absolutes and public acts of denunciation. This all-embracing policy of anti-terrorism depoliticizes politics by always locating it outside of the realm of power and strips community of democratic values by defining it almost exclusively through attempts to stamp out what Michael Leeden, a former counter-terror expert in the Reagan administration, calls "corrupt habits of mind that are still lingering around, somewhere" (cited in Valentine, 2001).

The militarizing of community and the perpetuation of a harsh culture of fear and insecurity results in the narrowing of community and the ongoing appeal to jingoistic forms of patriotism in order to divert the public from addressing a number of pressing domestic and foreign issues; it also contributes to the increasing suppression of dissent and what Lewis (2002) has rightly called the growing escalation of concentrated, unaccountable political power that threatens the very foundation of democracy in the United States" (p. A27). This is evident in Attorney General John Ashcroft's decision to relax restrictions on the FBI's ability to conduct domestic spying as part of its stepped up counter terrorism campaign. Dispensing with probable cause restrictions in order to begin counter terrorism investigations, the new FBI regulations allow federal agents to search commercial databases, monitor the World Wide Web, tap phones, read private e-mail correspondence, examine library and book store customer records, and compile dossiers on people and groups, without the need to show that a crime has been committed. According to officials at the American Civil Liberties Union, the new guidelines "say to the American people that you no longer have to be doing something wrong in order to get that F.B.I. knock at your door" (Van Natta, 2002, p. A1).

At the core of Bush's notion of community and hyper-patriotism is a notion of temporality that detaches itself from a sense of public deliberation, critical citizenship, and civic engagement. Binde (2000) refers to this view of temporality as "emergency time" and describes it as a "world governed by short-term efficacy," which under the imperatives of utter necessity and pragmatism, eschews long-term appraisals, and gives precedence to the "logic of 'just in time' at the expense of any forward-looking deliberation" (p. 52). According to Binde, emergency time opens the way for what he calls "the tyranny of emergency." He explains:

> Emergency is a direct means of response that leaves no time for either analysis, forecasting, or prevention. It is an immediate protective reflex rather than a sober quest for long-term solutions. It neglects the fact that situations have to be put in perspective and that future events need to be anticipated. Devising any durable response to human problem . . . requires looking at a situation from a distance and thinking in terms of the future. (p. 52)

Lacking any reference to democratic collective aims, the appeal to emergency time both shrinks the horizon of meanings and removes the application of governmental power from the fields of ethical and political responsibility. Emergency time defines community against its democratic possibilities, detaching it from those conditions that prepare citizens to deliberate collectively about the future and the role they must play in creating and shaping the conditions for them to have some say it how it might unfold. Under such conditions, cynical reason replaces reasoned debate with the one-way gaze of power and popular resistance to the "war" is dismissed as "a demagoguery of the streets, while dictators are offered up to us as responsible representatives of their countries" (Hesse & Sayyid, 2001, p. 3). But, emergency time in the context of Bush's "war against terrorism" also rejects the radical secularism at the heart of a substantive democracy in favor of a religious vocabulary. The metaphysics of religious discourse dispenses with the task of critically engaging and translating the elaborate web of historical, social, and political factors that underscore and give meaning to the broader explanations for terrorism. Instead, the complexity of politics dissolves into the language of "crusades," "infidels," "goodness," and "evil." Under such conditions, as Lukes and Urbinati (2001) point out: "A rhetoric of emergency has arisen in which a Manichean impulse is given free range, in which 'our' (American? Western?) values are seen as threatened by an enemy that is seen as the incarnation of evil and variously identified as 'fundamentalist' and 'Islamist' as embodied in Al-Quaida and personified by Osama bin Laden" (p. 1), Saddam Hussein, and others.

It is the displacement of politics and the weakening of democratic public spaces that allows for religious ideology and excess to define the basis of community, civic engagement, and the domain of the social. Against this notion of emergency time, educators, cultural workers, and others need to posit a notion of public time. According to democratic theorist Castoriadis (1991), public time represents "the emergence of a dimension where the collectivity can inspect its own past as the result of *its own actions,* and where an indeterminate future opens up as domain for its activities" (pp. 113–114). For Castoriadis, public time puts into question established institutions and dominant authority. Rather than maintaining a passive attitude toward power, public time demands and encourages forms of political agency based on a passion for self-governing, actions informed by critical judgment, and a commitment to linking social responsibility and social transformation. Public time legitimates those pedagogical practices that provide the basis for a culture of questioning, one that provides the knowledge, skills, and social practices that encourage an opportunity for resistance, a space of translation, and a proliferation of discourses. Public time unsettles common sense and disturbs authority while encouraging critical and responsible leadership. As Simon (2002) observes, public time "presents the question of the social—not as a space for the articulation of pre-formed visions through which to mobilize action, but as the movement in which the very question of the possibility of democracy becomes the frame within which a necessary radical learning (and questioning) is enabled" (p. 4). Put differently, public time affirms a politics without guarantees and a notion of the social that is open and contingent. Public time provides a conception of democracy that is never complete and determinate and constantly open to different understandings of the contingency of its decisions, mechanisms of exclusions, and operations of power. At its best, public time renders governmental power explicit, and in doing so it rejects the language of religious rituals and the abrogation of the conditions necessary for the assumption of basic freedoms and rights. Moreover, public time considers civic education the basis, if not essential dimension, of justice because it provides individuals with the skills, knowledge, and passions to talk back to power while simultaneously emphasizing both the necessity to question that accompanies viable forms of political agency and the assumption of public responsibility through active participation in the very process of governing.

Against Bush's disregard for public discussion of his policies, his fetish for secrecy, his clamoring for a notion of patriotism that is synonymous with a mindless conformity, and his flaunting of presidential power, public time gives credence to a notion of democracy that calls for the establishment of unbounded interrogation in all domains of public life. Democratic politics and viable notions of community are created and affirmed when public spaces are created that enable individuals and social movements to exercise power over the institutions and forces that govern their lives. Under such conditions, politics is not relegated to the domain of the other as a form of pathology, but is central to what it means to build vibrant public spheres and democratic communities (Castoriadis, 1997, pp. 85–98).

What has become clear both in Bush's State of the Union Address and in the policies enacted by his administration is that there is no discourse for recognizing the obligations a democratic society has to pay its debts to past generations and fulfill its obligations to future generations, especially the young who are being increasingly abandoned at all levels of government. His tax cuts privilege the commercial interests of the rich over public responsibilities to the poor, the elderly, the environment, and to children. His call for military tribunals for trying non citizens, his detaining of over 1,200 Arabs and Muslims, as well as two Americans, for extended periods in secrecy, and willingness to undermine the basic constitutional freedoms and rights by enhancing the power of the police and other enforcement groups pose a grave threat to those civil liberties that are fundamental to a democracy (see Sachs, 2002, p. A21). Said (2002) argues, more specifically, that:

> Bush and his compliant Congress have suppressed or abrogated or abridged whole sections of the First, Fourth, Fifth and Eighth Amendments, instituted legal procedures that give individuals no recourse either to a proper defense or a fair trail, that allow secret searches eavesdropping, detention without limit, and, given the treatment of the prisoners at Guantanamo Bay, that allow the US executive branch to abduct prisoners, detain them indefinitely, decide unilaterally whether or not they are prisoners of war and whether or not the Geneva Conventions apply to them—which is not a decision to be taken by individual countries. (p. 2)

Most importantly, Bush's "war against terrorism" camouflages how democracy is being undermined through its relentless attempts to depoliticize politics itself. What began as the demonization of political Islam has now been extended into the demonization of politics itself as Bush and his cohorts put forth policies that attempt to erase the possibility of imagining a democratic future, the democratic space of the social, the meaning of democratic community, or the practices that anchor democratic life. As Hesse and Sayyid (2001) insightfully observe:

> Through such processes, politics seems exiled. While the centre is reoccupied by a naturalized world order, politics is proscribed from the domain of order itself. Paradoxically, cynical reason becomes a dominant ideology within an apparently post-ideological West. In a Western world apparently deprived of political alternatives to corporate capital-

ism, neoliberalism and global social inequalities, what once passed for
politics has been exclusively transposed to the space occupied by those
discontented with the West, and dispossessed by it. (p. 3)

By depoliticizing politics, the "war on terrorism" becomes both an empty
abstraction and a strategic diversion. It is empty because terrorism cannot be
either understood or addressed through the discourse of moral absolutes and
religious fervor. Militarism does not get at the root of terrorism; it simply expands the breeding grounds for the conditions that give rise to it. Military intervention may overthrow governments controlled by radical fanatics such as the
Taliban, but it does not address those global conditions in which poverty thrives,
thousands of children die every day from starvation or preventable diseases,
where *250* million are compelled to work under harsh conditions, or some 840
million adults are without adequate shelter and access to health care (see Pogge,
2000, pp. 37–43). As long as such inequalities exist, resistance will emerge and
terrorism will be the order of the day. Not only is this a problem that will not be
solved by dropping thousands of bombs on poor countries (with or without accompanying packets of food), it also suggests rethinking how U.S. policies actually contribute to these conditions through its support of military dictatorships,
its unilateral disregard for international coalitions, and its ongoing support for
the ruthless policies of global neoliberalism. The rhetoric of "anti-terrorism"
cleanses Bush and his cohorts of the obligations of political and ethical responsibility on a global level by ignoring the complex bonds that tie the rich and the
powerful to the poor and the powerless. Such ties cannot be explained through
the language of a rabid nationalism, hyped-up patriotism, or religious zeal. As
Butler (2002) points out, fatuous moralism is no substitute for assuming responsibility for one's actions in the world:

> Moralistic denunciation provides immediate gratification, and even has
> the effect of temporarily cleansing the speaker of all proximity to guilt
> through the act of self-righteous denunciation itself. But is this the
> same as responsibility, understood as taking stock of our world, and
> participating in its social transformation in such a way that nonviolent,
> cooperative, egalitarian international relations remain the guiding
> ideal? (p. 19)

Moralism may offer Bush and his cohorts the ground of innocence, but it
does nothing to further the dynamics of democracy or civic engagement and
may, as Wideman (2002) suggests, even serve to "terrorize" those Americans it
claims it is benefiting:

> By launching a phony war [Bush] is managing to avoid the scrutiny a
> first-term, skin-of its teeth presidency deserves. Instead, he's terrorizing

Americans into believing that we require a wartime leader wielding un-
questioned emergency powers. Beneath the drumbeat belligerence of
his demands for national unity, if you listen you'll hear the bullying,
the self-serving, the hollowness, of his appeals to patriotism. Listen
carefully and you'll also hear what he's not saying: that we need, in a
democracy full of contradictions and unresolved divisions, opposition
voices. (pp. 33–38)

If Wideman is correct, and I think he is, then Bush's innocent posturing
wrapped in the righteousness of the rhetoric of anti-terrorism also provides a
massive diversion from addressing those political issues at the heart of what it
means to measure the reality against the promise of a substantive democracy.
Bush commits us to the dark world of emergency time, a world divided between
good and evil, one in which "issues of democracy, civil comity and social justice—let alone nuance, complexity and interdependence simply vanish" (Barber,
2002, p. 17). In this world of emergency time, politics assumes a purity that
posits only one right answer, one side to choose. Not only does emergency time
provide Bush with a political identity that closely resembles a kind of martyr-
dom, it certifies him as the proper authority for speaking the only admissible
language and holding down the only acceptable position. Emergency time not
only refuses to question its own assumptions, it also refuses to acknowledge its
glaring absences—those issues or points of view it either ignores or marginal-
izes. Hence, in the name of "fighting freedom's fight," Bush threatens to wage
war against Iraq and a host of other infidels while constructing a worldview for
public consumption in which a hypermilitarism is coupled with a mode of social
amnesia that conveniently forgets important domestic problems. One result is
that the growing gap between the rich and the poor is ignored, massive unemployment is disregarded, the war against youth marginalized by class and color
does not exist, poverty and racial injustice becomes invisible, the folly of attack-
ing the public sector is passed over, the shameful growth of the prison-industrial
complex is overlooked, Enron is easily forgotten, and government-sanctioned
threats to the environment evaporate.

Bush's notion of community depoliticizes politics and makes a sham of
civic complexity and responsibility. If we are to challenge his policies, then educators must adopt a notion of politics and pedagogy that embraces a notion of
public time, one that fosters civic engagement and public intelligence. This
means, at the very least, creating the conditions for rendering governmental
authority accountable for its actions while also mobilizing the conditions for
citizens to reclaim the power necessary to shape the regimes of power and politics that influence their lives on a daily basis. The greatest struggle Americans
face is not terrorism, but a struggle on behalf of justice, freedom, and democracy
for all of the citizens of the globe, especially youth. This is not going to take
place, as Bush's policies will tragically affirm, by shutting down democracy,

eliminating its most cherished rights and freedoms, and deriding communities of dissent. On the contrary, the struggle for democracy has to be understood through politics, not moralism, and if politics is to be reclaimed as the center of individual and social agency, it will have to be motivated not by the culture of fear but by a passion for civic engagement and ethical responsibility, and the promise of a realizable democracy.

The invocation of emergency time profoundly limits the vocabulary and imagery available to us in developing a language of critique, compassion, and possibility for addressing the relationship between the crisis of democracy and the crisis of youth. Limiting civil liberties, cutting back social programs, and defining democracy as expendable as part of the discourse of emergency time and the appeal to the culture of fear shuts down the opportunity for adults to both focus on young people as a symbol of the future and to create the symbolic and material conditions for increasing the scope of those values and freedoms necessary for them to become active and critical citizens willing to fight for a vibrant democracy.

THE CHALLENGE TO EDUCATORS

The events of September 11 provide educators with a crucial opportunity to re-claim schools as democratic public spheres in which students can engage in dia-logue and critique around the meaning of democratic values, the relationship between learning and civic engagement, and the connection between schooling, what it means to be a critical citizen, and the responsibilities one has to the larger world (see *Rethinking Schools*, 2001/2002).

Defined largely through an appeal to fear and a call to strengthen domestic security, the space of the social has been both militarized and increasingly commodified. As such, there is little public conversation about connecting the social to democratic values, justice, or what the public good might mean in light of this horrible attack as a moral and political referent to denounce mass acts of violence and to attempt to secure freedom and justice for all people. But such a task would demand, in part, addressing what vocabularies and practices regard-ing the space of the social and political were actually in place prior to the events of September 11th, and what particular notions of freedom, security, and citizen-ship were available to Americans—the legacy and influence of which might prevent them from assuming the role of critical and engaged citizens capable of addressing this national crisis. Instead of seeing the current crisis as a break from the past, it is crucial for the American public to begin to understand how the past might be useful in addressing what it means to live in a democracy in the aftermath of the bombings in New York and Washington, DC.

Public schools should play a decisive role in helping students configure the boundaries between history and the present, incorporating a critical understanding of those events that are often left out of the rendering of contemporary considerations that define the roles students might play as critical citizens. Of course, this will be difficult because many public schools are overburdened with high-stakes testing and harsh accountability systems designed to get teachers to narrow their curriculum and to focus only on raising test scores. Consequently, any struggle to make schools more democratic and socially relevant will have to link the battle for critical citizenship to an ongoing fight against turning schools into testing centers and teachers into technicians.

EDUCATION AND THE CHALLENGE OF REVITALIZING DEMOCRATIC PUBLIC LIFE

As the state is increasingly relieved of its welfare-providing functions, it defaults on its capacity to provide people with the most basic social provisions, extending from health care to public transportation, and simultaneously withdraws from its obligation to create those noncommodified public spheres in which people learn the language of ethics, civic courage, democratically charged politics, and collective empowerment. Within such a turn of events, schools are increasingly defined less as a public good than as sites for financial investment and entrepreneurial training—that is, as a private good.

As those public spaces that offer forums for debating norms, critically engaging ideas, making private issues public, and evaluating judgments disappear under the juggernaut of neoliberal policies, it becomes crucial for educators to raise fundamental questions about what it means to revitalize public life, politics, and ethics in ways that take seriously such values as patriotism, "citizen participation, . . . political obligation, social governance, and community" (Boggs, 2000, p. 17), especially at a time of national crisis when such terms become less an object of analysis than uncritical veneration. The call for a revitalized politics grounded in an effective democracy substantively challenges the dystopian practices of neoliberalism—with its all consuming emphasis on market relations, commercialization, privatization, and the creation of a worldwide economy of part-time workers—against its utopian promises. Such an intervention confronts educators with the problem as well as the challenge of analyzing, engaging, and developing those public spheres (e.g., the media, public education, and other cultural institutions) that provide the conditions for creating citizens who are equipped to exercise their freedoms, competent to question the basic assumptions that govern political life, and skilled enough to participate in shaping the basic social, political, and economic orders that govern their lives. It is precisely within these public spheres that the events of September 11th and military action against Afghanistan, the responsibility of the media, the civic obligation of educators, and America's role in the world as a superpower should be debated rather than squelched in the name of a jingoistic patriotism.

Two factors work against such a debate on any level. First, there are very few public spheres left that provide the space for such conversations to take place. Second, it is increasingly difficult for young people and adults to appropriate a critical language, outside of the market, that would allow them to translate private problems into public concerns or to relate public issues to private considerations. For many young people and adults today, the private sphere has become the only space in which to imagine any sense of hope, pleasure, or possibility. Reduced to the act of consuming, citizenship is "mostly about forgetting, not learning" (Bauman, 1998, p. 82). The decline of social capital can be seen in research studies done by the Justice Project in 2001, in which a substantial number of teenagers and young people were asked about what they thought democracy meant. The answers testified to a growing depoliticization of the social in American life and were largely along the following lines: "Nothing," "I don't know," or "My rights, just like, pride, I guess, to some extent, and paying taxes" or "I just think, like, what does it really mean? I know it's like our, like, our government, but I don't know what it technically is" (Greenberg, 2001, p. 15). Market forces focus on the related issues of consumption and safety, but not on the economic, cultural, and political meaning of a vibrant democracy.

When notions of freedom and security are decoupled and freedom is reduced to the imperatives of market exchange, and security is divested from a defense of a version the welfare state distinguished by its social provisions and "helping functions," not only does freedom collapse into brutal form of individualism, but also the state is stripped of its helping functions while its policing functions are often inordinately strengthened. Even as the foundations of the security state are being solidified through zero tolerance policies, anti-terrorist laws, soaring incarceration rates, the criminalization of pregnancy, racial profiling, and anti-immigration policies, it is crucial that educators and scholars take up the events of September 11th not through a one-side view of patriotism that stifles dissent and aids the forces of domestic militarization, but as part of a broader effort to expand the country's democratic rather than repressive possibilities.

Unlike some theorists who suggest that politics as a site of contestation, critical exchange, and engagement has either come to an end or is in a state of terminal arrest, I believe that the current, depressing state of politics points to the urgent challenge of reformulating the crisis of democracy as part of the fundamental crisis of vision, meaning, education, and political agency. If it is possible to "gain" anything from the events of September 11th, it must be understood as an opportunity for a national coming together and soul searching—a time for expanding democratic possibilities rather than limiting them. Politics devoid of vision degenerates into either cynicism, a repressive notion of patriotism, or it appropriates a view of power that appears to be equated almost exclusively with the militarization of both domestic space and foreign policy initiatives. Lost from such accounts is the recognition that democracy has to be struggled over— even in the face of a most appalling crisis of political agency. Educators, schol- ars, and policymakers must redress the little attention paid to the fact that the struggle over politics and democracy is inextricably linked to creating public spheres where individuals can be educated as political agents equipped with the skills, capacities, and knowledge they need not only to actually perform as autonomous political agents, but also to believe that such struggles are worth taking up. Central to my argument is the assumption that politics is not simply about power, but also, as Castoriadis (1996) points out, "has to do with political judgments and value choices" (p. 8), indicating that questions of civic educa- tion—learning how to become a skilled citizen—are central to both the struggle over political agency and democracy itself. Finally, there is the widespread re- fusal among many educators and others to recognize that the issue of civic edu- cation—with its emphasis on critical thinking, bridging the gap between learn- ing and everyday life, understanding the connection between power and knowl- edge, and using the resources of history to extend democratic rights and identi- ties—is not only the foundation for expanding and enabling political agency, but also takes place across a wide variety of public spheres through the growing power of a mass mediated culture (Giroux, 2001).

For many educational reformers, education and schooling are synonymous. In actuality, schooling is only one site where education takes place. As a per- formative practice, pedagogy is at work in a variety of educational sites (includ- ing popular culture, television and cable networks, magazines, the Internet, churches, and the press) where culture works to secure identities; it does the bridging work for negotiating the relationship between knowledge, pleasure, and values, and renders authority both crucial and problematic in legitimating par- ticular social practices, communities, and forms of power. As a moral and politi- cal practice, the concept of public pedagogy points to the enormous ways in which popular and media culture construct the meanings, desires, and invest- ments that play such an influential role in how students view themselves, others, and the larger world. Unfortunately, the political, ethical, and social significance of the role that popular culture plays as the primary pedagogical medium for young people remains largely unexamined by many educators and seems almost exclusively removed from any policy debates about educational reform. Educa- tors also must challenge the assumption that education is limited to schooling and that popular cultural texts cannot be as profoundly important as traditional sources of learning in teaching about important issues framed through, for ex- ample, the social lens of poverty, racial conflict, and gender discrimination. This suggests not only expanding the curricula so as to allow students to become critically literate in those visual, electronic, and digital cultures that have such an important influence on their lives, but it also suggests teaching students the skills to be cultural producers as well. For instance, learning how to read films differently is no less important than learning how to produce films. At the same time, critical literacy is not about making kids simply savvy about the media so they can be better consumers, it means offering them the knowledge, skills, and tools to recognize when the new technologies and media serve as either a force for enlarging democratic relations or when it shuts down such relations. Becoming media literate is largely meaningless unless students take up this form of literacy within the larger issue of what it means to be a critical citizen and engaged political agent willing to expand and deepen democratic public spheres. Within this expanded approach to pedagogy, both the notion of what constitutes meaningful knowledge, as well as what the conditions of critical agency, might point to a more expansive and democratic notion of civic education and political agency.

Educators at all levels of schooling need to challenge the assumption that either politics is dead or that any viable notion of politics will be determined exclusively by government leaders and experts in the heat of moral frenzy to impose vengeance on those who attacked the Pentagon and the World Trade Center. Educators need to take a more critical position, arguing that critical knowledge, debate, and dialogue grounded in pressing social problems offers individuals and groups some hope in shaping the conditions that bear down on their lives. Public engagement born of citizen engagement is urgent if the concepts of the social and public can be used to revitalize the language of civic education and democratization as part of a broader discourse of political agency and critical citizenship in a global world. Linking a notion of the social to democratic public values represents an attempt, however incomplete, to link democracy to public action, and to ground such support in defense of militant utopian thinking (as opposed to unadorned militancy) as part of a comprehensive attempt to revitalize the conditions for individual and social agency, civic activism, and citizen access to decision making while simultaneously addressing the most basic problems facing the prospects for social justice and global democracy.

Educators within both public schools and higher education need to continue finding ways of entering the world of politics by both making social problems visible and contesting their manifestation in the polity. We need to build on those important critical, educational theories of the past in order to resurrect the emancipatory elements of democratic thought while also recognizing and engaging their damaged and burdened historical traditions. We need to reject both neoliberal and orthodox leftist positions, which dismiss the state as merely a tool of repression in order to find ways to use the state to challenge, block, and regulate the devastating effects of capitalism. On the contrary, educators need to be at the forefront of defending the most progressive historical advances and gains of the state. French sociologist Bourdieu (1998), is right when he calls for collective work by educators to prevent the right and other reactionaries from destroying the most precious democratic conquests in the areas of labor legislation, health, social protection, and education. At the very least, this would suggest that educators defend schools as democratic public spheres, struggle against the deskilling of teachers and students, and argue for a notion of pedagogy grounded in democratic values rather than those corporate-driven ideologies and testing schemes that severely limit the creative and liberatory potential of teachers and students. At the same time, such educators must resist the reduction of the state to its policing functions, while linking such a struggle to the fight against neoliberalism and the struggle for expanding and deepening the freedoms, rights, and relations of a vibrant democracy.

Postcolonial theorist Amin echoes this call by arguing that educators should consider addressing the project of a more realized democracy as part of an ongoing process of democratization. According to Amin (2001), democratization "stresses the dynamic aspect of a still-unfinished process," while rejecting notions of democracy that are given a definitive formula (p. 12). Educators have an important role to play here in the struggle to link social justice and economic democracy with the equality of human rights, the right to education, health, research, art, and work. On the cultural front, teachers as public intellectuals can work to make the pedagogical more political by engaging in a permanent critique of their own scholasticism and promoting what a critical awareness to end oppression and forms of social life that disfigure contemporary life and pose a threat to any viable notion of democracy. Educators need to provide spaces of resistance within the public schools and the university that take seriously what it means to educate students to question and interrupt authority, recall what is forgotten or ignored, make connections that are otherwise hidden, while simultaneously providing the knowledge and skills that enlarge their sense of the social and their possibilities as viable political agents capable of expanding and deepening democratic public life. At the very least, such educators can challenge the correlation between the impoverishment of society and the impoverishment of intellectuals by offering possibilities other than what we are told is possible. Or, as Badiou (1998) observes, "showing how the space of the possible is larger than the one assigned—that something else is possible, but not that everything is possible" (pp. 115–116). In times of increased domination of public K–12 education and higher education it becomes important, as Lipsitz (2000) reminds us, that educators (as well as artists and other cultural workers) not become isolated "in their own abstract desires for social change and actual social movements. Taking a position is not the same as waging a war of position; changing your mind is not the same as changing society" (p. 81). Resistance must become part of a public pedagogy that works to position rigorous theoretical work and public bodies against corporate power and the militarization of visual and public space, connect classrooms to the challenges faced by social movements in the streets, and provide spaces within classrooms and other sites for personal injury and private terrors to be transformed into public considerations and struggles. This suggests that educators should work to form alliances with parents, community organizers, labor organizations, and civil rights groups at the local, national, and international levels to better understand how to translate private troubles into pubic actions, arouse public interests over pressing social problems, and use collective means to more fully democratize the commanding institutional economic, cultural, and social structures of the United States and the larger global order.

In the aftermath of the events of September 11, it is time to remind ourselves that collective problems deserve collective solutions, and what is at risk is not only a generation of minority youth and adults now considered to be a threat to national security, but also the very promise of democracy itself. As militarism works to intensify patriarchal attitudes and antidemocratic assaults on dissent, it is crucial for educators to join with those groups now making a common cause against those forces that would sacrifice basic constitutional freedoms to the imperatives of war abroad and militarism at home.

REFERENCES

Amin, S. (2001, June). Imperialization and globalization. *Monthly Review, 12*.

Anton, A. (2000). Public Gods as Commonstock: Notes on the Receding Commons. In A. Anton, M. Fisk, and N. Holstrom (Eds.) *Not for sale: In defense of public goods*. Boulder, CO: Westview.

Badiou, A. (1998). Ethics: An essay on the understanding of evil. London: Verso.

Barber, B. (2002). Beyond Jihad vs. Macworld: On terrorism and the new democratic realism," *The Nation*.

Bauman, Z. (1998). *Globalization: The human consequences*. New York: Columbia University
Press.

Bauman, Z. (2001). *Community: Seeking safety in an insecure world*. Cambridge, UK:
Polity.

Binde, J. (2000). Toward an ethic of the future. *Public Culture, 12*, 1.

Boggs, C. (2000). *The end of politics*. New York: Guilford.

Bourdieu, P. (1998). *Acts of resistance*. New York: The Free Press.

Butler, J. (2002). Explanation and exoneration, or what we can hear. *Theory & Event, 5*, 4.

Castoriadis, C. (1997, May). The crisis of the identification process. *Thesis Eleven, 49*.

Castoriadis, C. (1991). The Greek polis and the creation of democracy. *Philosophy, politics, autonomy: Essays in political philosophy*. New York: Oxford University Press.

Castoriadis, C. (1996). Institution and Autonomy. In P. Osborne, *A critical sense: Interviews with intellectuals*. New York: Routledge.

Critchley, S. (2002). Ethics, politics, and radical democracy—The history of a disagreement,. *Culture Machine*. Retrieved from
http://www.culturemachine.tees.ac.uk/frm

George, S. (2002, February 18). Another world is possible. *The Nation*, p. 12.

Giroux, H. (2001). *Public spaces. Private lives: Beyond the culture of cynicism*. Latham, Md: Rowman & Littlefield.

Greenberg, A. (2001, February 11). What young voters want. *The Nation*.

Hesse, B. & Sayyid, S. (2001). A war against politics. *Open Democracy*.
Retrieved November 28, 2001 from
http://openDemocracy@opendemocracy.net

Hobsbawm, E. (1994). *The age of extremes*. London: Michael Joseph.

Lapham, L. (2002, January). American Jihad. *Harper's Magazine*.

Lapham, L. (2002, June). Innocents abroad. *Harper's Magazine*.

Lewis, A. (2002, March 9). Taking our liberties. *The New York Times*.

Lipsitz, G. (2000). Academic politics and social change. In J. Dean, (Ed.). *Cultural studies and political theory.* Ithaca, NY: Cornell University Press.

Lukes, S. & Urbinati, N. (2001). Words matter. *Open Democracy.* Retrieved November 27, 2001 from
http://www.openDemocracy@opendemocracy.net

Pogge, T. (2000). The moral demands of global justice. *Dissent* (Fall).

Rethinking Schools. (2001/2002). 16:2, titled "War, Terrorism, and America's Classrooms."

Rich, F. (2002, March 30). The wimps of war. *The New York Times.*

Sachs, S. (2002, May 30. Judge rejects U. S. policy of secret hearings. *The New York Times.*

Said, E. (2002b). Thoughts about America. *Counterpunch.* Retrieved , March 5, 2002, from http://www.counternunch.org/saidamerica.html

Simon, R. (2002). On public time. Unpublished manuscript. Ontario Institute for Studies in Education.

Valentine, D. (2001). Homeland Insecurity. *Counterpunch.* Retrieved November 8, 2001 from. http://www.countereunch.org/homelandl.html

Van Natta., D. Jr. (2002, May 20). Government will ease limits on domestic spying by F.B.I. *The New York Times.*

Wideman, J. (2002, March). Whose war? *Harper's Magazine.*

Chapter 12

Looking Back to See Ahead: Some Thoughts on the History of Civic Education in the United States

Benjamin Justice
Rutgers University

Consider this observation from a governor of Massachusetts:

> The good citizen, who is not willing to be the slave of a party because he is the member of it, must make up his mind for himself . . . or he cannot exercise the right of suffrage with intelligence and independence. . . . The whole energy of the state should be directed to multiply the numbers of those capable of forming an independent and rational judgment of their own, and to diminish as much as possible the numbers of the opposite class, who, being blinded by ignorance, are at the mercy of any one who has an interest and the skill to delude them.

Or, how about this one from a prominent school reformer?:

> The work of public education is destined in the near future to be one of the most important lines of work which our republic has to do. Its importance in a government such as ours can scarcely be overestimated. Each man with us is the captain of his own fate and the carver of his own destiny . . . To decide righteously and to act wisely he must know. Knowledge and training, if of the right type, can hardly be provided too extensively.

In the first quote, Governor Edward Everett lectured a common school convention in 1838 on the vital linkage between education and a healthy civil society, especially in light of expanded voting rights, urban growth, and poverty

(Everett, 1838/1965, p. 212). In the second, from the conclusion of a popular 1909 book on school reform, Elwood P. Cubberley (1909, p. 67) identified the need for education to meet the demands of a new economy, with new kinds of immigrants, a new global marketplace, and new forms of technology reordering American society. Despite the generations separating them, and between them and us, the rhetoric sounds familiar: America is in danger, the rising generation of citizens are inept, and only a massive reform of public education can save the republic (Nash, Crabtree, & Dunn, 1997; *A Nation at Risk*, 1983). From their inception nearly 200 years ago, public schools have been a lightening rod for stormy rhetoric over the ills of American society, and at the same time, a magnet for hopeful pronouncements that they are a panacea for social ills (Perkinson, 1991; Zimmerman, 2002).

Saying that concern over the quality of civic education in public schools is nothing new is not, in itself, anything new either. But, it does suggest that there might be much to be gained by understanding how the concerns of the past have related to civic education. If this generation's rhetoric is not new, then is the crisis any different? Does the perception of a republic in danger reflect enduring tensions in American society, or the particular problems of our own time? Are our solutions any more novel than our talk? Looking back might help make some connections among the various chapters in this volume, and provide some foundation for others who seek to understand the challenges of civic education.

Rather than focus on one particular effort at civic education in the past, or provide a comprehensive history of civic education, this chapter traces three recurring themes in the long history of civic education in the United States: tradition versus truth, conflict versus compromise, and rhetoric versus reality. Since the creation of the American republic in the late 18th century, leaders of many stripes have focused on educational efforts at civic education; and the Founding Fathers were no slouches themselves when it came to holding up mass education (although the modern meaning of the term *public* would be anachronistic) as the cure for sociopolitical ills. Benjamin Rush, John Adams, James Madison, Thomas Jefferson, Noah Webster, and other leading figures also devised various plans for educating American citizens. Looking at the educational ideas of some of these luminaries is a good introduction to three major themes that run through the history of civic education. Like us, they sought to re-envision civic education for the new millennium.

THE CHALLENGES OF CIVIC EDUCATION IN A FREE SOCIETY

After breaking away from the one of the world's great powers, American revolutionaries of the late 17th century had a problem. They won independence through blood and sacrifice. Then they fashioned a constitution through deliberation and compromise. But how could they sustain that constitution, and the nation it embodied, over the long haul in 13 vast, sparsely populated, culturally unsophisticated colonies? On the one hand lurked the Scylla of old European society and politics—corrupt churches and oppressive aristocracies. On the other hand loomed the Charybdis of faction, discord, and social disorder. The answer many founding leaders identified to navigate the new nation between the two dangers was the creation of an informed, virtuous citizenry (R. D. Brown, 1996).

But mass education in a free society involved certain challenges. For one thing, America had no national mythology (comparable to other classical republics) on which to build icons to desirable character traits. Webster and Rush advocated the elevation of Revolutionary leaders into flawless heroes, even if that meant glossing over the truth. Jefferson attempted to link America to the "natural" history of North America (Holland 2001). Although the founders cherished the notion of rational decision making and free speech, and considered their new form of government to be the obvious choice for America both scientifically and morally, Rush, Webster, and Jefferson did not trust that others would reach the same conclusion. Nor did they agree with each other about which truths were appropriate. Some wanted the nation's educational focus to be political, others religious, still others utilitarian (R. D. Brown, 1996, p. 105–107; Tyack, 1996, p. 2; 1999, p. 925).

The inconsistency of these founders on the issue of how much freedom there should be in American education marked the long and enduring tension between what the Greek philosopher Plato once called noble lies, and what contemporary scholars might call critical inquiry (what the founders would have called "science" or "reason"), which is to say, the tension between teaching state-approved truths that inculcate desirable behaviors, values, and beliefs (even when these "truths" are not necessarily true) *versus* teaching people methods for finding their own "truth" from multiple perspectives, based on good evidence, even when that truth or those decisions do not reflect favorably on the government, leaders, or a group's sense of identity. The tension between tradition and truth has often been most obvious in clashes over the teaching of evolutionary theory in the 20th century, but it has shaped civic education, usually in the form of history, as well.

A second problem that faced the founder's plans for civic education was the extremely limited connection between their lofty rhetoric and the reality of educational practice in the early national period. The federal constitution made no mention of education, and neither the states, nor the federal government, had the resources, manpower, or the political will to go as far as some of the founders proposed or hoped. True, the federal government had set aside blocks of land for schools in the Northwest Ordinance, and New York State, Massachusetts, and Connecticut used various combinations of land and law to encourage common schools. But these plans did not create state "systems" of education that men like

Rush and Jefferson had hoped for, and movement toward mass education was incremental at best (Kaestle, 1983). Revolutionary leaders had ridden a wave of distrust of distant government and resistance to taxation. How could they now create state-run systems of education and get the people to pay for them (Kaestle, 1983, p. 9; Onuf, 1991)? What mechanism would determine which plans and purposes would prevail?

As states began to develop systems of tax-supported mass education in the 19th century, this problem of reform remained: How could diverse civic education crusaders shape quintessentially local, *common* institutions? The theme of conflict and compromise over the civic curriculum of public schools endures, much to the frustration of grand planners from the Founders onward (Tyack & Hansot, 1981). Whereas they have often been lightning rods to the political and cultural storms of the outside world, public school classrooms have been largely insulated from the electric rhetoric of would-be reformers and have, instead, reflected a slow process of change that has consistently resisted classroom-level controversy.

The third problem of civic education comes when we consider what the founders meant by such concepts as freedom, citizenship, and virtue. How could the creators of the U.S. government espouse and encourage a common education based on natural rights and free thought when they also condoned slavery and severely constrained rights of suffrage to White men of property? When Rush proposed making "the people" more homogeneous through education, he referred to the White masses—girls as well as boys. But Rush wrote at a time when many of these same masses, especially women, could not vote. Jefferson excluded girls in his educational plans for Virginia and excluded Native Americans and African slaves from his vision of the rights of man, including basic citizenship (Finkelman 1993; Wallace, 1997). (He suspended this narrow view of humanity when it came to his sexual conduct, however.) Good citizenship in that context, when a small percentage of the governed voted on behalf of the whole, when citizenship had strict racial and sexual boundaries, meant learning to obey laws, not engage issues. Suffrage did not reach the masses until after the deaths of Rush, Jefferson, Webster, and most of the founding generation. And, even then, voting regulations in most cases excluded women and people of African descent. This problem, the mismatch between the democratic nature of mass education and the limited imagination of the founders in creating a democratic polity, brings us to the third theme of civic education: the meaning of civic education in the context of changing notions of citizenship.

Despite the consistency of tensions between noble lies and critical inquiry, or the consistent disparity between hot rhetoric and the cool reality of classroom instruction, the relationship between "the people" and their government has remained *inconsistent*. Historians of citizenship have identified several distinct phases in American history of what it meant to be a good citizen. Because of this changing relationship, the standard by which one might evaluate civic instruction in public schools has changed over time as well. Viewing the very notion of a "good citizen" as a moving target may daunt civic education reformers, but it also opens up the potential for richer understandings about the limitations and possibilities of using schools to make citizens.

The following sections explore each of these themes—noble lies versus critical inquiry, conflict and compromise, and changing notions of citizenship— in more depth. I then conclude by examining how they relate to various issues raised by other authors in this book. If there is truth in advertising, then this analysis should offer some ways for researchers, practitioners, policymakers, and the public to "re-envision" civic education for the future.

NOBLE LIARS? NATIONAL MYTHOLOGY VERSUS CRITICAL INQUIRY IN CIVIC EDUCATION

At a September 2002 Rose Garden reception, President George W. Bush un-veiled several new history and civic education initiatives to the nation. His speech made it clear that the two—history and civics—were virtually synony-mous. "To properly understand and love our country," he said, "we must know our country's history." He continued,

> Today, I am announcing several initiatives that will improve students' knowledge of American history, increase their civic involvement, and deepen their love for our great country. . . .
>
> Children reflect the values they see in their parents, and in their heroes. And this is how a culture can be strengthened and changed for the bet-ter. . . .
>
> American children are not born knowing what they should cherish—are not born knowing why they should cherish American values. A love of democratic principles must be taught. (Bush, 2002)

Rush and Webster, in particular, would have approved of this use of history to cultivate civic virtues. Rush (1786/1973) once wrote that "the science of gov-ernment, whether it relates to constitutions or laws, can only be advanced by a careful selection of facts, and these are to be found chiefly in history" (p. 250). Above all, however, he placed the notion of virtue: republican virtue (Rush, 1786/1973).

Not all history, of course, was appropriate to the cause, nor were all facts. Careful selection was the key. Rush agreed with Webster's approach to writing history textbooks that glorified revolutionary leaders. "Every child in America,"

Webster (1790/1965) wrote, "as soon as he opens his lips . . . should rehearse the history of his own country; he should lisp the praise of liberty and of those illustrious heroes and statesman who have wrought a revolution in her favor" (p. 64). Webster even wrote a federal catechism for schoolchildren, and tried re-create the English language in a distinctly American mode. Could reason and science exclude or distort facts? Webster and his subsequent defenders argued that there need be no contradiction between education for virtue and education for truth, so long as the virtues themselves were true. The state had an obligation to teach children the right ideas. Rush even went so far as to argue that, "our pupils must learn that there can be no durable liberty *but in a republic*, and that government, like all other sciences, is of a progressive nature. The chains which have bound this science in Europe are happily unloosed in America [emphasis added]" (Rush, 1786/1973, p. 250).

Two hundred years later, George W. Bush, a true politician, tried to have it both ways as well, saying that, "Our history is not a story of perfection. It's a story of imperfect people working toward great ideals. This flawed nation is also a really good nation, and the principles we hold are the hope of all mankind. When children are given the real history of America, they will also learn to love America" (Bush, 2002). What this real history was, the President declined to say, although throughout his speech it became clear that it could only be the history that heralded the great triumphs of American ideals, a history in the service of virtue. Anything else could not, by definition, be *real* history, just as for Rush and other founders, any conclusion that questioned the moral primacy of the American republic could not be a reasonable one.

During the centuries separating Rush and Bush, the question of teaching virtues *versus* teaching truth continued to shape the curriculum that children learned in common, and later public, schools. For most of the 19th century, text-books determined what children learned in school, while teachers monitored students' progress and behavior, on an individual basis. Civic education in common schools came down to what was in the text, or in a more indirect fashion, what was on the walls—in the North, portraits of Washington and, later, Lincoln. What was in these textbooks? The titles of two leading studies of 19th-century textbooks are revealing in themselves: Elson's *Guardians of Tradition* (1964) and Tyack's "Monuments Between Covers" (1999). As Tyack writes, "Designed to commemorate and re-present emblematic figures, events, and ideas—and thus to create common bonds—they may instead arouse dissent" (p. 922). What exactly the truth was, of course, was up for grabs—different regions, different religions, each had their own noble lies. For most of the 19th century, southern schools, private and public, were forced to rely on textbooks written in the North as well, but sheltered children from offensive passages that threatened the noble lies of the South, especially over the issue of slavery (Elson, 1964, pp. 7–8, 98–100; Tyack, 1999, pp. 922–932).

In the early 20th century, professional scholars and their textbooks faced sharp criticism from groups who opposed their expert presentation of history when that history offended some cherished belief or virtue. Lippmann (1928/1993) famously referred to these grassroots groups as "American inquisitors." The Scopes Monkey Trial focused national attention on the teaching of evolution in high school biology, but arguments over the civic effects of history textbooks were no less heated. During the late 1920s, for example, anticommunist crusaders targeted textbooks that were too critical (meaning critical at all) of the capitalist economic system. In *Whose America,* historian Zimmerman cites one telling exchange between two distinguished history textbook authors and the Superintendent of New York City Public Schools. After blasting the textbook for bias, the Superintendent put his criticism this way. It "was not a question of historical facts," but "a question [of] whether all the true statements in the book aught to be taught to school children." Later, the Superintendent explained, "The schools of New York are interested in historical accuracy, but they are far more interested in Americanization" (Zimmerman, 2002, pp. 59–60). The great progressive intellectual movement of the 1910s and 1920s, which focused on scientific approaches to social phenomena (including such matters as history and civics), brought the unscientific, un*reasonable* calls for the maintenance of myths into sharp relief, but the founding fathers would have related to the superintendent's dilemma: Making good Americans required the suppression of the truth about America itself.

Civic education in schools has also come in more subtle forms beyond what the textbook might have taught. Reformers throughout public school history have noted the educational effects of going through the motions of school itself. Horace Mann, in the 1840s, and later William Harris in the 1870s and 1980s extolled the virtues of a common school education: punctuality, obedience, order, and delayed gratification (Reese, 2000, pp. 13–31). Mann, in particular, worried about rising crime, poverty, and the need for social control and economic uplift (Cremin, 1957; Reese, 2000). Likewise, penal reformers in the late 19th and early 20th centuries saw school attendance itself as fostering good citizenship skills, regardless of the content (Justice, 2000). By the late 1960s and 1970s, radical scholars excoriated public schools for these very same characteristics, labeling them a "hidden curriculum" that emphasized docility, passivity, and conformity, not to mention racism, sexism, and class-ism. In a cry to "de-school" society, Illich (1970/1983) accused schools and other bureaucratic social institutions as causing "physical pollution, social polarization, and psychological impotence" (p. 2). Jackson (1968), a researcher far less radical than Illich, compared children's learning experience in school to inmates' experiences in prisons and mental institutions, and noted the intellectual passivity and stagnation that the hidden curriculum could produce. Whatever the liberal or intellectually evocative aspects of the formal curriculum might be, a number of scholars from the late 1960s and 1970s argued that the act of schooling itself often conflicted with the supposed aims of public schooling in a free society. In Illich's words, schools were "anti-educational" (1983, p. 11).

The tension over teaching noble lies continues into the 21st century. During the 1990s, professional historians and a few conservative politicians and populists sparred over a proposed set of voluntary national standards for American history in public schools. Conservatives, led by Lynne Cheney and Rush Limbaugh, charged that the standards failed to pay proper homage to the Founding fathers and what Webster might have called their "supposed virtues." Cheney, former head of the National Endowment for the Humanities, wrote a scathing review of the standards for the *Wall Street Journal* that accused the standards, falsely, of excluding important American ideals and icons and focusing, instead, on the nation's failings (Nash, 2000, pp. 240-241). Opening a second front, Limbaugh told his TV audience: "When you bring [students] into a classroom and you teach them that America is a rotten place... and they don't have a chance here...you have a bunch of embittered people growing up, robbing and stealing and turning to crime because they've been told all their young lives that there's no future for them" (as quoted in Nash, 2000, p. 5). Was this not Horace Mann's nightmare as well (Mann, 2001/1848)? Advocates for the standards, including a large number of professional historians, countered that the standards reflected the best historical scholarship and a broad-based, moderate interpretation of history. Republican leaders seized on the rancorous debate to introduce a damning resolution in the Senate. Republican Senator Slade Gordon led the rhetorical charge, claiming that the standards were a liberal attempt to "Destroy our nation's mystic chords of memory." In an astonishing show of bipartisan showmanship, the U.S. Senate condemned the standards in a 99–1 vote (Nash, 2000, p. 234).

Seven years later, Lynne Cheney sat in the audience at George W. Bush's Rose Garden ceremony, now as the wife of the Vice President. Bush (2000) made a special note of her presence, lauding her efforts to help children "understand history." His endorsement of Cheney's version of historical understanding—especially in the wake of her vicious, politicized attack on the national standards—tied his own citizenship initiative to the long tradition of noble lies in American civic education: History in the service of politics; truth in the service of cherished myth.

CONFLICT AND COMPROMISE IN COMMON SCHOOLS

One of the problems with state-approved truths in a democratic society is figuring which truths to tell. The previous section pointed to one theme of civic education: the cultivation of a national mythology at the expense of what is known or believed to be factually or reasonably true. But between outright truth (which

is rare) and outright lies (which are also rare), lies a wide grey area where different groups fight for access to the hearts and minds of children. Because they sit
at the epicenter of American attempts to shape the attitudes and beliefs of the
next generation, public schools (their textbooks, their teachers, their traditions)
naturally attract controversy. Each interest group has its own set of noble lies,
behind which are virtues it holds to be true.

And, as the founding generation discovered, having an ideological reform
agenda for mass education is one thing, but enacting it is quite another. Webster
enjoyed the greatest success of that generation by writing popular textbooks.
Jefferson's plans for mass education in Virginia fizzled famously (Wagoner,
2004, chaps 2–4). Although state law and leadership have played important roles
in the history of common schools, for most of their history these institutions
have been built, financed, and managed at the local level. And, at *that* level,
Americans have avoided controversial issues—buying textbooks, when possible,
that did not offend local sensitivities; creating policies, when possible, that
found middle ground in contested turf; or, as was often the case of African
American history, simply ignoring the fact that the turf was even contested
(Nash, 1995). Mann urged schools to avoid controversial issues (Kaestle, 1983,
p. 80). Throughout American history, the civic education that students have encountered in common/public schools has been the polar opposite of the politics
surrounding that education. Whereas religious, political, and ethnic leaders have
engaged in nearly two centuries of "culture wars" over the common school curriculum, the schools themselves have plodded along slowly, under a flat pedagogy of banal rituals and ever-growing textbook lists of filleted American heroes—with all bones of contention removed.

Recall that textbook authors have historically sought to create virtuous versions of American history and culture. These versions have been sharply contested for nearly as long as they have been written; but, the process by which
textbook authors (or their editors) in the 19th and 20th centuries responded to
criticism is telling. In the 19th century, when Irish groups complained about
anti-Irish texts, or Catholics about anti-Catholic (or pro-Protestant) texts, publishers gradually responded by removing or revising offensive passages, and
adding, when possible, new heroes to the growing pantheon (Tyack, 1999, p.
924). When African Americans challenged textbook biases in the 1960s and
1970s, they got token heroes of their own—sidebars, photographs, and vapid
vignettes (Fitzgerald, 1979, pp. 71–145). Textbook publishers did not always
respond in the way that groups asked or hoped them to react. They generally
have written their noble lies to the greatest common denominator, but not at the
expense of a surprisingly narrow spectrum of possible expressions of the monolithic American principles that Rush, and Bush, cherish. Thus, most children of
the late 20th century have learned about Helen Keller's early life, but they do
not know about her adult role as a socialist and political activist (Loewen, 1995,
chap. 1). These same children have learned that Rosa Parks was a poor Black

woman with tired feet—a passive heroine whose arrest sparked a spontaneous bus boycott—but not that she, too, was a longtime activist and that African Americans in the North and South had been organizing and fighting for years (Kohl, 1995). In the case of textbooks, publishers have tended to respond to conflict by including critics' heroes into the circle of the triumphant "we," but have not seriously examined their criticisms or changed their master narrative, because that might be too controversial.

Aside from textbooks, public school pedagogy itself has emphasized passive approaches to civic education. In describing the relationship between over heated policy talk and actual teacher practice, historian Cuban has used an extremely useful metaphor of a hurricane blowing over the ocean. In the air, a furious maelstrom of theories clash, tossing up waves on the surface. A fathom below, the storm moves waters to a lesser extent, resulting in some new or revised courses of study and curriculum materials, while deep under the ocean there is calm, as classroom instruction remains largely as it did before (Cuban, 1979; 1993, pp. 1–2). During the late 19th and early 20th centuries, how teachers taught changed slowly from a textbook-centered classroom to a teacher-centered classroom. But, both teachers and textbooks remained fairly consistent in the 19th and 20th centuries as sources of a single pedagogical tradition: direct instruction in which a unified, unquestionably correct body of knowledge passes from textbook and teacher into student (Cuban, 1993; Finkelstein, 1989). In that context, children have learned about American history and culture in what Seixas (2000) has called the "best story" mode. Facts and interpretation have been indistinguishable and unquestionable: the noble lies unassailable. In the 20th century, the pledge of allegiance has been a similar form of civic education: rote, passive, and without comment.

How public schools have responded to religion—one of the most contentious issues in school history—is a good example of their controversy-killing power. Religion, like history, has figured large in the history of civic education, or at least, the history of rhetoric about civic education. Adams and Rush, and even Jefferson, ranked religion high among the subjects that little republicans needed to learn in school (R. D. Brown, 1996, p. 106). For them and others, religion was a cornerstone of republican virtue. During the common school movement in the decades before the Civil War, Protestant ministers led major common school reform movements in the East, and actually built common school systems in the West (Tyack, 1996; Tyack & Hansot, 1982). After the Civil War, and again during the 1890s, the 1920s, and the 1950s, religion in the public school cycled through American politics as pious (usually Protestant) crusaders captured public attention with millennial rhetoric about making America a Godly nation (Justice, 2005, pp. 1–25). In the year following the September 11, 2001, terrorist attacks, George W. Bush often repeated the phrase "God bless America" in his speeches, and drivers on the nation's highways could not miss the flag-adorned vehicles with "God Bless America" bumper stickers. The message was clear: America is God's nation.

The devil has been in the details. After the Civil War, many religious leaders called for expanded religious instruction. "Piety is not to be put on like a holiday dress, to be worn on state occasions, but it is to be exhibited in our conduct at all times," wrote Cardinal Gibbons in *Our Christian Heritage* (1889). "Our youth must practice every day the Commandments of God, as well as the rules of grammar and arithmetic" (pp. 489–495). To that end, Gibbons demanded public money to support his church's schools. The National Teacher's Association (later the NEA) resolved in 1869: "The Bible should not only be studied, venerated, and honored as a classic for all ages . . . but devotionally read, and its precepts inculcated in all the common schools of the land" (as cited in Tyack & Hansot, 1982, pp. 74–75). But others were not so enthusiastic about religious instruction in a common school—either out of religious scruple, in the case of Baptists, or recognition of religious pluralism within the classroom. Henry Ward Beecher, the most famous 19th century American minister, admitted that the Bible ought not to be read in front of children whose parents objected (Beecher, 1875). In still other cases, leaders complained that the public school's need to cater to a large common denominator cheapened and vulgarized religious instruction. "It is my opinion," countered a superintendent from Medina, New York, "that the mere perfunctory reading of the Scriptures at the morning exercises has no ethical value whatever. In fact, it lessens the respect of pupils for the Sacred Book" (Annual Report, 1903).

The Medina superintendent's opinion pointed to an obvious problem with one size-fits-all religious exercises. Even when they were successful, religious crusaders rarely achieved the kinds of reforms that their lofty rhetoric would suggest. As many states enacted compulsory Bible reading laws in the late 19th century, for example, they simultaneously outlawed any "sectarian" instruction (S. W. Brown, 1912). In practice, the actual religious instruction children received during public school has been, at best, symbolic, brief, and banal. In the 19th and early 20th centuries, religious instruction usually meant no more than 15 minutes, total, of one or more of the following: reading without comment, prayer without comment, and a song without comment (Justice, 2005, pp. 107–139, 157–187). In the mid-20th century, religious reformers enjoyed some success at more thorough instruction through released-time for weekday religious instruction—programs in which students left school and attended religious instruction off campus (Justice, 2005; Zimmerman, 2002, pp. 131–159). Nevertheless, these programs, by their nature, required students to leave their schools. With minor exceptions, genuine religious instruction has barely scratched the surface of the common (public) school curriculum for at least the last 150 years, possibly longer.

The common school's need to compromise has resulted in a strangely ironic kind of civic education in America. Over the last half century alone, Americans

have waged spectacular rhetorical and legal battles over tiny bits of curriculum—a Supreme Court decision over one paragraph of prayer in New York
City, months of congressional hearings and "culture wars" over proposed voluntary history standards, and periodic court decisions and (Senate resolutions con-
demning them) over two words, "under God" in the Pledge of Allegiance.
Meanwhile, high school students continue to rate their social studies and history
classes as boring and irrelevant, and school curricula, measured by textbooks, at
least, continue to eschew real controversy or live issues (Loewen, 1995, pp. 12–
17). In that sense, a much more interesting and important civic education goes
on *about* schools than *in* them.

THE CHANGING MEANINGS OF CITIZENSHIP

When George W. Bush addressed the Rose Garden crowd to unveil his history
and civics initiatives, he argued that the history of the United States has been,
essentially, the story of a single set of static, immutable beliefs that have consistently triumphed over "evil." In three brief paragraphs, he deftly summarized
this triumphant story, including, of course, his own presidency:

> To be an American is not just a matter of blood or birth; we are bound
> by ideals, and our children must know those ideals.
> They should know about the nearly impossible victory of the Revolu-
> tionary War, and the debates of the Constitutional Convention. They
> should know the meaning of the Declaration of Independence, and how
> Abraham Lincoln applied its principles to fight—to fight slavery. Our
> children should know why Martin Luther King, Jr., was in a Birming-
> ham city jail, and why he wrote a magnificent letter from that place.
> Our children need to know about America's liberation of Europe during
> World War II, and why the Berlin Wall came down. At this very mo-
> ment, Americans are fighting in foreign lands for principles defined at
> our founding, and every American—particularly every American
> child—should fully understand these principles. (Bush, 2002)

Whether or not Bush's version of history reflected good "historical thinking," it contained a clear antihistorical assumption: The past was the present writ
small.

Historians of citizenship tell a different story. What defined a citizen in
1802 did not in 1902, which in turn did not in 2002. Thus, whether or not
Americans cherished the same exact set of national values in those times (and on
this score historians do not agree), it is clear that such principles had very differ-

ent meanings in different historical contexts (Early, 1993; Gerstle, 1993; Gerstle, 1993; Higham, 1993; Ruiz, 1993). Citizenship has changed over time.

European observers of American society have long argued the existence of an "American creed," from J. Hector St. John de Crevecour in the late 18th century to Alexis de Tocqueville in the mid 19th to Gunner Myrdal in the mid-20th century. Americans, in their views, were bound not by blood or birthright, but by ideals. One question recent historians ask, however, concerns what particular ideals make up the American creed, whether there is in fact a single set of them, and whether they have changed over time. If there is to be meaningful civic education, then surely it should be guided by a unified set of ideas.

During the so-called culture wars of the 1980s and 1990s, Schlesinger Jr. and Higham, two well-respected American historians, argued that until the late 20th century, Americans did indeed cling to a unified set of beliefs built around concepts of individual liberty, limited government, and social opportunity. Not until the advent of "multiculturalism" did long-cherished liberalism give way to a particularist, group-rights focus (Higham, 1993; Schlesinger, 1998). Yet, other respected scholars have increasingly demurred from this argument. Smith (1997), for example, has argued that there have been multiple traditions of liberal and conservative in American politics—both liberal and republican and illiberal and exclusionary. American history has not been marked by a steady march of expanded rights of citizenship, but periods of inclusion and exclusion, expansion and contraction of civil rights. Still others point to changing meanings of the federal constitution over time, or to a fractured ideology of citizenship inherent from the beginning of the republic (Ackerman, 1991; Brandon, 1998; Holland, 1989). Constitutional issues aside, Hunter (1991), a well-known contemporary sociologist, has argued that Americans are fundamentally divided by separate, irreconcilable worldviews. In still another vein, Miller (2002) has shown the unique effects of 20th-century institutional thought, particularly through the existence of a large standing army, on the nation's collective understanding of citizenship. In all of these cases, the intellectual gloss of a single, consistent American creed covers a deeper reality of faction and change over time.

Whatever ideas may or may not have formed a unified American creed, visions of citizenship have long rested on shifting sands of identity politics. Throughout its history, American society has denied full membership—explicitly and implicitly—to different groups at different times. The most obvious has been the long tradition of anti-African racism in American society. How could Frederick Douglass buy into an American creed when the color of his skin barred him from meaningful civic participation? In 1847, he told a group of abolitionists, "I have no love for America, as such; I have no patriotism. I have no country. What country have I?" (as cited in Berns, 2001). Those in power have, throughout the 19th and 20th centuries, consistently excluded non-whites, women, and the poor from the rights of full citizenship by law and practice. The

civil rights movement of the 1950s and 1960s made great strides toward expanding full citizenship, but then met with increasing retrenchment, particularly in
the area of school segregation, by the 1980s and 1990s. President Bush himself
had campaigned with strident criticism of racism in American government, yet
his victory in the 2000 presidential election was the direct result of a U.S. Supreme Court's support of the actions of the state of Florida, systematically dis-
counting votes from predominantly Black voting districts (*36 Days*, 2001).

The ability to vote is one important measure of "good" citizenship. Yet, as
Schudson (1999) has shown, even that act has had differing meanings in different time periods. During the early years of the American republic, Jefferson and
Rush would have recognized the voting process as orderly, gentlemanly, and
deferential to elites. Property requirements limited the electorate—as did slavery
and widespread (although not universal) prohibitions of female and non-White
suffrage. By the late 19th century, with the advent of nearly universal White
male suffrage, voting rates peaked at their highest level ever. Yet, voting behavior was, by today's standards, poor citizenship indeed. Voting days were chaotic, occasionally even drunken or violent affairs. Candidates offered jobs, cash
payments, and alcohol in return for party loyalty (there was no secret ballot). At
the end of 19th century, progressive reformers began to "clean up" voting, re-
forming campaign finance, introducing civil service reforms and sterilizing election days. Voting rates plummeted. The progressive vision of a good citizen
(i.e., one who makes independent, rational choices on election day) differed
from the intensely partisan or deferential visions of earlier generation (Schudson, 1999).

And surely good citizenship extends well beyond the single, annual act of
voting. School reformers of Mann's generation saw the primary civic aim of
schools as producing moral citizens, as opposed to informed ones (although they
wanted that, too). The ballot box paled in comparison to their concerns over
rising poverty, crime, and immigration. The good citizen was a good Christian, a
hard worker, and a dedicated republican. The mass education they envisioned
was civic in the sense that it could instill the necessary virtues to lift any child
out of poverty, offering an equal chance at advancement to all (Mann,
2001/1848). At the end of the 19th century, Progressive reformers, on the other
hand, sought to differentiate civic education, channeling children into different
stations in society, with strong, often explicit correlations between subordinate
races, classes, and genders and subordinate futures. In the rhetoric (and school
reforms) of many Progressive Era educational leaders, the meaning of good citizenship varied by the social station of the citizen, and reflected a widespread
belief that civic education required scientific management (Tyack, 1974). This
was not the same American creed that guided the lofty rhetoric of the Founders.
This was people as cogs in the machinery of the republic rather than independent republican machines in their own right. Civically motivated school reforms

have changed over time in response to changing notions of good or effective citizenship.

What makes a good citizen in the early 21st century? Voting remains an important component of American civic life. But it is by no means the only or, arguably, the most effective means of civic engagement. Schudson argues that the great expansion of the judiciary in the late 20th century demands that good citizens be aware of their civic rights, and that activism along the lines of rights consciousness constitutes a major force in American civic life. Chapters in this volume by Margaret Smith Crocco (chap. 1) and Carole Hahn (chap. 3) make a similar case for tolerance of social diversity as a hallmark of civic competence. In these and other formulations, good citizenship is contextual. Good citizenship education, then, needs to recognize and adapt itself to those changing contexts.

CONCLUSIONS: RE-ENVISIONING CIVIC EDUCATION

For would-be reformers, these themes—noble lies versus critical inquiry, controversy-phobic classrooms, and changing meanings of citizenship—offer cautionary tales about the challenges of civic education in the United States. By the same token, however, they also suggest that the directions pointed to by scholars in this volume hold the potential to make substantive, transformative changes to how children learn to be citizens.

Noble Lies

Most chapter in this volume do not directly address the first of my themes; the question of telling noble lies in order to foster a sense of civic pride. Indeed, one of the challenges of even talking about this theme is the label itself. There seems to be agreement at the academic level that broad interpretations of American history should reflect research and evidence—academics of all political stripes are, almost by definition, not in the business of telling lies or creating myths. For example, Ravitch (1978, 1988), a respected senior scholar on history and civic education, is a strident critic of liberal historical revisionism *and* inaccuracy and poor pedagogy in K–12 history education. On the other hand, another conservative protagonist in the culture wars, Hirsch (1988), argues that the point is less the accuracy of the cherished myths, but that all citizens cherish the same ones. Not all interpretations, or myths, are created equal, however. As we have seen, in practice, the goal of emphasizing the "triumphs" of American democracy have led to the consistent and systematic exclusion of pertinent facts, obfuscation of others, and the creation of a fairly narrow, oftentimes misleading view of American history and American democracy. This has come about, in part, because using the past as cause for celebration is an inherently biased project, regardless of the particular political agenda: Those who celebrate the triumph of capitalism tend to downplay its failings and ignore, or vilify, its opponents; those who celebrate an afro-centric view of history tend to do the same with anachronistic conceptions of race (Schlesinger, 1998). Perhaps the trouble is in the aim itself: To trumpet history as a herald of present political agendas cheapens both the discipline of history and the aims of civic education. Could it be time to separate civics and history, for the sake of both?

The Founders recognized that the nation had no history as such, but that it desperately needed cohesion. If they were going to have to literally create a history, then why not build in virtuous heroes and stories? But they lived in a different time and place. Over 200 years later, the nation *does* have a history, and is, politically at least, in no danger of falling apart. Why do we still strive to celebrate the founding's "supposed virtues?" A number of researchers in this volume have demonstrated the very limited effectiveness of this traditional strategy for making good citizens. Students in public schools may learn how to behave in a mythological republic, but have very little preparation for living in a real one. How could they, if their lived experience with America bears little resemblance to the America in their texts? Instead, several chapters herein propose new strategies centered on an alternative course: effective citizenship in the context of realistic, contextual, social, and political processes.

Controversy and Consensus

As many of the authors here have noted, the relative failure of today's civic education begs new ways of understanding civic education and new approaches to teaching it. John Hibbing and Alan Rosenthal (chap. 8) lament the democracy education that American students typically receive, and link it to widespread voter apathy and cynicism. Rather than teach students how democratic government really works, they argue, schools set up unrealistic expectations. Likewise, Joseph Kahne and Joel Westheimer (chap. 9) have found a gap between the civics that students learn in schools and the actual process of effective social action in the broader society. They call for an invigorated civic education emphasizing a realistic view of politics and collective action for social change. According to the cross-national study by Wendy Richardson and Judith Torney-Purta (chap. 5), the mismatch between civic instruction in schools and civic realities extends to nations beyond the United States, although these authors also express optimism that schools have the potential to have a far greater impact.

In their unique charter school setting in Oakland, California, Bernadette Chi and Tim Howeth have fashioned a school that addresses at least part of these critiques of public civic education. Students at the East Bay Conservation Corps (EBCC) Charter School encounter a service-learning curriculum that encourages individual social action and service within the school community. Yet, the school does not address the kind of controversy-based political education that Hibbing and Rosenthal and Westheimer and Kahne propose. Moreover, the authors describe a challenging gap between the school setting and the larger society, between individual service within the school and collective action for social justice beyond its walls.

If history is a guide, advocates of controversial civic education—either for content about controversy, content that is controversial, or socially transformative curricula that address topics threatening the socioeconomic status quo—face an uphill battle in school reform. In general, American school boards, administrators, teachers and textbook companies do not like controversy, and they never have. On the other hand, those who focus on a civic education that stresses social, rather than political, action, may face fewer obstacles. Crocco (chap. 1), for example, reminds us that a central theme within the traditional "triumphant" story of American society is greater social inclusion. Moreover, although she cites troubling evidence of the continued exclusion of homosexuals, she nevertheless sees hope in the fact that multiculturalism has become mainstream in American popular culture. As the broader society accepts more forms of social diversity, civic education programs embracing interpersonal or social interaction will themselves be less likely to attract controversy.

Even those civic education strategies that focus on extra-political or social processes may face frustration, however. In the case of history textbooks, greater inclusion of social diversity has not led to major paradigm shifts in the narrative logic, or equal recognition of the actual points of view and agendas of members of those groups. Textbooks include the likes of Helen Keller, Rosa Parks, and Christopher Columbus in terms that do not threaten the status quo or attract the ire of powerful interest groups. In short, expanding the "circle of we" is not the same as recognizing the different political agendas that marginalized groups and individuals hold. Moreover, a civic education that is "realistic," even if it eschews politics *per se*, will necessarily include the same kinds of unpleasant, potentially controversial facts that political leaders have long resisted in public schools. African American students here in New Jersey today learn that their nation overcame racial prejudice during the civil rights movement, beginning with *Brown vs. Board of Education*, but do so while sitting in appallingly underfunded, racially segregated schools. Religious groups nationwide continue to express frustration over public school curricula that they see as excluding their unique perspectives, and American children living in poverty (who, at the time of this writing, account for 15%–20% of the total) may well wonder what, exactly, is the triumph of capitalism (Semple, 2003)? Now that the nation is mature and secure, these are indeed issues that future citizens ought to grapple with; whether shortsighted politicians or those with a vested interest in the status quo will allow such questioning is another matter.

The historical challenges that will continue to face civic education in the next century need not be grounds for pessimism, however. The results of public

schooling in the United States have historically been far more subtle and complex than explicit measures of civic competence might suggest. Common school
education in the 19th century created a remarkably literate nation (male and female) despite the very limited nature of systematic state control. During height-
ened periods of immigration, especially around the turn of the 20th century, public schools provided necessary, rudimentary language instruction, literacy, and
basic socialization to millions of immigrants. Yet, at the same time, whereas
Progressive reformers greatly expanded public education (increasing average
attendance, expenditures, teacher training, and explicit civic instruction) actual
voting rates plummeted. In short, the role of the school has been important, but
limited, especially in its connection to explicitly political, as opposed to more
broadly civic, behavior. Perhaps new paradigms for understanding civics and
civic education can increase the connection between schools and society.

Citizenship Education in an Ever-Changing Society

Regardless of one's opinion of the thesis that the American polity is defined by a
single creed, it is clear that the demands placed on tomorrow's citizens will be
different from those of the past. And to that end, several of the scholars in this
book have challenged the traditional, static view of citizenship that views it in
terms of virtuous adherence to immutable, abstract concepts, proposing new
conceptions that link to specific contexts of time and place, or to points of view.
This flowering of good thinking and research about civic education is grounds
for optimism, as is any movement to revise, complicate, and redirect a stale
paradigm. Their ideas fall into two general categories. The first is citizenship as
it relates to sociopolitical groupings that are not simply a nation-state: local
communities, to the "public" (as opposed to the state) and to the entire globe.
The second relates civic education to individual perspectives, of gender, sexual
identity, and adolescence.

Eric Davis (chap. 7) and William Cahill (chap. 6) call for understandings of
citizenship that transcend the narrow focus on one's nation-state. Clarifying
what is in the public interest, as opposed to what is in the interest of those in
power, opens up real possibilities for civic education that enables positive social
and political change. In their call for global civic education, Davis and Cahill
also break away from the confines of the nation-state centric view of civic education. They challenge the desirability of the isolationist, parochial view of
American national civic identity that characterized a widespread pre 9/11
American mind-set, and point to a long tradition of universalizing tendencies in
the history of American education—a legacy of immigration, but also of the
realities of America's economic, intellectual, and social ties to the outer, usually
Western, world. The long tradition of American exceptionalism that undergirds
so much of the rhetoric about American civic identity—from Benjamin Rush to

George Bush—appears in this light to be but one side of the coin, the flip of which is international and cosmopolitan.

The chapters by Margaret Smith Crocco (chap. 2), Carole Hahn (chap. 4) and Beth Rubin (chap. 10) reconceptualize citizenship (and thus civic education) in quite a different way. Comparing the place of gender and sexuality in social studies *as it is*, to *as it should be,* Crocco cites the enduring exclusion of sexuality from purportedly "multicultural" instruction, and calls for a place for sexuality at the multicultural table of public school social studies. Likewise, Hahn urges us to maintain a focus on gender equality in notions of citizenship. Teachers, textbook writers, and policymakers must recognize that gendered notions of citizenship continue to run through K–12 curricula, despite the improvements in the wake of the women's movement of the late 20th century. In both cases, the authors note the consequences of curricula that create narrow historical views of civic leadership and life, and demand more expansive, inclusive conceptions of social studies curriculum. Otherwise, the preparation of future citizens will fall short of the ideals of freedom and equality that appear, to most commentators, to characterize American civil identity. Rubin's chapter asks a different question. Rather than focus on the failings of the formal civic educational curriculum, she peers into students lives to try and understand how they experience civic life and, consequently, what they make of the curricula they experience in schools. Such an approach may well yield still more conceptions of citizenship, and potential focuses for effective in-school education.

We should take it as a healthy sign of our democracy that there can be so many robust approaches understanding citizenship. Paradoxically, the very health of our free society is indicated by the rancorous, at times paralyzing, politics of public education. The fact that Americans can and *do* argue about the content of their schools results in the same curriculum that, on the whole, offers such a paltry civic education. Scholarship can provide an important, leading role in these debates, however. High quality research on civic education can lead scholars and reformers alike toward a more nuanced, mature understanding of these questions and their answers than the Founders, for all their "supposed virtues," could ever have achieved. The lack of consensus over the meaning of civic education is a good thing. Indeed, if there truly is an American creed, it may best be described not by the particulars of what we think or teach about citizenship, but by the dynamic processes by which we say it.

REFERENCES

36 days: The complete chronicle of the 200 presidential crisis (2001). New York: Times Books.

Ackerman, B. (1991). *We the people: Foundations*. Cambridge: Belknap Press.

Annual Report of the State Superintendent. (1903). New York State.

Beecher, H. W. (1875). *"No. 16." 25 Pamphlets on Education*. Department of Special Collections, Milbank Memorial Library, Teachers College, Columbia University.

Brandon, M. E. (1998). *Free in the world: American slavery and constitutional failure*. Princeton, NJ: Princeton University Press.

Berns, W. (2001). *Making patriots*. Chicago: University of Chicago Press.

Brown, R. D. (1996). *The strength of a people: The idea of an informed citizenry in America*. Chapel Hill: University of North Carolina Press.

Brown, S. W. (1912). *The secularization of American education*. New York: Teacher's College Press.

Bush, G. W. (2002, September 17). *Bush remarks on history and civics education*. Office of the Press Secretary. Retrieved June 6, 2006 from http://www.whitehouse.gov/news/releases/2002/09/20020917-1.html.

Cremin, L. (Ed.). (1957). *The republic and the school: Horace Mann on the education of free men*. New York: Teacher's College Press.

Cuban, L. (1979). Determinants of Curriculum Change and Stability, 1870–1970. In J. Schafferzick & G. Sykes (Eds.), *Value conflicts and curriculum issues* (pp. 139–196). Berkeley, CA: McCutchan,

Cuban, L. (1993). *How teachers taught: constancy and change in American classrooms, 1880–1990*, (2nd ed.). New York: Teachers College Press.

Cubberley, E. P. (1909). *Changing conceptions of education*. Boston: Houghton Mifflin.

Early, G. (1993). American education and the postmodern impulse, *American Quarterly, 45*, 220–229.

Elson, R. (1964). *Guardians of tradition: American schoolbooks of the nineteenth century*. Lincoln: University of Nebraska Press.

Everett, E. (1965). Orations and speeches on various occasions. In R. L. Vassar (Ed.), *Social history of American education. Vol. I: Colonial times to 1860* (pp. 212–213). Chicago: Rand McNally. (Original work published 1838)

Finkelman, P. (1993). Jefferson and slavery: Treason against the hopes of the world. In P. S. Onuf (Ed.), *Jeffersonian legacies* (pp. 181–221). Charlottesville: University Press of Virginia.

Finkelstein, B. (1989). *Governing the young: Teacher behavior in popular primary schools in the nineteenth century United States*. New York: Falmer.

Fitzgerald, F. (1979). *America revised: What history textbooks have taught out children about their country, and how and why those textbooks have changed in different decades.* New York: Vintage.

Gerstle, G. (1993). The limits of American universalism, *American Quarterly, 45,* 230–236.

Gibbons, J. (1889). *Our Christian heritage.* Baltimore: J. Murphy.

Hewitt, N. (1993). A response to John Higham. *American Quarterly, 45,* 237–242.

Higham, J. (1993). Multiculturalism and Universalism: A history and critique. *American Quarterly, 45,* 195–219.

Hirsch, E. D. (1988). *Cultural literacy: What every American needs to know.* New York: Vintage.

Holland, C. (2001). *The body politic: Foundings, citizenship, and difference in the American political imagination.* New York: Routledge.

Hunter, J. D. (1991). *Culture wars: The struggle to define America.* New York: Basic Books.

Illich, I. (1983). *Deschooling society.* New York: Harper & Row. (original work published 1970)

Jackson, P.W. (1968). *Life in classrooms.* Chicago: University of Chicago Press.

Justice, B. (2000). "A college of morals": Educational reform at San Quentin prison, 1880–1920. *History of Education Quarterly, 40 (3),* 279–301.

Justice, B. (2005a). Release Time. In *Encyclopedia of New York State* (pp. 1291–1292). Syracuse, NY: Syracuse University Press.

Justice, B. (2005b). *The war that wasn't: Conflict and compromise in the common schools of New York State.* Albany: State University of New York Press.

Kaestle, C. (1983). *Pillars of the Republic: Common schools and American society, 1780–1860.* New York: Hill & Wang.

Kohl, H. (1995). *Should we burn Babar? Essays on children's literature and the power of stories.* New York: New Press.

Lippmann, W. (1993). *American inquisitors.* New Brunswick, NJ: Transaction. (original work published 1928)

Loewen, J. (1995). *Lies my teacher told me.* New York: Touchstone.

Mann, H. (2002). Twelfth annual report. As cited in J. W. Fraser (Ed.), *The school in the United States: A documentary history* (pp. 54–61). New York: McGraw-Hill. (original work published 1848)

Miller, C. R. (2002). *Taylored citizenship: State institutions and subjectivity.* Westport, T.: Praeger.

Nash, G. B. (1995). American history reconsidered: Asking new questions about the past. In D. Ravitch & M. A. Vinovskis (Eds.), *Learning from the past: What history teaches us about school reform* (pp. 135-163). Baltimore: Johns Hopkins Press.

Nash, G. B., Crabtree, C., & Dunn, R. E. (2000). *History on trial: Culture wars and the teaching of the past.* New York: Vintage Books.

A nation at risk: the imperative for educational reform.(1983). *A report to the nation and the secretary of education, U.S. Department of Education by the National Commission on Excellence in Education.* Washington, DC: U.S. Government Printing Press.

Onuf, P. S. (1991). State Politics and Republican Virtue: Religion, Education, and Morality in Early American Federalism. In P. Finkelman and S. E. Gottlieb (Eds.), *Toward a Usable Past: Liberty Under State Constitutions* (pp. 219–223). Athens, GA: University of Georgia Press.

Perkinson, H. J. (1991). *The imperfect panacea: American faith in education 1865–1990.* New York: McGraw-Hill.

Ravitch, D. (1978). *The revisionists revised: A critique of the radical attack on the schools.* New York: Basic Books.

Ravitch, D. (1988). *What do our 17-year olds know?: A report on the first national assessment of history and literature.* New York: HarperCollins.

Reese, W. J. (2000). Public schools and the elusive search for the common good. In L. Cuban & D. Shipps (Eds.), *Reconstructing the common good in education: Coping with intractable dilemmas* (pp. 13–31). Stanford, California: Stanford University Press.

Ruiz, V. L. (1993). "It's the people who drive the book": A view from the West. *American Quarterly, 45,* 243–248.

Rush, B. (1973). Thoughts upon the mode of education proper in a republic. In W. Smith (Ed.), *Theories of education in early America 1655-1819* (pp. 243–256). New York: Bobbs-Merrill. (original work published 1786)

Schlesinger, A., Jr. (1998). *The disuniting of America: Reflections on a multicultural society* (Rev. ed.), New York: Norton.

Schudson, M. (1999). *The good citizen: A history of American civic life.* Cambridge, MA: Harvard University Press.

Seixas, P. (2000). Schweigen! Die Kinder! Or, Does Postmodern History Have a Place in the Schools. In P. N. Stearns, P.Seixas, & S.Wineberg (Eds.). *Knowing, teaching, and learning history: National and international perspectives* (pp. 19–37). New York: New York University Press.

Semple, K. (2003, September 26). Number of people living in poverty in U.S. increases again, *New York Times.*

Smith, R. (1997). *Civic ideals: Conflicting visions of citizenship in U.S. history.* New Haven, CT: Yale University Press.

Tyack, D. (1966a). Forming the national character: paradox in the educational thought of the revolutionary generation. *Harvard Educational Review, 36 (1),* 29–41.

Tyack, D. (1966b). The kingdom of God and the common school: Protestant ministers and the educational awakening in the West. *Harvard Educational Review, 36*(4).

Tyack, D. (1974). *The one best system: A history of American urban education.* Cambridge, MA: Harvard University Press.

Tyack D., & Hansot, E. (1981). Conflict and consensus in American public education. *Daedalus, 110*, 1–25.

Tyack, D., & Hansot, E. (1982). *Managers of virtue: Public school leadership in America, 1820–1980.* New York: Basic Books.

Tyack, D. (1999). Monuments between covers: The politics of textbooks, *American Behavioral Scientist, 42*, 922–932.

Wallace, A. F. C. (1997). "The obtaining lands," Thomas Jefferson and the Native Americans. In J. P. Ronda (Ed.), *Thomas Jefferson and the changing West: From conquest to conservation* (pp. 25–42). St. Louis: Missouri Historical Society Press.

Wagoner, J. (2004). *Jefferson and education.* Monticello: Thomas Jefferson Foundation.

Webster, N. (1965). On the education of youth in America. In F. Rudolph (Ed.), *Essays on education in the early Republic* (pp. 41–77). Cambridge, MA: Harvard University Press. (original work published 1790)

Zimmerman, J. (2002). *Whose America? Culture wars in the public schools.* Cambridge, MA: Harvard University Press.

Author Index

Subject Index

R